D0731670

THE THEOLOGICAL DEVELOPMENT OF

EDWARDS AMASA PARK:

LAST OF THE "CONSISTENT CALVINISTS"

THE THEOLOGICAL DEVELOPMENT OF

EDWARDS AMASA PARK:

LAST OF THE "CONSISTENT CALVINISTS"

by

Anthony C. Cecil, Jr.

III

Published by

American Academy of Religion

and

SCHOLARS' PRESS

DISSERTATION SERIES, NUMBER ONE

1974

Distributed by

SCHOLARS' PRESS
University of Montana
Missoula, Montana 59801

THE THEOLOGICAL DEVELOPMENT OF
EDWARDS AMASA PARK:
LAST OF THE "CONSISTENT CALVINISTS"

by

Anthony C. Cecil, Jr.
Department of Religious Studies
University of North Dakota
Grand Forks, North Dakota 58201

Ph.D., 1973   Advisor:
Yale University   Sydney Ahlstrom

Library of Congress Catalog Card Number: 74-83338

ISBN: 0-88420-118-X

Printed in the United States of America

Printing Department
University of Montana
Missoula, Montana 59801

SUMMARY

Associated with Andover Theological Seminary as either
student or professor for over fifty years, Edwards Amasa
Park (1808-1900) was a theologian of no small influence
upon evangelical Protestant opinion in nineteenth-century
America. That influence came not only from his many students,
but also from his wide-ranging labors in behalf of missions,
education, reform, and other evangelical causes. It came
as well from his extensive correspondence and his long
editorship of the influential quarterly Bibliotheca Sacra,
an organ based upon the German scholarly models his European
trips taught him to admire.

Such broad influence assured a wide hearing for Park's
"Consistent Calvinist" thought. Proudly identifying himself
with the intellectual lineage of Jonathan Edwards, Samuel
Hopkins, and Nathanael Emmons, he believed the New England
Theology was the most nearly perfect expression of the
Christian faith ever devised. In expounding that theology
for his age, he followed the paths of mediation and innovation,
looking toward empirical, scientific models, and using both
natural and revealed sources. His goal was a theology for
both pulpit and study, which would be viable in a milieu of
democratic humanitarianism but would not unduly abridge the
evangelical concern with sin, salvation, and sovereign divine
grace.

Strongly attracted to the rationalism and moralism of
the Scottish "Common Sense" Philosophy, Park viewed the doctrines

of human depravity and atonement through individualistic, voluntaristic glasses. Reason was not his only theological oracle, however. In a controversial address distinguishing "the theology of the intellect" and "that of the feelings," he combined rationalistic and romantic motifs to demonstrate the fundamental continuity between his own doctrinal concepts and the more "figurative" expressions of Scripture and Westminster. Displaying an incipient interpretive freedom and historical awareness, he pointed to a basic deposit of faith which formed a felt substance of agreement among Christian believers even though their intellectual expressions of that deposit varied.

Attacked for diverging from Scripture and strict Reformed orthodoxy by Charles Hodge of Princeton, and praised for his innovations by Unitarian and other liberal spokesmen, Park found himself in a difficult situation. As the leading theologian at New England's "West Point" of Congregational Orthodoxy, he increasingly felt the need to defend his position. And, in the end, he vainly opposed his own students on a new Andover faculty which was bringing to fruition ideas implicit in his intellect-feeling distinction. Nevertheless, though that distinction became an empty polemical device in Park's later career, it allowed him, for the most part, a posture of mediation vis-a-vis seemingly contradictory doctrinal positions and made his theological development a sensitive and revealing barometer of an era of revolutionary change in American religious thought.

Few would contend that Edwards Amasa Park was among the greatest or most creative intellectual figures of the nineteenth century. But his influence on the American religious scene cannot be discounted. And his development as a theologian sheds a considerable amount of light not only upon the fate of the New England Theology in the last century but also upon a number of important intellectual interrelationships in the area of American religious thought. It could be argued, for example, that despite his conservatism, Park's combination of romantic and rationalistic modes of thought to defend a non-literal reading of Scripture and the Westminster Catechism had a very real positive impact upon the later development of theological liberalism at Andover Seminary. Certainly his love for "Consistent Calvinism" did not prevent the devotion of much of his career to a labor of theological mediation between Congregational Orthodoxy and its Unitarian and other critics.

In short, Park is a figure worthy of attention not because of the intrinsic merit of his ideas but because of the revealing commentary he provides on what was

happening to the nineteenth-century American religious
mind. It is with the perspective of this commentary
in mind that the following study has been written. It
is admittedly almost exclusively an exercise in intellectual history. This is not to deny a relationship
between Park's thought and its social context. Rather,
in this case, to focus upon one side of that relationship seemed the more fruitful and revealing way to study
the Andover professor and the struggle of theological
and spiritual conscience that he reflects.

Any work of this sort begets considerable indebtedness. It would be impossible to acknowledge all that is
owed in this limited space. Certainly a heartfelt word
of appreciation is due my faithful and tireless advisor,
Professor Sydney Ahlstrom, without whose critical wisdom
the project could never have reached completion. Thanks
are also due Mr. Kenneth E. Rowe of the Drew University
Library for his invaluable bibliographic aid. Of the
many other librarians and archivists who aided me, those
of Phillips Academy, Andover Newton Theological School,
Oberlin College, and, of course, Yale University deserve
special mention. My overall thinking about Park and his
place on the New England religious scene received valuable
input from Professor Harold Y. Vanderpool of Wellesley
College and from Professor Thomas A. Schafer of McCormick
Theological Seminary, the latter of whom also directed

me to some exceedingly useful manuscript sources. But my greatest debt of gratitude rests with the Charles R. Park family of Nashville, Tennessee, who graciously allowed me to visit in their home and examine their priceless collection of family papers. The importance of these papers to this study would be difficult to overestimate, as the notes and bibliography should make clear. Finally, but by no means least in the realm of gratitude, come the long-suffering labor and support of my wife, Carolyn. Debts of this order, however, are word-defiant.

TABLE OF CONTENTS

Chapter I

THE MAKING OF AN EDWARDSEAN THEOLOGIAN:
THE FIRST THREE DECADES

Edwards Amasa Park, as his name implies, grew up in
a home where the name of Jonathan Edwards carried well-nigh
the same canonical weight as those of Paul and John. Born
in Providence, Rhode Island, in December 1808, he was the
second of four sons, all of whom became Congregational
clergymen, to bless the family of the erudite Calvin Park,
Professor of Languages, and later, Professor of Moral
Philosophy and Metaphysics at Brown University.[1] One of

---

[1]Calvin Park (1774-1847) came from a family very much
aware and proud of its staunch Puritan-Reformed heritage
/see Frank Sylvester Parkes, compiler, Genealogy of the
Parke Families of Massachusetts (Washington, D.C.: Presswork of the Columbia Polytechnic Institute Printing Office,
1909)/. His father, though a farmer, had great respect for
the family's academic and ministerial traditions and was
extremely proud that two of his sons, Calvin and Thomas,
chose to attend Brown and become clergymen. The reasons
behind the choice of Brown over Harvard are not clear,
since the family lived near the latter and had ties there-
with through relatives. Whatever this motivation, however,
Calvin's matriculation at Brown and his membership in the
Pacific rather than the First Congregational Church of
Providence (the latter became Unitarian) assured the continued identification of his family with Reformed Orthodoxy
in New England. This was true despite the fact that his
marriage to Abigail Ware in 1805 endowed him with such
liberal relatives as Henry Ware, Sr., whose election in
that same year to Harvard's Hollis professorship of divinity
marked the Unitarian conquest of that venerable institution.
See "Calvin Park, D.D." in William B. Sprague (ed.), Annals
of the American Pulpit (New York: Robert Carter and
Brothers, 1859), II, 460-463. Also see Richard Salter

Park's biographers, who spoke from personal experience, well described the household of Calvin Park:

> He /E. A. Park/ was born, of course, into
> scholarly surroundings, and into as intense
> a theological atmosphere as probably ever
> was encountered in the world; where the
> subjects of God's sovereignty, of His decrees,
> and of the way of harmonizing with these the
> obligation of man, were the supreme, almost
> the sole, topics of reflection and talk.[1]

Not surprisingly, when Park later reflected on his childhood, he was led to remark, "I was at ten years of age somewhat of a theologian, and a rigid Calvinist; had a great reverence for Dr. Emmons and Dr. Hopkins."[2] This reverence was later to mature into two full-scale "Memoirs" of these famed Edwardsean theologians. But already in his early youth, those important biographies were, in a sense, taking shape, as he perused the sermons and other

---

Storrs, Edwards A. Park: Memorial Address (Boston: Press of Samuel Usher, 1900), pp. 17-20; and Frank Hugh Foster, The Life of Edwards Amasa Park (New York: Fleming H. Revell Company, 1936), pp. 24ff.

[1]Storrs, Memorial Address, p. 21.

[2]Park, "Autobiographical Fragments," in Foster, Life, p. 31. The complete ms. of these "Fragments" is now lost. The Emmons mentioned here was, of course, Nathanael Emmons (1745-1840), pastor-theologian of the small community of Franklin, Massachusetts, and one of the most daring and creative of the Edwardsean disciples in New England. His fellow disciple to whom Park also refers, Samuel Hopkins (1721-1803), served first a frontier pastorate in Great Barrington, Massachusetts, and later a thriving seaport church in Newport, Rhode Island. He gave his name to an important later recension of Edwardsean theology, which included among other trademarks, the famous doctrine of "disinterested benevolence." His career was marked by numerous reform activities and publications, including an early biography of Edwards, for whom Hopkins acted as a sort of literary executor.

writings of Hopkins and as he actually listened to the
sermons of Emmons in the nearby Massachusetts town of
Franklin. Emmons was, in fact, a not infrequent visitor
in the Park home in Providence. In the interim between his
graduation from Brown and his assumption of teaching duties
there, Park's father had studied theology with the distinguished Franklin divine, and the two developed a rather
close relationship. One of Park's brothers testified to
that relationship through his theologically weighty name:
Calvin Emmons. Park himself stood in awe of this great
follower of Edwards, into whose presence he was privileged
to be introduced while still a young boy. Through Emmons,
in effect, he gained early first-hand access to Edwardsean
theology in living, breathing form--an access which made a
more decisive impact upon his thinking than books alone
could ever have achieved.[1]

Reinforcing this impact was, of course, his father's
own intellectual example. Calvin had the same difficulty
as his son Edwards would later manifest in deciding between
the vocations of teaching and preaching. At Brown he did
both, but it was his sermons which seemed to move and
influence the young Edwards more than the father's home
tutoring.[2] This was undoubtedly because the sermons

---

[1]cf. Park, "Miscellaneous Reflections of a Visitor
upon the Character of Dr. Emmons," in The Works of Nathanael
Emmons, ed. Jacob Ide (Boston: Crocker and Brewster, 1842),
I, cxxvii-clxxii.

[2]cf. Park, "Autobiographical Fragments," in Foster,
Life, p. 30.

brought Edwardsean doctrine home to the emotional as well
as the intellectual nature of the young Park. Nonetheless,
it was the latter nature which his parents sought most to
cultivate.

Park described himself, in his youth, as being of a
"meditative...cast of mind" and as being "a great castle-
builder."[1] He was given to long melancholy ruminations on
the state of his soul. But the rigid intellectual discipline
to which he was early subjected seemed to preclude, in his
view, any significant emotional outlet for these ruminations.
He once said that he could not remember a time when he had
not been in school.[2] And the type of schooling he received
provided few avenues of imaginative or emotive expression.
At age nine, he took up the study of Latin, followed soon
thereafter by Greek. Play and other "idle" pursuits were
strictly limited in the well-disciplined Park household.
"If my mother had allowed me to read novels, or such poetry
as Byron's," Park once speculated, "I know not what would
have become of my imagination. But she cultivated the
prudential traits of my character and repressed the
imaginative."[3]

Mixed in with his early classical education was, of
course, a demanding regimen of theological instruction

[1] Ibid., p. 31.

[2] Storrs, Memorial Address, p. 25.

[3] Park, "Autobiographical Fragments," in Foster, Life,
p. 31.

administered by his father. It was indeed no idle claim
on Park's part that he was "somewhat of a theologian" by
age ten; for at that age, his father comprehensively
examined him in the doctrines of the Reformed faith and was
extremely pleased with his answers.[1] Not long after this
revealing theological examination, Park was sent to his
maternal grandfather's home in Wrentham, Massachusetts, to
attend the Academy there in final preparation for college.
But there seemed little the Academy could teach him that
he had not already learned at home.[2] Thus, by the time he
was thirteen, he had acquired a formidable store of classical
and theological learning and was deemed ready for matriculation at Brown.

                    *   *   *

The choice of Brown was practically a foregone conclusion, given his father's long-standing connection with
that institution. Though founded and controlled by Baptists,
the University required no religious tests for its professors and provided for a fixed representation of Congregationalists and members of other denominations on its

----

[1] cf. George R. W. Scott, "Professor Edwards Amasa Park:
A Biographical Sketch," in Professor Park and His Pupils,
ed. D. L. Furber, et al. (Boston: Press of Samuel Usher,
1899), p. 12.

[2] cf. Foster, Life, p. 31.

governing boards.[1] One was thus not likely to be indoc-
trinated in a particular faith at Brown in the 1820's, but
one would certainly find himself in a more orthodox
religious milieu there than at Harvard, for example.

The Brown student of Park's day was subjected to a
relatively thorough classical curriculum, including
readings from Cicero, Horace, Vergil, Sallust, Xenophon,
and Homer. Considerably more attention was paid to Latin
than to Greek works; and the emphasis in much of the Latin
study, as might be expected, was upon style and argument
rather than upon ideas as such. Logic, rhetoric, elocution,
grammar, and criticism occupied major space in the "Course
of Instruction" outlined by the Brown catalogues of the
1820's. In English, as in Latin, the student learned to
prize the well-turned phrase, the effective illustration,
the cogent argument: qualities Park would later emphasize
in his own teaching and practice of "sacred rhetoric."[2]

"My college course was not a very liberal one," Park
declared in retrospect; and if he meant this as a criticism

---

[1]This and much of the ensuing information and comment
about Brown University in the early nineteenth century
are based upon Walter C. Bronson, The History of Brown
University: 1764-1914 (Providence: Published by the
University, 1914), entire; especially chap. V.

[2]cf. his "Lectures on Style" as recorded by an
unidentified student, 1845 (one-vol. ms., Brown University
Library).

of the limited areas of instruction, he was certainly
right.[1] Modern language instruction was not to be had.
His later mastery of German thus came largely from his
study in Germany itself. Brown exposed him to almost no
history and to severely limited amounts of mathematics,
science, geography, and political theory. Greek was
taught more for New Testament than for classical studies.
The depths of Greek philosophy and Greek tragedy were thus
left largely unplumbed. Yet despite all these limitations,
the Brown curriculum decisively shaped Park's future
intellectual development. It immersed him in a matrix
of theological and philosophical ideas that would form the
bedrock of his thinking for the rest of his life.

The attention paid to logic, rhetoric, and the classics
at Brown was certainly equaled, if not surpassed, by that
lavished upon Scottish "Common Sense" Philosophy[2] and
rational apologetic theology. When Park was not writing
style-oriented compositions on "The Emotion of Sublimity"
or "The Road to Literary Eminence," he was penning carefully
reasoned orations and essays on the "Theoretic Errors of
Eminent Philosophers" or the theological conundrum "Does

---

[1]See "Autobiographical Fragments" in Foster, *Life*,
pp. 37-38. The Brown faculty, in many cases, displeased
Park as much as the curriculum: see his letter of
reminiscence to Professor /C. W.?/ Parsons, April 8, 1881,
Drew University Library.

[2]This philosophy and the exponents thereof mentioned
below are discussed more fully in a later chapter.

Reason Teach That God Is the Author of Moral Evil?"[1]   His

junior oration (delivered in the spring of 1825) detailing

where "eminent philosophers," particularly the medieval

"schoolmen," had gone astray would have warmed the heart

of Thomas Reid (1710-1796), the father of the Scottish

Philosophy. It was essentially an enthusiastic and rather

uncritical student reading of the history of philosophy

through Reid's eyes. Over three decades later, however,

Park was still willing to endorse this youthful treatise

with the following note: "At the time of writing this

composition I was sixteen years...old. I have made no

improvement since."[2]

Park's attachment to Common Sense Philosophy was

undoubtedly inspired and reinforced by his father's

intellectual commitments. Reid and his disciple Dugald

Stewart (1753-1828) were central figures in the elder Park's

reading and teaching.[3] Their ideas were common topics of

discussion in his home, and it is likely that young Edwards

was already reading Stewart's Mental Philosophy before he

entered Brown.[4] Certainly, as his junior oration on

---

[1]The mss. of these and other college compositions are in the C. R. Park Family Papers (private collection, Nashville, Tennessee).

[2]Composition with note of endorsement in C. R. Park Family Papers.

[3]See the letter from Jacob Ide in Sprague, Annals, II, 462.

[4]Park's early interest in this book is mentioned in Alexander McKenzie, Memoir of Professor Edwards Amasa Park (Cambridge, Massachusetts: John Wilson and Son, 1901), p. 6.

philosophy implies, the literature of the Scottish
Philosophy formed a major part of his reading, both
curricular and extracurricular, throughout his college
years. Important items in that reading included Reid's
Works and Harvard Professor Levi Hedge's Elements of
Logick (1816), a standard "Common Sense" text.[1] Since Park
lived at home during his freshman year and since his father
continued to teach at Brown during most of the son's tenure
there, the elder Park undoubtedly gave personal and decisive
direction to his son's selection and study of these and
other philosophical works in the "Scottish mold."

But there was another class of literature to which
Calvin Park was equally committed and in which he
enthusiastically tutored his precocious son. This was,
broadly speaking, the literature of eighteenth-century
British rational apologetic, particularly that directed
against Deism.[2] Samuel Clarke's Boyle Lectures on The
Being and Attributes of God received considerable attention from the young Park, particularly during his last

---

[1]Park's use of the library copies of these works
was particularly noticeable during the spring of 1825
when he was preparing his philosophical oration. Old
Brown library records indicate that he checked out volumes
of "Reid's Works" on March 5 and 25, and "Hedge's Logick"
on April 1 and 22.

[2]cf. John J. Dahm, "Science and Apologetics in
the Early Boyle Lectures," Church History, XXXIX, 2
(June, 1970), 176-186.

year of college.[1] In addition, his father and the Brown
curricular requirements saw to it that he was thoroughly
immersed, during his junior and senior years, in the major
works of William Paley (1743-1805): The Principles of
Moral and Political Philosophy (1785), Natural Theology
(1802), and especially the famous View of the Evidences of
Christianity (1794). Paley's utilitarian moralism and his
external, mechanical view of revelation made a lasting and
highly significant impression upon Park's mind. Finally,
in contrast to the somewhat popularizing tendencies in
Paley's thought, the profound arguments of Bishop Butler's
Analogy of Religion (1736) occupied a major portion of
Park's senior-year studies. He found himself in fundamental
sympathy with Butler's goal of establishing an analogy or
conformity of the truths of religion with what is observed
in nature. But the extent of his comprehension of the
subtle distinctions and qualifications involved in the
principle of analogy is not at all certain. What is certain
is that Park's early study of Clarke, Paley, and Butler left
him with a lasting conviction of the well-nigh unlimited

---

[1]According to Brown library records, Park checked out
"Clarke on the Attributes" on three separate occasions
during the summer and fall of 1825. Clarke (1675-1729), a
Cambridge-educated latitudinarian divine strongly influenced
by Isaac Newton, delivered these lectures in 1704. Though
critical of the Deists, he was in sympathy with some of
their teachings and had controversial Unitarian tendencies as
well. The ideas on free will which he expressed in his famous
correspondence with Leibnitz and in his attack on the
determinism of the Deist Anthony Collins gave decisive shape
to the "Arminian" position whose destruction Jonathan Edwards
sought in his weighty treatise on the Freedom of the Will.

value of reason and science in proving and expounding the
Christian faith.

*   *   *

In the nineteenth century, as in the eighteenth, that
faith, particularly in its orthodox Reformed expression, was
under increasing attack from devotees of reason and science.
Thus it was well, perhaps, that the young Park was able to
sharpen his apologetic wits in dialogue with the likes of
Clarke and Butler before he felt called upon to provide his
own reasonably "scientific" defense for American Congregational Orthodoxy. The most visible enemies of that
Orthodoxy during Park's years at Brown were called neither
"Deists" nor "Arminians" but "Unitarians."

Through his Enlightenment-oriented education, which
was very typical of the age, Park actually came to share
much of the philosophical outlook of the Unitarians and
found himself in sympathy with certain aspects of their
critique of Orthodoxy, particularly in regard to the doctrine
of native depravity.[1] But his family background and
religious training made any serious adherence to Unitarian
doctrine on his part well-nigh impossible. With his Brown
classmates, he debated at length the doctrinal issues raised

---

[1]See Chap. VIII.

by Unitarianism.[1]   He also joined with a large number of
these classmates in their "rebellion" against the administration of President Asa Messer, a Baptist whose reputed
Unitarian sympathies had alienated many influential
Providence residents and Brown alumni.   Before that
"rebellion" (Messer's term) came to an end, both Park's
father and the President had resigned their posts, and Park
had had his first personal brush with the painful divisiveness of the Unitarian controversy.   But his motives for
involvement in the Brown phase of that controversy and the
effects of that involvement on his later thinking are not
at all clear.

The trouble at Brown took early and repeated turns
toward violence.   Large numbers of students, no doubt
encouraged by their elders, began to damage college property
and to disrupt classes during Park's junior and senior
years.   Unlike previous instances of essentially non-
malevolent student rowdyism, these new disorders were
"deliberate, organized, and protracted."[2]   Their aim
seemed clearly to be the removal of President Messer from
office.   Messer used strict disciplinary measures to halt
the disturbances and, as a result, incurred increasing
student hostility; for he then came to be labeled both

---

[1]See Foster, Life, p. 45; Storrs, Memorial Address,
p. 28.

[2]cf. Bronson, History, p. 188; for a detailed account
of the entire anti-Messer affair and its theological
ramifications, see pp. 186-192.

"Unitarian" and "tyrant." Park's part in the anti-Messer revolt was apparently limited to deliberate absence from senior recitations. And this he seemingly did as much from the pressures of group conformity as from any strong conviction of President Messer's theological or disciplinary errors.[1] Yet the President, deliberately misled by some of Park's own classmates,[2] singled him out as a leader of the disruptions and forced him to sign a special confession of guilt. This so infuriated Park that he refused to accept his valedictory appointment or even to attend commencement. That refusal in turn made him, willy-nilly, a leader in a major commencement boycott which led to Messer's resignation and to his replacement by the able Francis Wayland.

Park's father, whose recent resignation may have reflected his own problems with the Messer administration, supported his son in this commencement disruption; and so, too, did a majority of the townspeople and Brown alumni, who doubted Messer's orthodoxy. Park was seen as a kind of student hero who had delivered his college from heterodoxy. But his action was probably motivated as much by accidental circumstances and personal pique, both with his fellow students and with Messer, as by serious doctrinal

---

[1] See Scott in Park and Pupils, pp. 13-14, upon which the following account of Park's motives and actions in the Messer dispute is largely based.

[2] cf. Foster, Life, p. 47.

14

conviction.[1]   Nevertheless, the whole Messer affair caused
him to begin to think more seriously about the theological
commitments inherited from his family. What did such commitments imply in terms of vocational goals? This was, understandably, the major question troubling him when he left
Brown in the summer of 1826 (he received his degree despite
his absence from commencement) to take a temporary teaching
position with the classical school of Weymouth Landing,
Massachusetts.

Park had held such positions even before his college
graduation and had acquired an enviable reputation for
effective pedagogy.[2] But at Weymouth, his mind was on much
more than teaching college preparatory requirements. For
it was there that he undertook the intensive self-examination
which led to his decision to enter the ministry.[3] He could

[1]Park's attitudes toward Messer and his reputed
heterodoxy were curiously ambivalent, at least as they
appear in his later reminiscences. On one occasion, he
accused the Brown president of outright duplicity in secret-
ly holding Unitarian beliefs while maintaining an orthodox
front for the sake of the college: see Park to "Dr. Stockbridge" (identity uncertain), October 13, 1888, Brown
University Library. However, in another context, no less
conducive to candor than the first, Park unreservedly
endorsed the sincere good faith and effective leadership
of the Messer administration (see his comments in Bronson,
History, p. 197). For more on this matter, see Park's
appraisal of Messer in Sprague, Annals, VI, 327-333.

[2]See Park, "Rules and Directions to Instructors"
(8-p. ms., undated, probably 1824-26, in C. R. Park Family
Papers), in which he summarizes, for the benefit of others,
some of the practical wisdom gleaned from his teaching
experience in the Providence area.

[3]cf. Scott in Park and Pupils, p. 16; and Storrs,
Memorial Address, pp. 27-30, upon which the ensuing account
of Park's "conversion experience" is largely based.

not remember a time when he had not been interested in the "subject of religion." But that interest, he feared, was more intellectual than experiential. He had never experienced an "overwhelming sense of sin" with an ensuing "sharp point of crisis," during which he was brought "out of previous darkness into...marvelous light."[1] In other words, he had never been "converted" and, for that reason, was not only wary of committing himself to the ministry, but was not even sure he could sincerely call himself a Christian and apply for full church membership.

This concern with the state of his soul had plagued his childhood and had increased markedly in college as he came more and more to consider himself beyond the pale of grace.[2] At Weymouth, with the choice of a lifework weighing heavily upon him, the question of personal salvation became almost an obsession with him. He gave serious consideration to the professions of law and medicine as means of avoiding that all-important question. But, he reasoned, "If I could not preach honestly, I could not do anything honestly."[3]

He therefore decided to test himself in order to discover once and for all what his true inner attitude

---

[1]cf. Storrs, Memorial Address, p. 29.

[2] See his address (dated June 26, 1824) before the Brown Theological Society examining what for him had become a burning personal question: "Can Anyone Be Saved Without a Change of Heart in This Life?" (ms. in Park Family Papers, Yale University Library).

[3]From Storrs, Memorial Address, p. 30.

16

toward the doctrines of Christianity really was. Toward this
end he put himself through a rigorous doctrinal examination.
His purpose, in good Edwardsean fashion, was to learn not
only whether he believed, but also "whether he loved the
doctrines of the Bible, especially those which are commonly
disliked and opposed by men, concerning God's character
and sovereignty, His decrees of election, His attitude
toward sin."[1] His conclusion was that he did indeed
believe and love these doctrines and was willing to spend
his life preaching and defending them. Thus the commitment
to Congregational Orthodoxy which he inherited from his
father in a formal, intellectual sense became at last
a seriously examined, personally appropriated vocational
commitment.

As a result of this commitment, Park's tenure at
Weymouth lasted only six months. He then spent a year
studying theology with his father, who had assumed pastoral
duties in Stoughton, Massachusetts, after his resignation
from Brown. In retrospect, Park felt that he "learned
more of theology than ever anywhere else" during his year
at Stoughton.[2] He studied "Clarke on the Attributes" with
renewed interest under his father's careful direction. He
also studied the ever-increasing literature of the Unitarian
controversy and actually contributed to that literature

[1]Ibid.

[2]"Autobiographical Fragments," in Foster, Life, p. 53.

through an article in the Spirit of the Pilgrims entitled
"Which Society Shall You Join, the Liberal or the Orthodox?"[1]

This was Park's first theological publication, and it
reflected the growing seriousness with which he had come to
view the issues raised by Unitarianism since he left college.
The article purported to be an "impartial inquiry" into the
means by which one might test the validity of the two
opposing "systems" of Liberalism (Unitarianism) and
Orthodoxy. Its suggestions were not very original, but
they indicate the direction Park's thinking was beginning
to take. In order to decide between the Liberal and
Orthodox "societies," Park argued, one must "endeavor,
first, to ascertain which is the true, and which the false
system; and, secondly, which is the beneficial, and which
the injurious, system."[2] Here Park was combining criteria
valued by both sides in the Unitarian controversy in a
manner which forecasted the mediating apologetic stance
characteristic of many of his later writings. His test of
truth or falsity was Scripture, the last resort for much
of the anti-Unitarian polemic on the part of the Orthodox.
But Scripture was obviously not enough to clinch one's
decision between the two opposing parties. One must still
determine which system better promotes piety and morals,

---

[1]Subtitled "A Letter to a Friend," Spirit of the
Pilgrims, I, 5 (May, 1828), 234-248; reprinted that same
year as a pamphlet by Peirce and Williams, Boston.

[2]Ibid., p. 236.

or good character (i.e., is more beneficial). And in that kind of utilitarian determination, the Unitarians tended to be more at home than the Orthodox.

Park did not state openly which system passed his twin tests, but there were enough hints in the article to leave few readers in doubt. In effect, he was calling for the defense of Orthodoxy not only through traditional Scriptural appeals but through the acceptance and use of the Unitarians' own favorite moralistic (and rationalistic) presuppositions and arguments. Given the theological commitments evident in this article, it is scarcely surprising that within three months of its publication its author was standing in the grave presence of Leonard Woods (1774-1854) to be examined for admission to Andover Theological Seminary. Little did Woods know that the young man he was examining would one day succeed him in the influential Abbot Chair of Christian Theology.

*   *   *

The Abbot Chair was one of the original professorships established when Andover was founded in 1808 as an adjunct to Phillips Academy.[1] Taking advantage of certain legal

---

[1]The following summary account of Andover history is based upon Leonard Woods, History of the Andover Theological Seminary (Boston: James R. Osgood and Company, 1885), and Henry K. Rowe, History of Andover Theological Seminary (Newton, Massachusetts: For the Seminary, 1933).

and financial provisions for a theological school at the
Academy, a group of "Old Calvinist" clergy and laymen
decided to counter the heterodoxy of Harvard by establishing
a "West Point" of Congregational orthodoxy in Andover.
After considerable negotiation and deliberation, a group
of "Consistent Calvinists," or "Hopkinsians," decided to
make common cause with their Congregational brethren to
present a united orthodox front against the Unitarians.

There were, however, significant theological differences
between these two groups. The "Old Calvinists" were
content to have the Westminster Shorter Catechism as the
sole doctrinal standard of the new seminary. The Hopkinsians,
on the other hand, wanted to make clear their dissent from
such irrational and "inconsistent" Westminster doctrines
as the imputation of Adam's sin and Christ's righteousness
to a helpless humanity. This faction of Andover's constituency, known as the "Associate Founders" since they
joined an already initiated endeavor, drew up a carefully
worded "Associate Creed" to protect their specific "New
Divinity" doctrinal interests. The Creed, though nominally
a compromise document representing the views of both
founding groups,[1] tended to emphasize an individualistic
understanding of sin and righteousness based upon acts of
personal responsibility.

---

[1] cf. Leonard Bacon's "Commemorative Discourse" in
A Memorial of the Semi-Centennial Celebration of the
Founding of the Theological Seminary at Andover (Andover,
1859), pp. 95-101.

Faculty subscription to this Creed was to be required
at five-year intervals. The Associate Founders were dis-
trustful of the Phillips Academy trustees, to whom the
original Old Calvinist founders had entrusted the over-
sight of the seminary. By a complicated and portentous
legal arrangement, they therefore established a three-
man Board of Visitors, whose primary responsibility proved,
in practice, to be the evaluation of faculty adherence to
the Creed. Naturally, the Abbot Professorship, because of
its sensitive character vis-à-vis Andover's doctrinal
standards, received close Visitorial scrutiny, even though
it was not endowed by the Associate Founders. Later it
would become the center of controversy as Trustees and
Visitors vied for authority at the seminary. But its
first occupant, Leonard Woods, had the confidence of
both groups.

*   *   *

Woods had been an influential mediating force in
the founding of Andover. He stood in the Edwardsean
theological line of Hopkins and Emmons, but a degree of
ambiguity surrounded his true theological commitments.[1]
Though perhaps advantageous in view of the sensitive
professorship he held, that ambiguity, coupled with his

---

[1]See F. H. Foster, A Genetic History of the New
England Theology (Chicago: The University of Chicago
Press, 1907), pp. 357ff.

poor showing against Harvard's Henry Ware (1764-1845) in the "anthropological phase" of the Unitarian controversy, made Park somewhat suspicious of this important Andover professor. Nevertheless, Park boarded with Woods and learned a great deal from him both in and out of the seminary classroom. The young Brown graduate's theological acumen, in turn, made a lasting and highly significant impression upon the mind of his teacher.

In addition to Woods, the Andover faculty of Park's day was dominated by two other luminaries. One of these was Moses Stuart (1780-1852), the father of modern critical biblical scholarship in America. This remarkable scholar was called to Andover in 1810 as Professor of Sacred Literature after a revival-filled, four-year pastorate at New Haven's Center Church. Self-taught in Hebrew and German, he became living proof that the evangelical spirit of Timothy Dwight, under whose spell he fell at Yale, and the best German critical scholarship could coexist amicably in the same person. This combination of knowledge and vital piety made a lasting impact upon Park's thinking. He was inspired by the missionary scholars who left Stuart's classroom to convert the heathen and to translate the Scriptures into numerous strange tongues. The respect for linguistic erudition learned from his father made Park marvel at a man who made up his own Hebrew and Greek grammar texts to replace inadequate European models, and who had just completed a remarkable exegetical-critical

commentary on Hebrews (1827-28) when Park entered Andover.
But Park seemed even more impressed with the way in which
Stuart's immense scholarly labors appeared to enhance,
rather than to impair the effectiveness and popularity
of his preaching, lecturing, and conversation.

In sum, one could argue that the most important
thing Park learned from Stuart was a healthy appreciation
for critical biblical study in the German mode. An
orthodox Congregationalist, Park came to believe, had
little to fear and much to gain from the proper application
of such study. In turn, he accepted a number of Stuart's
general hermeneutical assumptions about the Scriptures.
For example, Stuart's rejection of literal or verbal
inspiration in favor of a less rigid understanding of the
"plenary" authority of the Bible exerted an important
influence upon Park's own developing notions of biblical
interpretation.[1] He agreed with Stuart that many parts
of the Bible, when literally interpreted, contained a
number of problems and contradictions. But, like Stuart,
he also believed that many of these could be reduced or
eliminated through a more holistic reading of the Scriptures.
In other words, it was the whole, not the parts, which
should ultimately be viewed as the inspired and perfect
rule of faith and practice. In addition, it was religious,

---

[1]Stuart's notions of inspiration were not always
pleasing to his more conservative colleague Leonard
Woods: see Woods, History, pp. 153-154.

not scientific truth which formed the content of this inspired rule, in the eyes of both Stuart and Park.

Park did not accept the precise manner in which Stuart blended the canons of dogma, spirit, and reason in his hermeneutics. He did not share Stuart's caution in regard to the effects of a priori dogmatic conclusions (such as those in Andover's "Associate Creed") upon impartial, critical exegesis. And his reading of Scripture tended to be less open to the "inspiration of the Spirit" and more rationalistic than Stuart's. But, on the whole, he could appreciate the value of Stuart's exegetical methods, particularly when applied to doctrinal disputes. Such a dispute flared up during his senior year at Andover when Stuart and the ultraconservative Charles Hodge of Princeton found themselves at odds over the doctrine of imputation of original sin. The controversy focused particularly upon the proper interpretation of Romans 5:12-21, where a typological parallel is drawn between the sin of all men in Adam and the possibility of salvation for all in Christ.[1]

Following the text in his usual close manner, Stuart admitted that the passage in question assumed a relationship between Adam's sin and the sin of all mankind, but he felt that the precise nature of that relationship was left

---

[1]This famous pericope is well summarized in v. 18 as follows: "Therefore as by the offence of one judgment came upon all men to condemnation; even so by the righteousness of one the free gift came upon all men unto justification of life." (KJV)

unexplained. He preferred to believe that the passage assigned no guilt without personal responsibility for actual sin. And his exegesis rather effectively brought out the Pauline emphasis (so dear to the revivalist) upon the blessings procured by Christ for all men, at least potentially, as opposed to the universal evils of Adam's transgression. Hodge, on the other hand, tried to read a more pessimistic and juridical confessional position into the Pauline pericope. In the eyes of God, all men were regarded as sinners before any personal transgression of their own. The sin of Adam was "imputed" to his descendants in a divine transaction which was basically unrelated to their actual moral character.[1] This dispute left neither side convinced of error, but Stuart's position tended to be stronger than his opponent's because he kept his eyes on the text and tried to avoid reading dogmatic presuppositions into it.[2] His methods and his doctrinal

---

[1] The above treatment of the Hodge-Stuart imputation controversy owes much to Stephen J. Stein, "Stuart and Hodge on Romans 5:12-21: An Exegetical Controversy about Original Sin," Journal of Presbyterian History, XLVII, 4 (December, 1969), 340-358.

[2] This, of course, is not to say that Stuart had no presuppositions of his own. He may have admired German biblical scholarship more than did Hodge, but he was not completely willing to let the exegetical chips fall where they might. He and Hodge, after all, represented the partisan Reformed theological interests of "New School" evangelicalism and "Old School" confessionalism, respectively. Though they disagreed over the rigidity with which one should adhere to the letter of Scripture or creed, they both feared the German-style "neologies" that seemed to flow from unrestrained biblical criticism. In addition, Stuart shared with his Andover colleagues and with Hodge the intellectual outlook of the Scottish Philosophy. Thus, when he attacked Hodge's

conclusions did not go unnoticed by Park. They would prove
particularly useful to him in his own future conflict with
Hodge.[1]

Reinforcing the influence of Stuart upon Park were
three Andover-trained biblical scholars, all of whom Park
came to know as a seminarian, but whose lives and careers
continued to impinge upon his long after his student days
at Andover. One of these was Calvin Stowe (1802-1886),
translator and biblical critic, who was Assistant Instructor
in Sacred Literature at Andover when Park was studying
there and who later, after his marriage to the famous
Harriet Beecher, became Park's neighbor and colleague on
the Andover faculty. Another was Edward Robinson (1794-
1863), skilled philologist, librarian, and Professor
Extraordinary of Sacred Literature during Park's senior year
at Andover. Later, as Professor of Biblical Literature at
Union Theological Seminary in New York, Robinson became
known for his biblical research in Palestine and founded
(in 1843) the influential quarterly Bibliotheca Sacra.
Modeled after the scholarly European theological journals

---

doctrine of imputation by appealing to a "universal sense"
of justice and fairness, a concept of divine benevolence
based on that sense, and an equation of all guilt with
personal responsibility, he was, in effect, adopting the
"Common Sense" interpretation of Paul.

[1]The foregoing account of Stuart and his relationship
to Park's theological development is chiefly indebted to
John Herbert Giltner, "Moses Stuart: 1780-1852" (Yale
University: unpublished Ph.D. dissertation, 1956); and to
Park's Discourse Delivered at the Funeral of Professor
Moses Stuart (Boston: Tappan and Whittemore, 1852).

of the day, this remarkable serial "sacred library," under
the editorship of Park and his colleagues, became the Andover
"house organ" for some forty years. One of the most
important of Park's editorial collaborators on the
Bibliotheca Sacra was still another Stuart-trained biblical
scholar, Bela Bates Edwards (1802-1852). Edwards and Park
first met as students at Andover and later received faculty
appointments there within a year of each other. Their
children intermarried, and their families developed a very
close and long-lasting relationship.[1] In short, throughout
most of his long association with Andover, first as student
and later as professor, Park would find himself surrounded
by the ideas, the scholarship, and the disciples of Moses
Stuart. Such a pervasive intellectual presence and influence
could scarcely fail to make a decisive, long-term impact
upon his thought.

A third dominant figure on the Andover faculty during
Park's student days was the venerable Ebenezer Porter (1772-
1834), Professor of Sacred Rhetoric, President of the seminary, and founder of the important Porter Rhetorical Society,
before which some of the most significant theological figures
of the day were invited to lecture. Porter, a pupil of the
Edwardsean John Smalley, occupied a patriarchal position
on the faculty which symbolized Andover's strong evangelical

---

[1]This relationship is revealed in countless letters in
the C. R. Park Family Papers. See also Park's "Life and
Services of Professor B. B. Edwards," Bibliotheca Sacra,
IX, 36 (October, 1852), 783-821.

commitments. He was the resident teacher and practitioner of that art so dear to American evangelicals: the art of revival preaching. His well-known Letters on Revivals and other like works stressed the practical effect of doctrines, such as divine sovereignty, when preached to unconverted sinners.[1] His writings were avidly read and annotated by Park, whose presidency of the Rhetorical Society during his senior year placed him in a close and admiring relationship to the great "Dr. Porter."[2] Later when Park himself was called upon to instruct Andover's rhetoric classes, he would rely heavily upon the works and example of his former teacher.[3]

Under the influence of Porter and other like-minded faculty members, the Andover of Park's student days was

---

[1]cf. Ebenezer Porter, Letters on the Religious Revivals Which Prevailed about the Beginning of the Present Century (Boston, 1858, c1832), p. 111 (on divine sovereignty).

[2]See Storrs, Memorial Address, p. 31; also see letter of F. R. Shipman to O. H. Gates, November 6, 1928 (Andover Newton Theological School Library) which describes some of the books (and their annotations) in Park's library.

[3]Porter's widow actually donated her husband's lecture notes to Park when he was appointed to teach Sacred Rhetoric at Andover. In her letter accompanying the notes, she expressed the hope that Park would "more than fill" the position vacated by her late husband. See Mrs. Lucy P. Porter to E. A. Park, probably fall, 1836, in C. R. Park Family Papers. The notes themselves (3 vols., ms. dated 1823; also in C. R. Park Family Papers) indicate that Porter combined instruction in the practical arts of preaching with extensive consideration of important doctrinal questions (original sin, free will, etc.)--a practice Park would continue and expand.

alive with evangelical zeal. Swollen by a flood of converts
from successive waves of campus revivals at such colleges
as Williams and Amherst, the enrollment had increased
dramatically since the seminary's founding in 1808. With
the increased enrollment had come a corresponding growth
in the seminary's influence and prestige. The quality and
enthusiasm of both faculty and student body were high.
So, too, was the degree of their involvement in home and
foreign missionary activity, Sunday School work, and the
like. Andover's future seemed to lie in the harvest of
revivalism, and thus far, that future seemed bright indeed.

   To this haven of evangelicalism, on the eve of Park's
graduation (in 1831), came the man who would inspire and
dominate the "Third" Great Awakening of the 1830's: Charles
Grandison Finney (1792-1875). Naturally, this peripatetic
evangelist from the "burned-over district" of upstate New
York was welcomed with open arms by students, faculty, and
townspeople alike. His growing reputation had preceded
him and was not marred in the least by the controversial
nature of his methods and doctrines, which had once
threatened his entry into New England. Religious feeling
was running so high at the seminary during Finney's visit
that the anniversary (graduation) exercises were canceled
so that nothing would interfere with the "work of the Lord."
Park described his own first encounter with Finney's
preaching with enthusiasm:

          The house was crowded, and I was given a seat
          with a number of men on a bench against the

> back wall. I was absorbed by the pathos of
> the preacher. After a time I felt the bench
> tremble beneath me, and I looked around to
> ascertain the cause. The men on the bench
> were all crying; and then I discovered that
> I was crying too![1]

If the emotional side of his nature had been suppressed in

childhood, it was now given full vent in the religious

fervor aroused by a great evangelist.

                    *   *   *

Rejecting an invitation to teach Biblical Literature

at Bangor Theological Seminary, Park left Andover in the

summer of 1831 to accept a pulpit call to the town of

Braintree, near Boston. Braintree was a parish of farmers

and mechanics, not greatly unlike those in upstate New

York among whom Finney had held his first successful

revivals. The town had in fact been stirred for some time

by the waves of evangelical zeal created by Finney and

others. Park was actually called there to be a temporary

replacement for the eminent Richard S. Storrs II, an old

friend of the Park family whose evangelical sympathies had

led him to take a five-year leave of absence to become a

traveling agent for the American Home Missionary Society.

Already accustomed to an emotive and animated style of

preaching, the congregation was deeply moved by the fresh

and earnest appeals of the young seminarian. In no time

---

[1] Quoted in Foster, Life, pp. 59-60.

30

at all, a revival of sorts was under way. Following the
example of Finney, Park preached continually, on Sunday
and during the week, in his church and in local school-
houses (in some of which he had once taught during his
college days). Also inspired by Finney were his efforts
to preach without notes, to dramatize the Scriptures, and
to mingle "logic and tears" in his attempts to win souls.

The revival lasted about four months, was moderately
effective in producing converts, and served to establish
Park's reputation, in neighboring parishes and beyond, as
a preacher of uncommon skill and power.[1] But it marked the
climax of his active participation in anything resembling
Finneyite evangelism. For Park's destiny lay with the
lecture desk rather than the pulpit. His inner religious
experience, despite all his prayerful self-examination,
came ultimately through a gradual, spiritual and intellectual
maturation, not through a sudden burst of emotion. And his
encounter with Finney, despite its emotive impact, did not
really change this fundamental aspect of Park's nature.
This is not to say, however, that Park ceased to believe in
the value of revivals or failed to support them. He was
convinced that they were an effective deterrent to Unitarianism. But an improved Orthodox theology could, he felt, be
even more effective in this regard. And it was the construction of such a theology which would consume most of his

---

[1]cf. Storrs, Memorial Address, pp. 36-37.

active career.

Nevertheless, Park always felt that good theology would serve and promote good evangelical preaching. And though his Braintree revival was his last, he never lost interest in writing and preaching good sermons. When the revival at Braintree was over, he settled down to write a series of about thirty sermons based upon the final scenes in the life of Christ. He labored long and hard over this series, and some of his results were masterpieces. Two of these, the so-called "Judas" and "Peter" sermons, were so highly regarded by preacher and congregation alike that they remained in Park's file for decades, were revised and repreached on countless occasions, and were selected by his daughter Agnes to appear in her Memorial Collection of his best sermons.

Both reveal Park's early skill in making the Scriptures personally relevant and alive with dramatic imagery and psychological insight. For example, after a vivid, imaginative recounting of Jesus' betrayal, which produced a steady buildup of listener interest, the "Judas" sermon reached a sudden and dramatic climax when the minister cried:

> Is there or is there not some Judas Iscariot
> in this church? There are to be found many
> Judases at the last--is there one of them
> here? Are you unsuspected in your Christian
> walk? So was Iscariot honored and trusted
> until that evening when the generous woman
> wasted the ointment. Is the question going

32

                    around the seats, Who then is the faithless
                    disciple? Let us determine who it is.[1]

The sermon then concluded with a pointed recitation of

some of the common sins of churchgoers.

                    *   *   *

     Sermons like this gave Park a wide and lasting

reputation for pulpit oratory. He began to receive calls

to larger parishes, including Boston's Old South Church.

He also was urged to teach rhetoric at the Presbyterian

seminary in Auburn, New York. But periodic health problems,

particularly deteriorating eyesight, were beginning to make

an extended vacation seem essential. He therefore declined

all offers of new positions and left Braintree in August

of 1833 for a year of rest and travel. His professional

future again lay heavily upon his mind. If his two years

at Braintree had allowed him to develop the confidence and

skill to become an effective preacher, they had also con-

vinced him that preaching alone was not enough to provide

him with complete vocational fulfillment. He was not

altogether sure how to achieve such fulfillment, but he

decided to accept the next good offer of a teaching position

he received.

     Coupled with this vocational quandary was a theological

_____

     [1]Park, "Judas," in Memorial Collection of Sermons,
Agnes Park, compiler (Boston: The Pilgrim Press, 1902),
p. 71.

one. Park was becoming increasingly dissatisfied with the
theological training he had received from Leonard Woods. As
a result of this dissatisfaction, he journeyed to New Haven
in the winter of 1834-35 to hear the lectures of Yale's
Nathaniel W. Taylor (1786-1858).[1] His mind could scarcely
have been better prepared for what he heard. He had just
spent more than a year in rest, travel, and serious thought.
His thoughts turned not only to his own future but to the
future of Orthodox Congregationalism as well. That future,
he felt, was seriously jeopardized by the inadequate
apologetic position of Woods.

The Unitarians, he believed, were essentially correct
in demanding that their Orthodox opponents reconcile traditional Reformed notions of native depravity with the benevolent character of God. He was dismayed that Woods, in his
debate with Ware, had, on the whole, avoided this issue

---

[1]Graduate of Yale College, intimate friend of Lyman
Beecher, and protégé of Yale's revival-minded president
Timothy Dwight, Nathaniel William Taylor became perhaps
the chief theological architect of the Second Great Awakening and the "Evangelical United Front" in America. Exposed
to both "Old Calvinist" and "New Divinity" influences, he
sought to make the New England theological tradition
preachable and understandable in an optimistic, democratic
age. While still in his twenties, he succeeded Moses
Stuart as pastor of New Haven's prestigious Center Church,
and there gained a reputation for both intellectual and
homiletical prowess. Largely on the basis of that reputation, he was appointed in 1822 to the Professorship of
Didactic Theology in the newly formed Yale theological
faculty. His many students and the Quarterly Christian
Spectator spread his revival-oriented "New Haven Theology"
far and wide. See Sidney Earl Mead, Nathaniel William
Taylor, 1786-1858: A Connecticut Liberal (Chicago: The
University of Chicago Press, 1942).

by taking refuge in a barrage of biblical texts.[1] He was
even more dismayed that Woods had later seen fit to attack
Taylor's famous Concio ad Clerum, preached at Yale in 1828
before the Congregational ministers of Connecticut. In the
Concio, Taylor had attempted to answer Unitarian objections
to the Orthodox anthropology by defining depravity as "man's
own act, consisting in a free choice of some object rather
than God, as his chief good," and by declaring that man's
nature was the "occasion, or reason" for sin, not its
inherently corrupt physical cause.[2] Woods found Taylor's
explanations of sin to rely too heavily upon the will of
man and not enough upon the will of God. He preferred to
see the existence of human depravity as a mystery bound up
in the inscrutable purposes of an omnipotent Deity.[3]

Park saw Woods' position as dangerously close to those
deterministic notions, attributed to the Orthodox by their
Unitarian opponents, which seemed to make God the author of
sin. He regarded Taylor's understanding of depravity as
more apologetically viable. His winter in New Haven was
thus an important intellectual experience for him. He

---

[1]On the famous "Wood'n Ware" debate of the early
1820's, see H. Shelton Smith, Changing Conceptions of
Original Sin: A Study in American Theology since 1750
(New York: Scribner's, 1955), chap. 4.

[2]Nathaniel W. Taylor, Concio ad Clerum. A Sermon
Delivered in the Chapel of Yale College, September 10,
1828 (New Haven: Hezekiah Howe, 1828), pp. 8 and 13.

[3]cf. Woods, Letters to Rev. Nathaniel W. Taylor
(Andover, 1830), p. 37.

took notes assiduously as Taylor defended the justice and
benevolence of the Orthodox God through such notions as
"moral government," "power to the contrary," and an ambiguous distinction between the "inevitability" and the "necessity" of sin.[1] In an age dominated by evangelicalism,
democratic optimism, and Scottish "Common Sense" Philosophy,
a theology which emphasized divine sovereignty and original
sin was a distinct liability. Taylor clearly realized this
and, despite the intra-Orthodox furor he aroused, perse-
vered in making conservative Reformed doctrine more amena-
ble to the times. His efforts in this regard found a
receptive ear in Park, who was finding less and less to
admire in the theology of his former teacher Leonard Woods.[2]

In the spring of 1835, Park left New Haven to take a
teaching position at Amherst. In addition to "Mental and
Moral Philosophy" in the Scottish mode, he was to teach
rhetoric, Hebrew, and a special exegetical course on the
Epistle to the Romans. His father's example and his
education at Brown and Andover well qualified him for his
new duties. And he welcomed the opportunity to influence
and train Amherst's young ministerial students, many of
whom were on their way to Andover. One of the periodic
college revivals which usually awakened ministerial

[1]Some of these notes are still extant in the C. R. Park
Family Papers.

[2]cf. Foster, Genetic History, pp. 473 and 483ff.,
regarding Park's shift in theological allegiance from Woods
to Taylor.

intentions was actually under way when Park arrived on
campus, but he assumed no active leadership in it.[1] He
did, however, preach regularly in the college chapel and
in neighboring churches during his brief tenure at Amherst.
And he found his more educated congregations to be as
deeply moved by his "Judas" and "Peter" sermons as were
the farmers and mechanics of Braintree. In general, he
seems to have been well received at Amherst as both teacher
and preacher, but he was not entirely happy there. His
real interests had come to lie in ministerial training,
and he found too much chaff mixed in with the wheat on the
college level.

He was, therefore, more than happy to accept an appointment to Andover's Bartlet Professorship of Sacred Rhetoric
in the fall of 1836. Leonard Woods had made a special trip
out to Amherst in the summer of that year to persuade Park
to come to Andover. But the trip was hardly necessary.
Park had been offered the position of his dreams, and he
was not about to reject it. In September he was married
to Anna Maria Edwards of Hunter, New York, a great-grand-
daughter of Jonathan Edwards and a great-grandniece of
Benjamin Franklin.[2] Thus began two long-lasting and highly

---

[1]See William S. Tyler, A History of Amherst College...
from 1821-1891 (New York: Frederick H. Hitchcock, 1895),
pp. 275-276; for the general "state of the college" when
Park arrived, see chap. V.

[2]See Timothy and Rhoda Ogden Edwards of Stockbridge,
Mass., and Their Descendants: A Genealogy, compiled by
William H. Edwards (Cincinnati: The Robert Clarke Company,
1903), pp. 97-98; and Scott in Park and Pupils, p. 24. Anna

significant marriages in Park's life: his marriage to
Andover, which consumed the remainder of his active career
(almost fifty years), and his marriage into the family of
Jonathan Edwards, whose last "lineal disciple" Park proved
to be.

Maria Edwards (1812-1893) was the eighth child of William
Edwards and Rebecca Tappan. Though born in Northampton,
she lived most of her unmarried life in Hunter. She was
educated at some of the best girls' schools in New England,
including Catherine Beecher's in Hartford. Since Park
himself was not an Edwards descendant, she was his only
genealogical link to that famous family.

Chapter II

THE ANDOVER YEARS:
PROFESSOR OF PREACHING AND THEOLOGY

Park arrived at Andover at a crucial time. Porter's
retirement in 1831 from the Chair of Sacred Rhetoric had
left a void which was difficult to fill. Other theological
schools--Union, Auburn, Yale, East Windsor, Bangor--were
beginning, with increasing success, to compete for students
with Andover. An effective preacher was desperately needed
in the Bartlet Chair, and Park was an excellent choice for
the job. He threw himself into his work with fervent
dedication, preparing lectures on preaching, preaching himself, incisively criticizing student sermons, and conducting
weekly Gesellschaften focusing upon the rhetorical benefits
of great literature. The goal and the achievement of all
this labor was, in the words of one admiring student, to
show "eloquence in the pulpit the noblest of fine arts...,
requiring a powerful enthusiasm in the soul, contemplating
the exhibition of loftiest themes, directed to the securing
of immortal results...."[1]

Park published extensively on homiletical method, both

---

[1]Richard Salter Storrs, Edwards A. Park: Memorial
Address (Boston: Press of Samuel Usher, 1900), p. 44.

during and after his Bartlet tenure.[1] Well representative
of his views in this area was an article describing the
acquisition of "Power in the Pulpit" which appeared
after his first decade at Andover.[2] Powerful preaching,
declared the Andover divine, possessed the following
essential elements: a sound "argumentative" approach;
a positive and certain conviction of the doctrinal
truths presented, which yet avoids controversy if
possible; a perspective and plan allowing for the presentation of important truths "singly" as well as in their
"proper combination"; a free expression of the minister's
heart which avoids repressing the "spontaneous out-
gushings of his soul"; and, in general, an "affectionate-
ness, a simplicity and an humbleness of Christian feeling."
Here one can see at work the interplay of intellect
and feeling which would decisively shape Park's

---

[1]Included in his contributions to the subject were the
following: "Plainness as a Quality of Sermons," Christian
Review, V, 20 (December, 1840), 481-510; "The Elocution of
the Pulpit," in William Russell, Pulpit Elocution (Andover:
Allen, Morrill and Wardwell, 1846), pp. 14-21; a long series
of essays under the general title "The Three Fundamental
Methods of Preaching," which included "The Writing of Sermons,"
Bibliotheca Sacra, XXVIII, 111 (July, 1871), 566-598, and
XXVIII, 112 (October, 1871), 707-739; "The Public Reading of
Sermons, and the Preaching of Them Memoriter," Bibliotheca
Sacra, XXIX, 113 (January, 1872), 157-195; and "Preaching
Extempore," Bibliotheca Sacra, XXIX, 114 (April, 1872), 339-
383, and XXIX, 116 (October, 1872), 720-770; and finally a
two-part article on "The Structure of a Sermon--the Text,"
Bibliotheca Sacra, XXX, 119 (July, 1873), 534-573, and XXX,
120 (October, 1873), 697-728.

[2]"Power in the Pulpit," Bibliotheca Sacra, IV, 13
(February, 1847), 96-117.

theological career. A good sermon had to appeal to both
heart and head, to both the poetic and the prosaic side of
man's nature.

In regard to the former side, Park continued throughout
his career to write and speak in support of revivalism and
evangelical piety. He was always concerned to find, in the
words of one of his later articles, "Methods of Perpetuating
an Interest in Hearing the Gospel."[1] One such method was
the writing and distribution of inspirational biography.
This might take any form from articles in reference works
to a full-scale "Memoir," as with that Park attached to his
edition of his friend Bela Bates Edwards' writings.[2] Or it
might involve the distribution of some of the many funeral
and memorial sermons preached by the Andover professor,
such as that at the funeral of Moses Stuart.[3] It might
also simply involve commendatory introductions to inspiring
biography.[4] But whatever form it assumed, the aim was

[1]Bibliotheca Sacra, XXVIII, 110 (April, 1871), 334-365.

[2]cf. Writings of Professor B. B. Edwards (Boston:
John P. Jewett and Company, 1853), I, 1-370; see also the
"Memoir" attached to the Writings of William Bradford Homer
(Andover: Allen, Morrill, and Wardwell, 1842), pp. 13-136.

[3]A Discourse Delivered at the Funeral of Professor
Moses Stuart (Boston: Tappan and Whittemore, 1852).

[4]See, for example, Park's "Introduction" to the
Autobiography of William G. Schauffler, for Forty-nine Years
a Missionary in the Orient (New York: Anson D. F. Randolph
and Company, 1877), pp. ix-xxxv; see also his "Introduction"
to Mary Lamson's Life and Education of Laura Dewey Bridgman,
the Deaf, Dumb, and Blind Girl (Boston: New England
Publishing Company, 1879), pp. i-xxx.

fundamentally the same: to interest the "heart" in the
gospel through the experience of some pious person. In
the final analysis, however, saintly lives were but
supplemental to the heart-directed "appeal" of a good
evangelical sermon. It was this which most effectively
won over the sinner and "perpetuated an interest in hearing
the gospel." And the Bartlet Professor, a connoisseur of
such appeals, saw to it that his students and the Andover
constituency at large were well acquainted with the best
specimens of the day, including his own.[1]

But preaching, in Park's eyes, included much more than
emotive entreaties to sinners. On appropriate occasions,
it could involve considerable political and social comment
as well. When, for example, the Andover divine was called
upon to deliver a Massachusetts election sermon, he felt
quite comfortable in describing the divine sanction of
government and the manner in which the church upheld the
state by promoting benevolent activities, political virtue,
and the like.[2] If the times seemed to demand it, he was
also capable of devoting one of his many ordination sermons[3]

---

[1]cf. Park's "Influence of the Preacher," in Henry Clay
Fish, Pulpit Eloquence of the Nineteenth Century...Contain-
ing Discourses of Eminent Living Ministers in Europe and
America, with Sketches Biographical and Descriptive (New
York: M. W. Dodd, 1857), pp. 13-30.

[2]Park, The Indebtedness of the State to the Clergy
(Boston: Dutton and Wentworth, 1851).

[3]In a letter to Brown librarian Harry Lyman Koopman
(November 13, 1894; ms. Brown University Library), Park
indicated that he had preached seventy such sermons.

to a political or social theme. As the Civil War began, he
preached such a sermon on "The Imprecatory Psalms Viewed in
the Light of the Southern Rebellion."[1] Though willing to
admit that there was "no joy in heaven at the misery of the
rebels," he yet insisted upon seeing the conflict as a holy
war waged to save America for her divine mission of spreading
liberty and Christianity throughout the world.[2] To support
such a providential view of the war, he turned to those
Psalms which described the enemies of the Lord and drew
what seemed to him obvious parallels. Could there be any
doubt of the reference when, for example, the Psalmist
found these enemies to be "confederate against thee"?[3]

To focus, however, upon Park's limited pulpit comment
on politics and society or his concern for the evangelical
appeal of a sermon is, in the end, to miss his primary
emphasis as a professor of "sacred rhetoric." This was his
effort to see that the preaching of his students reflected
a sound doctrinal foundation. While he occupied the Bartlet
Chair, he preached several series of elaborate doctrinal
sermons in the seminary chapel, ranging over such topics as
conscience, regeneration, natural and moral law, the divine

[1]Bibliotheca Sacra, XIX, 73 (January, 1862), 165-210.
First published as a pamphlet entitled A Discourse Preached
at the Ordination of Rev. Walter S. Alexander over the
First Congregational Church in Pomfret, Connecticut (Andover:
Warren F. Draper, 1862).

[2]Ibid., pp. 182,191,210.

[3]Ibid., p. 191; cf. Psalm 83:5b KJV.

44

decrees, and natural theology.[1] His colleague and former
teacher Leonard Woods took his place among the students to
hear the young professor expound his views on such controversial themes as the nature of sin, free agency, and the
like.

The venerable Abbot Professor was probably not entirely
pleased with what he heard. Park had a confidence in the
natural man with which Woods, remembering his debates with
the Unitarians, was no doubt uneasy. The new professor's
view of the relation of nature to revelation seemed harmless
enough: "Natural religion," said he, "waits upon the soul
as far as to the porch of the temple, and there gives up her
escort to the Bible...."[2] But he would not allow the Bible
to be used to prove total depravity. Such a pessimistic
anthropology simply could not be included among the revealed
mysteries which one had to accept on faith. It would undermine man's ability to know and act freely according to his
best reason and experience. Park was sure that, fundamentally speaking, "man was constituted right."[3]

---

[1]cf. Storrs, Memorial Address, p. 50. In one of his
"Annual Reports to the Board of Trustees of Andover
Theological Seminary," required of faculty members by the
constitution of the seminary, Park mentioned the months of
labor expended on these chapel sermons. He obviously
regarded them as integral to his training of young preachers
(cf. the "Report" dated September 2, 1844; ms. Phillips
Academy Archives).

[2]Park, "Natural Theology: Sermon 6," January 3, 1846
(ms. in C. R. Park Family Papers), p. 1.

[3]Park, "Natural Theology: Sermon 7," January 3, 1846
(ms. in C. R. Park Family Papers), p. 42.

*   *   *

Whether or not Woods approved the doctrinal foundation
being laid in these sermons for the preaching of the
Bartlet Professor's students, he could scarcely question
Park's effectiveness in chapel or lecture hall. And that
effectiveness was proving to be a significant spur to
Andover's enrollment. Park's influence was clearly on the
rise at the seminary, and two important events during his
tenure in the chair of sacred rhetoric aided that rise.
One of these was his first trip to Europe (mainly Germany)
in 1842-43. That trip introduced him first-hand to the great
German centers of theological learning at Berlin and Halle.
His writing and teaching thereafter would never be the same.

His landing in Hamburg produced considerable cultural
shock. A staunch New England Congregationalist could find
little to admire, for example, in the revelry of the Conti-
nental Sabbath. It was "not a day of spiritual rest to the
Hamburghers," he declared. "It was a day of pleasure,
parties, rides, dinners, and amusement of all kinds."[1] But
the intellectual "shock" of Berlin was even greater. He
engaged two young _Privatdocenten_, Philip Schaff and Karl
Kahnis, to instruct him in the theology of Schleiermacher
and the philosophy of Hegel. The two apparently had little

---

[1]Park, European Journal Notes (1842-43; ms. in C. R.
Park Family Papers), I, 1-2.

success, however, in leading their American pupil through the tortuous paths of German speculation.[1]   More to Park's liking, and understanding, were the exegetical methods of the evangelical Lutheran biblical scholar Ernst Wilhelm Hengstenberg. First introduced to those methods through his association with Moses Stuart, the Bartlet Professor admired the way in which the Lutheran exegete combined dogma, piety, and reason in his higher critical hermeneutics. Hengstenberg's lectures were one of the high points of Park's stay in Berlin.[2]   Also high in his esteem were the lectures of the great Berlin church historian J. A. W. Neander, though he failed fully to

---

[1]Ibid., II, 35-37; for Schaff's own account of his and Kahnis' encounter with Park in Berlin, see David S. Schaff, The Life of Philip Schaff (New York: Charles Scribner's Sons, 1897), p. 65. For Park's correction of this account, in regard to Kahnis, see George R. W. Scott, "Professor Edwards Amasa Park: Biographical Sketch" in Professor Park and His Pupils, ed. D. L. Furber, et al. (Boston: Samuel Usher, 1899), pp. 34-35. Also see Frank H. Foster, The Life of Edwards Amasa Park (New York: Fleming H. Revell Company, 1936), p. 122. Park's early personal association with Schaff in Berlin was destined to be continued when Schaff came to Andover in 1862-63 to fill an interim vacancy in the professorship of ecclesiastical history between the terms of W. G. T. Shedd and Egbert Smyth (see chap. VI). Park apparently developed considerable respect for the learning of his erstwhile Berlin tutor; for when the latter came to America, he became a frequent and not unsolicited contributor to the Bibliotheca Sacra. It should be noted that Park's initial interest in Schleiermacher, hardly a "safe" theologian in the eyes of New England orthodoxy, was probably sparked, not by Schaff and Kahnis, but by Moses Stuart's widely noticed translation (in 1835) of a work by Schleiermacher on the doctrine of the trinity /see the Biblical Repository and Quarterly Observer, V (April, 1835), 265-353; VI (July, 1835), 1-116/.

[2]cf. Foster, Life, p. 123.

comprehend Neander's historical methodology.[1]

Berlin's great academic resources did not impress Park, however, as much as those at Halle. There he met two "mediating" theologians who extensively influenced him: August Tholuck, pupil of Neander, and Julius Müller. Finding much of German Protestant theology and church life imprisoned in a "dry and rather paralyzing formalism," the Andover divine heard the warmly evangelical preaching of Tholuck with joy and relief.[2] Though he felt the Halle professor's bias against reason and dogma was a little too extreme, Park had high regard for the piety and moral emphasis of his sermons, lectures, and biblical commentaries.[3] Tholuck's concern for the moral dimension of the life of faith was strongly shared by Müller, his friend and

---

[1]Ibid. Neander's influence on Park is discussed in the next chapter.

[2]Ibid., pp. 120, 124. See also Park, "Journal Letters from Europe, 1842-43" (to wife): Halle, March 11-March 13, 1843, pp. 13-15; Halle, March 16, 1843, pp. 21-24; Halle, March 29-April 7, 1843, pp. 4-6 (mss. in C. R. Park Family Papers). Also see entry dated March 26, in European Journal Notes, Vol. IV, p. 1 (mss. in C. R. Park Family Papers).

[3]Even before he went to Germany, Park had translated some of Tholuck's sermons and written a sketch of his "life and character." For the sermons, which typify Tholuck's pietistic moralism, see Selections from German Literature, ed. and trans. B. B. Edwards and E. A. Park (New York: Gould, Newman, and Saxton, 1839), pp. 115-198. The "life and character" sketch, designed to be read with, and to increase the personal effect of the sermons, occupies pp. 201-226 of the same volume. Also in this volume is Park's translation of a Neander-like edificatory piece by Tholuck on "The Life, Character and Style of the Apostle Paul." This work and Park's translations of Tholuck's sermons may also be found in The Biblical Cabinet (Edinburgh: Thomas Clark, 1840), XXVIII, 33-51 and 85-98.

colleague on the Halle faculty. This was especially evident in Müller's understanding of sin as a free act on the part of each individual. Park's own concept of sin as act rather than state borrowed much supporting elaboration from this otherwise orthodox and highly conservative Lutheran theologian.[1]

Andover's Bartlet Professor returned from Europe with a healthy, if not uncritical, appreciation of German learning and culture. He made two other trans-Atlantic voyages later in his career (1863-64 and 1869-70), but neither matched the intellectual impact of his first venture abroad. On his later trips, he simply renewed old acquaintances, consulted Berlin physicians about his recurrent health problems, and, in general, spent more of his time as tourist than as visiting scholar.[2] His attitudes toward and use of German philosophy and theology were decisively and lastingly shaped by his initial first-hand encounter with them.[3] Nowhere was this shaping more apparent than in the second important, influence-building event of his Bartlet tenure: the beginning of his editor-

---

[1]cf. Foster, Life, p. 124. Of course, the influence of Moses Stuart in this regard is not to be discounted.

[2]Ibid., chaps. IX and XII; see also Scott, in Park and Pupils, pp. 35ff.

[3]cf. George P. Fisher, "Professor Park as a Theologian," The Congregationalist, LXXXV, 24 (June 14, 1900), p. 871.

ship of the Bibliotheca Sacra.[1] In 1844, just after his
return from Europe, he joined with his friend Bela Bates
Edwards in designing a German-style scholarly periodical
for the Andover community. The result was the quarterly
"house organ" Bibliotheca Sacra, whose influence spread
far beyond the seminary's constituency.

The fruits of Park's European studies began to appear
in the very first number of the new journal. He used his
much improved command of German to translate at length
from Tholuck's unpublished theological lectures.[2] Soon
thereafter came articles more directly related to the
Bartlet Professor's professional concern: expositions
and illustrations of homiletical and rhetorical principles
derived from such German masters in the field as Franz
Volkmar Reinhard and Heinrich August Schott.[3] Throughout

---

[1]On the general history and influence of this long-
lived journal, see Frank Luther Mott, "The Bibliotheca
Sacra," in his A History of American Magazines, Part I,
1741-1850 (Cambridge, Massachusetts: Harvard University
Press, 1938), I, 739-746. See also John Henry Bennetch,
"The Biography of the Bibliotheca Sacra," and Arnold D.
Ehlert, "Genealogical History of the Bibliotheca Sacra,"
Bibliotheca Sacra, C, 397 (January-March, 1943), 8-30 and
31-52. Also see Samuel L. Boardman, "The Bibliotheca
Sacra," New England Historical and Genealogical Register,
XXXVI, 3 (July, 1882), 339-340.

[2]August Tholuck, "Theological Encyclopedia and
Methodology," trans. Edwards A. Park, Bibliotheca Sacra,
I, 1 (February, 1844), 178-217; 2(May, 1844), 322-367;
3 (August, 1844), 552-578; 4 (November, 1844), 726-735.

[3]cf. Park, "Schott's Fundamental Principles of
Rhetoric and Homiletics," Bibliotheca Sacra, II, 5
(January, 1845), 12-48; "Schott's Treatise on the Subject-
Matter of Sermons," Bibliotheca Sacra, III, 11 (August,
1846), 461-499; "Schott's Treatise on the Structure of
a Sermon," Bibliotheca Sacra, V, 20 (October, 1848),

Park's four-decade editorship of Andover's serial "sacred
library," the latest "German theological intelligence"
continued regularly to grace its pages. When unable to
rely on his own knowledge of that "intelligence," the
editor employed various "foreign correspondents," many of
them his own students studying in Germany.

These were not always Congregationalists. Following
the German model, Park tried to make the Bibliotheca Sacra
a broad-based forum of free scholarly inquiry, which cut
across "sectarian," or "partisan," lines.[1] One of his
best German correspondents, for example, was Methodist
theologian William Fairfield Warren, a student of Park's
in the 1850's, who became an authority in the field of
comparative religion and was the first president of Boston
University. Episcopalians, Unitarians, and numerous other
denominational representatives also contributed to the
Andover journal. And the range of subjects treated was
broad, indeed. There were articles on missions and education,
on social issues (such as slavery), on non-Western languages
and religions, on biblical criticism and archeology, on
systematic and historical theology, and so on. In the
latter category, along with the expected material on the
New England Theology, were German items ranging from

731-750; and "Reinhard's Sermons," Bibliotheca Sacra, VI,
22 (April, 1849), 330-337, and VI, 23 (July, 1849), 507-
534.

[1]See the statement of editorial policy in Bibliotheca
Sacra, XIV (1857), 460.

Julius Müller on sin to Ferdinand Christian Baur on the atonement. Park himself contributed an average of one major signed article a year during his editorship, on topics ranging from Aristotle to American theological education. His reviews, most unsigned, ran into the hundreds.[1] Since substantial works like those he reviewed came infrequently from his own pen, it is not unfair to say that his career, as defined by publications, was principally bound up in the volumes of the Bibliotheca Sacra.

*   *   *

The contributions and influence of an editor of Park's caliber would be difficult to overestimate. He used his German learning and his increasingly respected "German" journal to form and speak to an audience of pastor-scholars. And that audience included a significant segment of America's evangelical Protestant leadership. A man who was doing as much as Park to increase Andover's enrollment and prestige could not long be denied the seminary's most coveted faculty appointment: the Abbot Professorship of

---

[1]See Bibliography for a representative sample of these. Park's "philosophy of reviewing" was formed early, as indicated by a "college exercise" he prepared as a student at Brown entitled "Effects of Critical Reviews" (1824; ms. in Brown University Library). Reviews, said the future editor ("Effects," p. 2), should be a self-revelation for the authors reviewed and should "correct the tastes and opinions of mankind in general."

Christian Theology. But the appointment did not come
without a degree of dissension. The Bartlet Professor's
relationship with the two senior members of the faculty,
Woods and Stuart, was not entirely harmonious. One source
of discontent was the cavalier manner in which Park
repeatedly rejected Stuart's proffered contributions to
the Bibliotheca Sacra.[1] Another stemmed from theological
differences between Woods, who wanted to please both the
Old Calvinist and the Hopkinsian constituency of Andover,
and Park, who wanted to commit the seminary more distinctly
to "Consistent Calvinism."[2] Coupled with these differences
were various personal and professional jealousies which
caused Park to wonder if he would ever be allowed to take
Woods' place.[3]

Nevertheless, though perhaps harboring reservations

---

[1] cf. letter of Park to Bela Bates Edwards (then in
London), Andover, June 14, 1846 (ms. in S. P. Scattergood
Family Papers; private collection, Philadelphia), wherein,
among other things, the conflict between Stuart and his
former pupil over these rejections is discussed.
The writer is indebted to Professor Thomas A. Schafer
of McCormick Theological Seminary for bringing this letter
to his attention.

[2] Woods' position in this regard is well outlined in
his Theology of the Puritans (Boston: Woodbridge, Moore,
and Company, 1851), entire, but especially pp. 13-14. In
this pamphlet, he attempted to prove the existence of a
common "Puritan theology" to which both "Old" and "New"
("Consistent") Calvinists adhered. Deviations from this
common Reformed theological standard among those claiming
to be orthodox New England Congregationalists either
involved non-essential doctrinal points or consisted
"chiefly in phraseology." Andover's "Associate Creed,"
he believed, was a good representative statement of this
common Puritan theology.

[3] See the letter of Park to B. B. Edwards (cited above),

on the matter, Woods finally invited the young professor
of preaching to teach the doctrines he had been proclaiming
from the chapel pulpit. In the academic year 1846-47,
Park replaced Woods on an interim basis; and in the summer
of 1847, the replacement became permanent with his formal
induction into the Abbot Chair. That induction did not
have the unanimous approval of the Andover Trustees.[1] One
of them, Daniel Dana, a conservative Presbyterian minister
from Newburyport who had served since the seminary's
founding, addressed a letter of protest to his fellow
trustees on the very day the new Abbot Professor was
officially to take office. In essence, he charged that
Park could not honestly sign the Westminster Catechism, as
the laws of the seminary required, because of the new
professor's heretical notion that "actual sin is the
character, and /that an/ evil nature is not, strictly
speaking, the character, of the being who sins."[2]

Failing to get a positive hearing from the other
trustees, Dana published his protest for the benefit of

---

in which he expressed concern for the future of Andover
if Woods remained entrenched in his position much longer.
Though events proved him wrong, he (Park) saw little
hope at the time (summer, 1846) that his elder colleague
would soon retire. See also Foster, Life, pp. 117-118.

[1]cf. Park to B. B. Edwards (cited above) in which
Trustee reluctance to allow Woods' retirement is discussed.

[2]Daniel Dana to the Trustees of Andover Theological
Seminary, Andover, June 2, 1847 (ms. in Phillips Academy
Archives).

the "religious public," but drew limited response.[1] The
doctrinal, legal, and historical issues which he raised
regarding the Abbot Professorship, though little noticed
at the time, were nonetheless proleptic of things to come
at Andover.[2] But on this occasion Park and his supporters
were in firm control of the situation and easily prevailed.
Intra-faculty jealousies and discord, though gradually
abating, did not end with Woods' retirement, however. It
was no easy task to get along with Park. Even his close
friend Bela Bates Edwards, who replaced Stuart the year
after Park's new appointment, frequently found himself in
a state of estrangement.[3] He and Park strongly disagreed,
for example, over the preaching role of the Abbot Professor.[4] Park felt that it should be large, and this

---

[1]cf. Daniel Dana, A Remonstrance Addressed to the
Trustees of Phillips Academy, on the State of the
Theological Seminary under Their Care, Sept., 1849
(Boston: Crocker and Brewster, 1853), 24p., and the
sympathetic Review of Dr. Dana's Remonstrance by an
anonymous "layman" (Boston: Crocker and Brewster, 1853),
40p. See also /George Allen/, The Andover Fuss: or, Dr.
Woods Versus Dr. Dana on the Imputation of Heresy Against
Professor Park Respecting the Doctrine of Original Sin
(Boston: Tappan and Whittemore, 1853), 31p., which
maintained that Park was no more heretical than Woods,
whom Dana supported. The "fuss" got some attention in
the religious press, especially in the pages of the newly
founded Congregationalist and the newly revived Panoplist
(see Bibliography); but it tended to be overshadowed by
Park's debate, on many of the same doctrinal points, with
Charles Hodge of Princeton (see following chapters).

[2]See chapter on "The Great Disruption."

[3]cf. Foster, Life, p. 118.

[4]cf. Park to B. B. Edwards (cited above), p. 3.

brought him into conflict with another good friend, Austin
Phelps, the new Bartlet Professor. Phelps' author-daughter
Elizabeth confessed years later to a degree of misgiving
on the occasions she heard Park preach. "I think I usually
began with a little jealous counting of the audience,"
said she, "lest it should prove bigger than my father's."[1]

Nevertheless, these differences between Park and his
colleagues were never very serious; for, in most cases,
they freely granted him the leadership role he determinedly
sought at the seminary. During the years 1853-68, the
peak of his career, he served as "President of the Faculty,"
a post roughly equivalent to the modern deanship. Little
that concerned Andover, whether great or small, failed to
receive his attention during this period. The school's
constituency seemed to regard him as the very embodiment
of what Andover stood for. Though he engaged in a broad
spectrum of activities, it was in his theological lectures
that this embodiment took its decisive and most influential
shape. "As a lecturer he had no superior," declared one
of his students; and this sentiment was echoed by countless
others.[2]

When one examines the notes of his students today,
however, it is sometimes difficult to believe they meant

[1]Elizabeth Stuart (Phelps) Ward, Chapters from a
Life (Boston: Houghton, Mifflin, and Company, 1897), p. 40.

[2]George B. Frost to Owen H. Gates (Andover-Harvard
librarian making inquiries about Park's lectures), Andover,
no date, probably fall, 1928 (ms. in Andover Newton
Theological School Library), p. 3.

this. They were quick to admit that, when read to the
class by others (e.g., when he was ill), the Abbot Professor's remarks were "logically compacted, free from
illustrations, and dry as bonedust."[1] But joined with his
"remarkable personality," Park's lectures were something
entirely different; and, as one of his admirers put it,
"it would be difficult to reproduce his system of theology
without the collateral part of their delivery."[2] Though
he always brought to class "a large black bag" from which
he drew "a voluminous pile of papers" and "several books,"
he did not simply read or dictate propositions to his
audience.[3] He had before him the "main heads" of what he
would say, but the "treatment under each head was left to
the inspiration of the hour."[4] That inspiration might at
times take strange turns: "Two students in Phillips
Academy," recalled one member of his class, "were involved
in a burglary during our middle year. The case attracted
wide attention, and for several days it was used as a

---

[1]Ibid., p. 2.

[2]William F. Slocum to Owen H. Gates, Newton Centre,
November 14, 1928 (ms. in Andover Newton Theological School
Library), p. 2.

[3]cf. Henry A. Stimson to Owen H. Gates, New York,
November 15, 1928, p. 1; Arthur W. Kelly to Gates, Auburn-
dale, Massachusetts, November 15, 1928, p. 1; and Frost to
Gates (cited above), p. 2 (mss. in Andover Newton Library).

[4]Charles F. Thwing to Owen H. Gates, Cleveland,
November 15, 1928 (ms. in Andover Newton Library), p. 2.

telling illustration of many points in the theological course."[1]

Thus, though Park's lectures were indeed "very systematically planned, with many numbered divisions and subdivisions," they were by no means "dry as bonedust" to those who flocked to hear him during the height of his career.[2] The annual theological feast laid before his enthusiastic classes began with "Preliminary Remarks" on terminology, sources of knowledge (e.g., nature and Scripture), and the like. It then moved on to topics appropriate to the methods of natural theology: the existence and attributes of God, immortality of the soul, prevention of sin in a moral system, and so on. Next came proofs of biblical inspiration, followed by expositions of such revealed truths as the Trinity, the person of Christ, and the divine decrees. Then came the heart of Park's system: anthropology, including treatments of sin and free will; and soteriology, which took in the atonement, regeneration, sanctification, and justification. Finally, the Abbot Professor rounded out the year with eschatology and ecclesiology, and made some concluding

---

[1] Kelly to Gates (cited above), p. 2.

[2] Ibid., p. 1.

comments on the "advantages" of his theological system.[1]

The reasoned movement of his lectures through that system, though designed to follow a fundamentally orthodox Reformed course, was nonetheless bold and provocative. When later critics were inclined to caricature Park's work as a theologian, one who had grown up in intimate contact with that work rose to defend it: "There is a scarecrow which 'liberal' beliefs put together, hang in the field of public terror or ridicule, and call it Orthodoxy. Of this misshapen creature we knew nothing in Andover."[2] Unfortunately, the "scarecrow" image has tended to prevail. And this is probably due, in large part, to the often prolonged and seemingly sterile polemics in which Andover was continually embroiled. Park's first major theological battle, pitting him against Charles Hodge of Princeton, arose from ideas which, as expressed by the Abbot Professor, were anything but sterile, however. The background and context of these ideas, their exposition, and the controversy they provoked will form the subjects of the next three chapters.

---

[1]For an outline of Park's lectures see Edmund Kimball Alden, Notes on Park's Lectures on Systematic Theology (1846-47; ms. in Oberlin College Library), pp. 13-16; also see David Dana Marsh's Notes (1866-67; ms. in Andover Newton Theological School Library), pp. 766ff.

[2]Ward, p. 53.

Chapter III

INTELLECTUAL RELATIONSHIPS: RATIONALISM,
IDEALISM, AND HISTORY

Park's fundamental metaphysical commitment, as
previously indicated, was to a philosophy known as
Scottish Common Sense Realism. He found that commitment
to be in perfect resonance with his theological heritage.
"New England divinity," he declared, "has been marked by
a strong, practical common sense."[1] The context of this
remark made it abundantly clear what sort of "common sense"
he had in mind. He proudly linked "our later /New England7
theologians" with the philosophy of men like Thomas Reid
and Dugald Stewart. Reid and Stewart were, in fact, Park's
intellectual patron saints, if one can judge by the number
of adulatory references he made to them. He was fascinated
by Reid's apparent skill in refuting Berkeley and Hume,
though he felt that Reid's attention to the former was
really a "work of supererogation" since Berkeleian
philosophy had few living disciples and was "harmless"

---

[1]Park, "New England Theology," Bibliotheca Sacra,
IX, 33 (January, 1852), 191.

within the Anglo-American "Aristotelian" milieu.[1] As for

the erudite works of Stewart, Park showered them with

some of his highest praise as a reviewer.[2]

The attention Park gave these two Scotsmen is hardly

surprising when one realizes how central they were to the

formulation and exposition of Common Sense Philosophy. At

Aberdeen, as a college regent and Philosophical Society

member,[3] and later at Glasgow, as Adam Smith's successor

in moral philosophy, Reid became in many ways the key

architect of the Scottish Philosophy. As a parish minister,

he was awakened from his idealistic slumbers by Hume's

Treatise on Human Nature (1738-40); but he eventually

developed an answer to Hume's skepticism through a

"realistic," as opposed to an "ideal," or "representational,"

theory of perception.[4] He found Hume's disturbing arguments

---

[1]See the translators' "Introduction" to Selections from German Literature, ed. and trans. B. B. Edwards and E. A. Park (New York: Gould, Newman, and Saxton, 1839), p. 3.

[2]See Park, "Review of Stewart's Active and Moral Powers," Bibliotheca Sacra, VII, 25 (January, 1850), 191-193.

[3]On the significance of the Aberdeen Philosophical Society, see James McCosh, The Scottish Philosophy (New York: Robert Carter and Brothers, 1880; c1874), pp. 227-229.

[4]A good brief introduction to (and some interesting criticisms of) Reid's somewhat confusing realistic theory of perception, posed as an alternative to the "ideal hypothesis," may be found in McCosh, pp. 208-213. See also the excellent critical treatment of this subject in A. D. Woozley's "Introduction" to Reid's Essays on the Intellectual Powers of Man (London: Macmillan and Company, 1941; c1785), pp. x-xxv.

to be based upon the false notion that "nothing is
perceived but what is in the mind which perceives it."
In other words, "we do not really perceive things that
are external, but only certain images and pictures of them
imprinted upon the mind...."[1]

To counter Hume's representational assumptions, Reid
studied the mental processes of sensation and perception
and came to the "common-sense" conclusion "that every
operation of the senses...implies judgment or belief,
as well as simple apprehension."[2] For example, the perception of a tree involves not merely a mental impression
but a judgment as to the real existence, shape, etc., of
the tree. Such a judgment is not arrived at by reasoning
or proof but is an "original" and "natural" outgrowth of
the perceiving faculty, "a part of that furniture which
nature /and the Almighty7 hath given to the human understanding."[3]

In arguing that sensation carries with it an
immediate, directly known judgment about external reality,
Reid was attempting to establish the validity of self-

---

[1]Thomas Reid, An Inquiry into the Human Mind on the
Principles of Common Sense (Edinburgh: Bell and Bradfute;
and William Creech, sixth edition, 1810; c1764),
"Dedication," p. vii.

[2]Ibid., ch. vii, p. 471; see also Reid, Intellectual
Powers, edited and abridged by A. D. Woozley, II, 5,
pp. 78-82.

[3]Reid, Inquiry, ch. vii, p. 472.

evident principles of universal human consciousness
("common sense") which lie at the base of all rational
proof and discourse. The reasoned denial of such
principles, which are actually anterior to experience,
Reid called "metaphysical lunancy."[1] Included on his list
of perceptual self-evidents were concepts like substance
and causality. But as he continued to survey the inner
landscape of man's conscious mind faculty by faculty, he
began to discover other self-evident principles besides
those revealed by perception.[2] For example, he found that
self-consciousness as a whole elevates mind over matter by
revealing "that such beings only as have some degree of
understanding and will can possess active power."[3] He also
found that "moral approbation implies a real judgment" based
upon objective principles known to universal human intuition.
To imply that such approbation is nothing but a subjective
(and changeable) feeling would, Reid felt, be a surrender

---

[1]Ibid. One should compare Kant on this point. See
Woozley's "Introduction" to Reid's Intellectual Powers,
pp. xxxii-xl.

[2]This "surveying" of the inner landscape of consciousness was a highly refined "empirical" art among the Scottish
Philosophers and their adherents. Park himself was a
skilled practitioner in the science (broadly defined) of
psychology, or "mental philosophy," as revealed, for
example, in his long, careful review of "/Francis/ Wayland's
Intellectual Philosophy," Bibliotheca Sacra, XXI, 46
(April, 1855), 403-415.

[3]Reid, "Essays on the Active Powers of Man," in The
Works of Thomas Reid, Vol. II, ed. William Hamilton
(Edinburgh: MacLachlan and Stewart, 1863, sixth edition;
c1788), I, v, p. 525.

to ethical relativism. And that position was as enveloped
in "metaphysical lunacy" as the "ideal theory" of perception,
which placed the existence of the external world in subjective doubt.[1]

Such was the Common Sense philosophy of Thomas Reid.
Its substance was little changed by its chief exponent
Dugald Stewart. From his position in the chair of moral
philosophy at Edinburgh, which he assumed in 1785, Stewart
gained an international following for the Scottish
Philosophy, particularly in France and America. That Park
found the philosophy of Reid and Stewart popular among
New England's "later theologians" is eloquent testimony
to the extent of this international hegemony of "Common
Sense." But not every American theologian who accepted
this hegemony would have considered himself Park's
"theological kin." For during the late eighteenth and
early nineteenth centuries, Scottish Realism managed the
philosophical conquest of a remarkably broad spectrum of
American theological endeavor, from the ultra-orthodoxy
of Princeton Presbyterianism to the ultra-liberalism of
Harvard Unitarianism.[2]

How did this conquest come about? The answer lies

[1]Ibid., V, vii, pp. 670-679. See also S. A. Grave,
The Scottish Philosophy of Common Sense (Oxford: Clarendon
Press, 1960), pp. 224-257.

[2]cf. Sydney E. Ahlstrom, "The Scottish Philosophy and
American Theology," Church History, XXIV, 3 (September,
1955), 257-272.

largely in the apologetic needs of the times. Faced with
the increasingly corrosive acids of secular rationalism,
many American Reformed theologians welcomed the opportunity
the Scottish Philosophy provided of proving the reasonableness of their orthodox tenets. This situation is not
without its irony, for Scottish Realism certainly did not
originate as a conservative effort to shore up a failing
orthodoxy. It arose during the eighteenth century as the
philosophical voice of the Unitarian-like "Moderate" party
within the strife-torn Church of Scotland. Molded by the
thought patterns of the Enlightenment, the Scottish adherents of this remarkable philosophy became the theological
liberals, not to say revolutionaries, of their day. Their
philosophy proved to be both simple enough for effective
communication in tracts and sermons, and yet intellectually
stimulating enough to conquer the major Scottish univer-
sities and to play a key role in the "Scottish Renaissance"
of the eighteenth and nineteenth centuries.

Apparently only American Unitarians were really at
home in this philosophical milieu. Yet, as indicated,
Common Sense Realism "came to exist in America...as a vast
subterranean influence, a sort of water-table nourishing
dogmatics in an age of increasing doubt."[1] The major
source of such dogmatic nourishment, from the point of
view of orthodox apologetics, seems to have been the

---

[1]Ibid., p. 268.

radical dualism--epistemological, ontological, and cosmological--of the Scottish Philosophy.[1] The clear subject-object distinction presupposed by Reid's theory of perception disallowed any heresy-supporting monistic view of the universe, whether idealistic or materialistic. Closely related to this anti-monistic posture was Reid's notion that mind alone is an active power or efficient cause, while matter is but an instrument in the hands of an intelligent being.[2] This dualism of active mind versus passive matter made possible an easy identification of human intellect and Divine Mind, and provided "arguments" for the existence of the soul and God as unassailable as the common-sense beliefs in a real external world and self-evident moral intuitions. For example, if a man like Reid chose to "argue for" belief in God, he simply proved the absurdity of non-belief. It is absurd not to accept God's existence, for such a position implies that no intelligence or will (active power) other than one's own actually exists.

One could go on to cite other orthodox theological advantages of the dualistic character of the Scottish Philosophy. For example, such a philosophy could be used to preserve God's transcendence over his creation, along with the consequent orthodox necessity of revelation.

---

[1]Ibid., pp. 267-268; cf. Reid's "Preface" to his Intellectual Powers, Woozley ed., pp. xlv-xlvi.

[2]cf. Grave, pp. 134-135.

At the same time, it allowed for an empirical affirmation
of science and a rationalistic concern for natural theology.[1]
It could be argued, however, that these apologetic
advantages came at a high price to an orthodox Reformed
theologian like Park. The optimistic, man-centered
rationalism of Scottish Realism would seem to co-exist
poorly with the theocentric, judgmental, paradoxical gospel
of Augustine, Calvin, and Edwards. But if the gospel were
to be heard at all in the nineteenth century, bold measures
were required. And Park's use of the Scottish Philosophy
to produce what amounted to a radical rationalization of
his Reformed heritage was just such a measure.

*   *   *

In shaping this rationalization, the Abbot Professor
relied not only upon the likes of Reid and Stewart, but
upon the eighteenth-century British apologists he had
learned to admire as a Brown undergraduate: Samuel Clarke,
William Paley, and Joseph Butler. From these sources he
fashioned a foundation of "natural theology" upon which
the revealed paradoxes of his Reformed faith could rest
securely. Through the reasoned light of nature man could

---

[1]Ahlstrom, "Scottish Philosophy," p. 268. An empirical,
or scientific, concern was evident from the very beginning
in Park's theological lectures. He urged his first Andover
theology class to "cultivate a delicate appreciation of
evidence." cf. Edmund Kimball Alden, Notes on Park's
Lectures on Systematic Theology (1846-47; ms. in Oberlin
College Library), p. 5.

discern the existence and many of the attributes of God.
He could discover basic ethical principles and note their
foundation in God's moral government of the universe.
He could even find evidence for the soul's immortality.[1]
But, most important, he could recognize the verity of
revelation.

In an age of rapid social and intellectual change,
marked by broad population movements and intercultural
contacts (including the missionary movement which Andover
heartily supported), Park believed the Christian revelation
had to be seen in the perspective of universal truth.[2]
Put another way, revelation had to be "reasonable." It
had to meet all men where they were, in such a way that
it could be recognized by all as authentic. Thus, people
who deprecated natural theology, Park told one of his
sacred rhetoric classes, were "sawing off the limb on
which they stand."[3] Finitude and depravity aside, man
had a basic natural ability to "distinguish truth from
falsehood in spiritual concerns." Without this ability,
he could not "discern the truth of the Scriptures" and

---

[1]See George Park Fisher, Notes on Park's Lectures on
Systematic Theology (1850-51; ms. in Yale University
Library), p. 83. Also see A Society of Clergymen /Park
and B. B. Edwards/, "Natural Theology," Bibliotheca Sacra,
III, 10 (May, 1846), 248.

[2]cf. Park and Edwards, "Natural Theology," pp. 244-
245.

[3]Cited from Robert Coit Learned, Notes on Park's
Lectures on Sacred Rhetoric (1840-41; ms. in Andover Newton
Theological School Library), p. 121*.

68

would be led into "the most fatal skepticism" vis-à-vis
revelation.[1]

This natural discernment of scriptural truth actually
began with a natural knowledge of God, since "the logical
order of our processes is to believe in the existence of
a being before we consider the truth or falsehood of his
declarations."[2] Not merely his existence, but his fundamental attributes as well, had to be demonstrated from
his works in nature before his "words" in scripture could
be authenticated. In particular, God's benevolence had
to be visible in his works before his words could be
believed. But a distinction could be made in this regard,
which allowed the words to be subsumed under the works,
thus having scripture prove itself, so to speak. The
Bible, Park averred, represented both a higher form of
the natural "wisdom of the world" and a decisive divine
revelation.[3] In its former capacity, it could be used
"as one of the signs or arguments furnished by natural
theology" to demonstrate the benevolence of the Creator
and, in consequence, to validate his revealed words.[4]

[1]Park and Edwards, "Natural Theology," p. 249.

[2]Ibid., p. 276.

[3]cf. F. H. Foster, A Genetic History of the New
England Theology (Chicago: The University of Chicago
Press, 1907), p. 478.

[4]Park and Edwards, "Natural Theology," p. 277.

Apologetics alone was not at stake here. The basic integrity of the divine-human encounter in revelation was also a factor in Park's concern for a sound natural theology. On the human side, this integrity involved the preservation of a degree of continuity between man's creaturely understanding and the divine message of revelation. Park heartily approved the theological maxim of Richard Baxter that "God never exacteth of men according to what they have not, but only requires a good use of what they have."[1] This meant, in the eyes of the Andover professor, that man's integrity as a creature of God would never be violated in his relationship with the Creator. Revelation did not totally contravene, but instead required a "good use" of, natural human powers of comprehension. On the divine side of things, the positive evaluation of these powers protected the integrity of God's judgment upon a sinful humanity in possession of more than enough knowledge to be left "without excuse."[2]

---

[1]cf. Park, "Richard Baxter's 'End of Controversy,'" Bibliotheca Sacra, XII, 46 (April, 1855), 368.

[2]Park often employed the well-known Pauline passages on this theme (e.g., Romans 1:18-25; 2:14-15) to defend his view of natural theology. cf., e.g., Park and Edwards, "Natural Theology," p. 251, and Park's sermon on "Conscience," in Discourses on Some Theological Doctrines as Related to the Religious Character (Andover: Warren F. Draper, 1885), pp. 260-261.

*   *   *

There were thus worthy apologetic motives and fundamental theological values involved in Park's rationalization of his Reformed heritage. But there were risks
involved as well. Important among these was the historyless tendency evident in many of his eighteenth-century
sources. Historical awareness was crucial to Park's
theological task if he were not to lose his Reformed moorings
in the process of getting his message across to his nineteenth-century audience. Yet, on the surface at least,
Common Sense rationalism was basically trans-historical
in outlook. It might thus appear that a more fruitful
metaphysical outlook for the nineteenth-century theologian
as rooted in a tradition as was Park lay in the realm of
romantic idealism.

The metaphysical flexibility of the Scottish Philosophy
should not be underestimated, however. It enjoyed an
eclectic versatility which enabled it, with varying success, to hold together an empirical viewpoint, symbolized
by men like Francis Bacon, and a rationalistic viewpoint,
derived in large part from Cambridge Platonism.[1] This
Platonic strain in the Scottish Philosophy was particularly
evident in the thought of Sir William Hamilton (1788-1856),

---

[1] cf. Torgny T. Segerstedt, The Problem of Knowledge in
Scottish Philosophy (Lund: C. W. K. Gleerup, 1935), pp. 3-
39. It was, of course, these two viewpoints—empirical and
rationalistic—which accounted for the apologetically
attractive dualism of the Scottish Philosophy.

a later adherent of the school who received cautious
approval from Park.[1] Given Hamilton's example, one could
argue that the French philosopher Victor Cousin (1792-1867)
was not, in principle, inconsistent in his attempt to
house Common Sense Realism and German idealism under the
same philosophical roof.

On the American scene, eloquent testimony to the
flexibility and versatility of Scottish Realism came from
the career of James Marsh (1794-1842) of the University
of Vermont. Marsh claimed to reject Common Sense thought
in favor of the idealism of Samuel Taylor Coleridge. But
he nonetheless combined rationalistic and romantic notions
in his theology. His aim was to recover the inner
spiritual vitality which he felt New England religion
had lost since the advent of Common Sense rationalism.
To do this, he placed heavy emphasis upon the subjective,
psychological basis of ethics and theology; and, almost
in spite of himself, he began to develop formulations
which sounded like a curious blend of Coleridge and Reid.

For example, his understanding of conscience lay
somewhere between Reid's original rational faculty, whose
judgments were based upon self-evident moral principles,
and Coleridge's more emotive feeling, or "sense," of
"moral responsibility," which arose from total human

---

[1]cf. Foster, Genetic History, pp. 472-473.

self-consciousness.[1] Marsh saw conscience as a rational
"power." And that power testified to the character of
human actions as judged against a "law of moral rectitude"
present to the consciousness of all. But he also saw it
as a "conscious feeling of obligation" which one should
"reverence" as a divine revelation.[2] A further example of
Marsh's combining a Common-Sense type of rationalism with
Coleridgean romantic tendencies can be found in his concept
of the atonement. He stressed the subjective, psychological
reference of the doctrine. And he felt he was consistent
in expressing that reference through both an emphasis on
the inward effect of the atonement upon the feelings (based
upon the organic relation between soul and incarnation) and
a regard for the vindication of God's moral government to
the rational mind.[3]

In formulating his understanding of conscience and of
the atonement, Marsh claimed to be recovering the idealistic

---

[1]cf. Reid, "Active Powers," in Works (Hamilton ed.),
Vol. II, Essay III, Pt. III, chs. vi-viii, pp. 589-599;
see also Samuel Taylor Coleridge, Aids to Reflection, ed.
James Marsh (New York: Gould, Newman, and Saxton, 1840;
c1829), p. 145.

[2]cf. James Marsh, "A Discourse on Conscience," in The
Remains of James Marsh, ed. Joseph Torrey (Boston: Crocker
and Brewster, 1843), pp. 403-411.

[3]cf. Marsh, "Review of Stuart on the Epistle to the
Hebrews," The Quarterly Christian Spectator, Ser. 3,
Vol. I (March, 1829), pp. 147-148; also see Coleridge, Aids
(Marsh ed., 1840), pp. 297-298. The "moral government"
theory of the atonement was not derived from Scottish
Philosophical presuppositions but was very congenial to
them.

inwardness of Cambridge Platonism, which he adopted as his key historical guide for the shape New England theology ought to assume. The fact that the rationalistic side of the Scottish Philosophy also had certain points of contact with Cambridge Platonism may at least partially explain Marsh's tendency to combine rationalistic and romantic modes of subjectivity. But the pervasive influence of Common Sense Realism in America, largely as the result of its eclectic adaptability to diverse theological needs, probably best explains Marsh's failure to break completely with Scottish-type thought. Marsh was clearly faced with a dilemma. He did not want to separate himself completely from the New England orthodoxy of his day. His aim was to revitalize, not to destroy or repudiate. He could thus not bring himself to discard Scottish thought patterns alto-gether. They were too firmly entrenched in his own thinking and in the orthodox theological circles with which he wished to maintain some semblance of identity, vis-à-vis transcendental radicalism and other forms of extreme theological liberalism. Thus, despite all the theological shortcomings which he saw in the Scottish metaphysic, he was able to accentuate its positive value as a rational model for subjective inwardness, which could be profitably conjoined with the more emotive model of romantic idealism.

What Marsh was able to do with Common Sense thought is discussed here not necessarily because Park may have been directly influenced by him. Rather, he provides some indication of the range of moderately orthodox theological possibilities that were opening up in nineteenth-century America as Scottish rationalism and Germano-British romantic idealism clashed and merged on the intellectual landscape. In Park's age, an American theologian's adherence to Common Sense presuppositions did not necessarily lead to "corpse-cold," ahistorical rationalism any more than a theological attachment to romantic idealism necessarily led to pantheism. The eclectic, adaptable character of Scottish Realism allowed for its association with a variety of philosophical and theological patterns.

*   *   *

Park's exposure to this variety was perhaps most significant in the realm of historical endeavor. Marsh's disciple William G. T. Shedd, who taught church history at Andover in the 1850's, creatively expressed his conservative Reformed theology in terms of organic and developmental concepts of self, history, and nature.[1] And that expression at least partially relieved some of Park's typically orthodox fears of "romantic" or "liberal"

---

[1]This and the ensuing comments on Shedd are based upon Cushing Strout, "Faith and History: The Mind of William G. T. Shedd," Journal of the History of Ideas, XV, 1 (January, 1954), 153-162.

ideas.[1] Shedd developed an idealistic philosophy of
history which allowed him to view Christian revelation
as organic growth rather than static given. In the role
of church historian, he saw himself as studying the
concrete ecclesiastical and doctrinal manifestations of
this revelatory growth. But he drew no skeptical or
unorthodox conclusions about the place of church history
vis-à-vis secular history. In fact, the latter represented
the growth of a sinful "germ" introduced by the Fall, a
growth which must be redeemed through the church's
development of the original "germ" of divine creative
power.

With his liberal-sounding but conservatively interpreted concept of the immanent, redemptive, historical
development of divine life and truth within the church,
Shedd opened up a whole new historical awareness at
Andover. Its skeptical tendencies overcome and its values
for orthodox doctrine made apparent, church history emerged
from its subordination to theological study to become a
serious independent discipline at New England's chief
bastion of Congregational orthodoxy. Park's first-hand
contact with German historical consciousness, especially
in the person of Neander, furnished the Abbot Professor

---

[1]One of Park's students once commented, "Professor
Park deals with transcendentalism as the sun does with
fog. He dries it up!" cf. "An Undergraduate," "Professor
Park in the Lecture Room," The Congregationalist, XII,
10 (March 9, 1860), p. 37, col. 6.

76

a potentially valuable resource in his attempts to come
to terms with Shedd's ideas.[1] Neander combined a
christocentric piety with a rather romantic, developmental
view of church history as progressive Incarnation. His
lectures opened new vistas for Park, whose previous
historical study had focused mainly upon Johann von
Mosheim's _Institutes of Ecclesiastical History_ (1755),
the standard text in the field in American theological
seminaries throughout much of the nineteenth century.
Mosheim's careful pioneering efforts at historical objec-
tivity placed more emphasis upon institutions than ideas
and left American theologians like Park without an adequate
understanding of their place in the living development of
Christian doctrine. Neander's idealistic viewpoint helped
supply his Andover pupil with such an understanding.

But it was the Berlin historian's piety which most
impressed Park. He did not fully comprehend and remained
somewhat suspicious of the philosophy of history espoused
by Shedd and Neander. As a result, he made few attempts

---

[1] cf. Frank Hugh Foster, _The Life of Edwards Amasa Park_
(New York: Fleming H. Revell Company, 1936), p. 123. It
is difficult to determine from Foster and other available
sources exactly how Park regarded Neander. Existing sources
frequently refer more to the personal habits and idiosyn-
crasies of Park's German teachers and acquaintances than
to their ideas or their possible intellectual influence
upon him. Nonetheless, there are broad hints in his
writings during and after his initial German visit that
seem to point to the influence of Neander as discussed
below. See Park, "Journal Letters from Europe, 1842-43"
(to wife): Berlin, November 18, 1842, p. 5; Berlin,
February 19, 1843, p. 9 (mss. in C. R. Park Family Papers).

to find points of contact between that philosophy and his
own Scottish metaphysic. His interest focused instead
upon Neander's broad practical distinction between piety
and doctrine. This distinction allowed the historian to
transcend doctrinal differences in a sympathetic appreciation of the men and movements of the past. The inspirational motives behind such transcendence, though often leading
Neander to an uncritical use of sources, drew Park's
admiration. He was very much in sympathy with the German
scholar's attempt to find in the Christian past a source
of edification for the present. Edification, however,
was not the only function of church history, in Park's
eyes. Awareness of the past could also reduce the fear
and misunderstanding of theological novelty which the
Andover divine detected among many adherents of orthodox
Reformed doctrine in America.[1]

Park was convinced that the youth and experimental
character of the country had produced a historyless
tendency among many American theologians. In overcoming
their excessive attention to the present, historical
study could teach them "that there is but little under
the sun which is really new and yet essentially dangerous."[2]
Knowledge of the changing "forms of doctrine" in various

---

[1] cf. A Society of Clergymen /Park and B. B. Edwards7,
"Thoughts on the State of Theological Science and Education
in Our Country," Bibliotheca Sacra, I, 4 (November, 1844),
747-750.

[2] Ibid., p. 747.

ages would help to make the present-day theologian
"diffident" in his own opinions and "catholic" in his
feelings toward past heretics and contemporary opponents.[1]
In short, following Neander's example, Park believed the
theologian should study history in order to become an
"advocate of comprehensive truth."[2] Such advocacy
balanced antiquity against novelty and one polemical
position against another in its search for that light of
truth which "often shines forth in its fulness from and
after the controversy rather than from either of the men
who controvert."[3]

Park celebrated the intellectual labor involved in
this dialectically comprehensive exercise, speaking
enthusiastically of the "invigorating discipline of our
Creator in giving us the raw material /of theological
truth7 and not the fabric ready-made."[4] There were,
however, definite limits to his catholicity and to his
historical sympathies. Since the church fathers "lived
before the rational processes of induction and the

[1]Ibid., pp. 749-750.

[2]Park, "The Duties of a Theologian," The American
Biblical Repository, II, 4, s. 2 (October, 1839), p. 352;
see also Alden, Notes, p. 2.

[3]"Duties of a Theologian," p. 353; cf. also Alden,
Notes, p. 1.

[4]"Duties of a Theologian," p. 354; see also Park,
"The Utility of Collegiate and Professional Schools,"
Bibliotheca Sacra, VII, 28 (October, 1850), p. 634.

fundamental laws of belief had been very distinctly explained," he once remarked that they "would better be
called the church babies."[1] Of course, "respecting the
fundamental principles of Christianity," the theologian
should "listen with deference to the voice of the faithful
in all past ages."[2] But he must carefully "discriminate
between their authority in regard to an essential doctrine,
and their authority in regard to an unessential one, or to
a refined speculation."[3]

Examples of essential doctrines for Park included "the
total depravity of the heart by nature, the need and fact of
regeneration by the Holy Ghost, our dependence on the Atonement," and the like.[4] Such doctrines fell "directly under
the cognizance of Christian feeling" and could "not have been
radically misunderstood by the mass of believers."[5] As to
unessential doctrine or "refined speculations," the Abbot
Professor commented:

> There are theories of doctrine more recondite and
> less distinctly revealed than the doctrine itself:
> they are not to be decided by the religious feel-
> ing, the authority of which is always venerable;
> their proof depends on a scientific discipline,
> such as the /church/ fathers never had....[6]

---

[1]"Duties of a Theologian," p. 349; cf. also Foster,
Genetic History, p. 476.

[2]"Duties of a Theologian," p. 348.

[3]Ibid., p. 349.

[4]Ibid.

[5]Ibid.

[6]Ibid.

Classed as "unessential" theories not meeting the
test of Park's "scientific discipline" were such sacramental
doctrines as the real presence and baptismal regeneration.
These were important to Roman Catholics and "Oxford
divines," against both of whom he, like many other American
Protestants, harbored a strong prejudice.[1] He asserted
that he could never follow the Catholic and Anglo-Catholic
example of submitting his faith "on obscure and subordinate
points to the dicta of any uninspired men, however ancient,
however unanimous."[2] In this separation of substance and
accidents in doctrinal history, Park was employing a
distinction of crucial significance to his theological
career: that between intellect and feeling. Through this
distinction, rationalistic, pietistic, and even romantic
motifs entered his theological methodology to varying
degrees. His major address of 1850 expounding this
distinction will form the subject of the next chapter.

---

[1]Ibid.; see also Park's Dudleian Lecture at Harvard on
"The Intellectual and Moral Influence of Romanism," Bibliotheca Sacra, II, 7 (August, 1845), 451-488. In that lecture
(cf. pp. 453-455), he sometimes distinguished Protestantism
and Romanism in much the same way that Philip Schaff did
in his Principle of Protestantism (1845); i.e., Protestantism
looks forward, while Romanism looks backward. The Andover
professor recognized the theological value of a dialectical
look in both directions, but his anti-Catholic, pro-
Edwardsean biases never really allowed him the historical
insight of Schaff in this regard.

[2]"Duties of a Theologian," p. 349.

Chapter IV

THE THEOLOGY OF THE INTELLECT AND
THAT OF THE FEELINGS

In September of the years 1848 and 1849, two important

lectures were delivered before the Porter Rhetorical

Society at Andover. In the former year, fresh from his

experience of "seeing the gospel," Horace Bushnell inspired

the Society with "A Discourse on Dogma and Spirit; or the

True Reviving of Religion."[1] As the title implies, Bushnell

---

[1]Published in God in Christ (Hartford, 1849), pp. 279-
356, along with a discourse on the work of Christ and one
on the Incarnation and the Trinity, given at Harvard and
Yale, respectively, in the summer of 1848--all prefaced by
the famous "Preliminary Dissertation on the Nature of
Language." Bushnell (1802-1876) was one of a distinguished
line of pastor-theologians whose works made a highly
significant contribution to American religious thought.
Educated at Yale College, he tried several vocations,
including teaching, journalism, and law, before experiencing
a quiet conversion that owed much to Coleridge's Aids to
Reflection. That experience sent him to the Yale Divinity
School and thence, in 1833, to the new North Church
(Congregational) in Hartford, Connecticut, where he spent
his entire active career (until 1859). His theology, which
attempted to preserve his Puritan heritage in a new
intellectual milieu, was marked by romantic motifs and
was conciliatory and comprehensive in spirit. In an age of
individualism and discontinuity, he stressed organic
continuities in history, communal relationships, salvation
(atoning union with Christ), and the like. His comprehensive
viewpoint did not, however, make him uncontroversial; and
his church had to withdraw from its consocation to save
him from possible heresy proceedings. He has been called
the "father of progressive orthodoxy" in America (see
chap. VI). cf. Barbara M. Cross, Horace Bushnell (Chicago,
1958).

was concerned with that perennial problem of religious depression in New England; but he did not give the traditional answers to it. No revival of conventional revivalism and no refinement of theology could give New Englanders the much desired religious awakening. What was needed was an inversion of the then prevalent "relations of dogma and spirit, so as to subordinate everything in the nature of science and opinion to the spirit, and thus to elevate everything in the nature of science and opinion into the region of spirit and life."[1] Dogma has certain pedagogic, apologetic, and other values, Bushnell affirmed, but it must be kept in its place as the servant of spirit.[2] Sterile dogmatic preaching and polemics had stifled New England spiritual life and left it confined within the narrow expectations of a mechanical revivalism.

This was not the first time Andover had been exposed to ideas of this sort. Nine years before, Bushnell had delivered an address on "Revelation" to the Society of Inquiry that effectively set the stage for his later

---

[1]Bushnell, God in Christ, p. 352. Conventional revivalism, in Bushnell's view, could not fully effect this necessary inversion because it limited the work of the spirit to extraordinary conversion or renewal experiences, often almost mechanically produced, and did not allow for gradual spiritual growth. For more on this subject, see Bushnell's "Spiritual Economy of Revivals of Religion," Quarterly Christian Spectator, X (1838), 131-148.

[2]cf. God in Christ, pp. 310ff.

discourse on dogma and spirit.[1] Hastily written but long

ruminated upon, the address set forth the rudiments of

Bushnell's famous theory of language, based upon the

supposed analogical relationship between the sense images

of the external world and the more abstract language of

thought. Because of this relationship, language, for

Bushnell, was always a partial, figurative, or indirect

vehicle of truth. The treasure of revelation was more

or less incarnate in the various earthen vessels of

language and dogma, but could be fully known only

intuitively, inwardly, or spiritually.[2]

To the inattentive, Bushnell's discourse on dogma

and spirit with its presupposition of linguistic skepticism

could easily become a call for the abandonment of the

theological enterprise altogether. It was apparently so

interpreted by the next Porter Society lecturer a year

later. In a wide-ranging address on "The Relations of

Faith and Philosophy,"[3] Henry Boynton Smith, soon to begin

---

[1]The address in ms. is in the Yale Divinity School
Library. For the circumstances of its delivery and some
notion of Bushnell's feelings and motivations relative to
it, see Mary Bushnell Cheney, ed., Life and Letters of
Horace Bushnell (New York: Harper and Brothers, 1880),
pp. 88ff.

[2]Bushnell's language theories apparently owed much to
one of his teachers at Yale Divinity School, Josiah Willard
Gibbs. For more on this, as well as on the combining of
Romantic and Puritan-Edwardsean elements in Bushnell's
concept of religious knowledge, see H. Shelton Smith, ed.,
Horace Bushnell, Library of Protestant Thought (New York:
Oxford University Press, 1965), pp. 27-37.

[3]Bibliotheca Sacra, VI, 24 (November, 1849), 673-709.

his career at Union Seminary as a major molder of the
New School Presbyterian mind,[1] defended "doctrinal theology"
against the objection "that language is inadequate to
embody spiritual truth." Calling language the "express
image of spirit," Smith asserted, "It may have had its
origin in the regions of sense; but by the action of the
soul upon it, it has been transfigured."[2] But Smith agreed
with Bushnell "that the letter kills if the spirit be not
there" and that a renewed emphasis upon inward experience
of the truth of Christianity could elevate New Englanders
"above those lesser controversies which have narrowed our
minds and divided our hearts."[3]

Like Park, Smith had spent some time in Germany with
such men as Tholuck and Hengstenberg. Reared a Unitarian
but converted to a kind of moderate orthodox faith which
he nourished in the seminaries of Andover and Bangor before
his European study, Smith was understandably impressed by
the German evangelical response to rationalism and could
even give qualified praise to Schleiermacher for his
reconciliation of faith and philosophy.[4] Concern for such

---

[1]For a good brief treatment of Smith and his signifi-
cance for American theology see W. K. B. Stoever, "Henry
Boynton Smith and the German Theology of History," Union
Seminary Quarterly Review, XXIV, 1 (Fall, 1968), 69-89.

[2]Smith, "Faith and Philosophy," pp. 694-695.

[3]Ibid., pp. 704-705.

[4]Ibid., pp. 700-701.

a reconciliation was at the heart of Smith's address at
Andover.

In that address, he affirmed a kind of christocentric
mediating theology "whose office it is to present the
substance of the Christian faith /i.e., Christ/ in a
scientific form, and in harmony with all other truth."[1]
Such a theology, Smith felt, "gives us all that philosophy
aims after,...in a more perfect form" and more besides
(i.e., salvation).[2] It allows for "a real inward experience as well as an objective reality."[3] Smith elevated
inwardly experienced substance over creedal, biblical,
or philosophical form in his theological method; but he
feared certain subjective tendencies evident in much of
New England theology, which he felt had become man-centered
rather than God-centered: "Christianity is viewed rather
as a system intended to cultivate certain states of feeling,
than as a revelation to build us up in the knowledge of God
and of Christ."[4] He added, "Some of our philosophical
tendencies are in the same line. Mental philosophy is
studied, as if all philosophy were in knowing the powers
of the mind; it is made the basis of theology."[5] In sum,

---

[1] _Ibid._, p. 706.

[2] _Ibid._

[3] _Ibid._, p. 705.

[4] _Ibid._, p. 703.

[5] _Ibid._

citing Christ-centered German evangelical theology as a guide, Smith wanted to redress the theological balance in New England between subjective human experience, or mental powers, and objective, but inwardly experienced revelation in Christ. When this was done, he felt, faith and philosophy could be truly reconciled.

*   *   *

Underlying both the Bushnell and the Smith address was a problem as old as theology itself--the problem of head versus heart, of intellect versus feelings. Both Bushnell and Smith believed that New England religious life had been adversely affected by an overly rationalized faith, though Smith appeared to have somewhat more confidence in reason than did Bushnell.[1] Nonetheless, Bushnell and Smith alike aroused the fears of New England orthodoxy by their apparent lack of regard for traditional creedal forms. These fears were hardly allayed when, less than a year after the Smith address, one who should have been a leader of the orthodox forces seemed to come out in favor of this new anti-creedalism. Standing before the Convention of the Congregational Ministers of Massachusetts gathered

---

[1]This can best be seen by comparing the relative amount of emphasis and attention given to defining and defending the enterprise of systematic theology in the two addresses. Of course, Bushnell did not always practice the ascetic attitude toward dogmatic speculation that he seemed to preach.

in May of 1850 in Boston's Brattle Street Meeting House,
the man who only three years before had succeeded Leonard
Woods as Andover's Abbot Professor of Christian Theology
set out to define the relationship between "The Theology
of the Intellect and That of the Feelings." The speaker,
of course, was none other than Edwards Amasa Park.[1] Before
him sat Old Calvinists and Hopkinsians, Trinitarians and
Unitarians.[2] It was a perfect occasion to continue the
theme of reconciliation evident in the addresses of
Bushnell and Smith. Commenting upon the latter's address
many years afterward, Park noted that the lecturer

> spoke to every one a word in season /and7 every
> one was delighted with it. The men who rejected
> faith, and the men who condemned philosophy;
> those who believed in Bushnell, and those who
> disbelieved in Schleiermacher; theologians who
> had a power to the contrary and theologians who
> had not much power of any kind, all crowded
> around the orator of the day, and thanked him
> for the lesson to their brethren, and praised
> his diversified gifts.[3]

Was this the kind of response Park sought to his
address? Perhaps, but Park could never be indifferent
toward his own Edwardsean heritage for the sake of

---

[1] The address, hereinafter cited as "Intellect and
Feelings," was first published in the *Bibliotheca Sacra*,
VII, 27 (July, 1850), 533-569. Page citations will be
to the original published article.

[2] The Convention antedated the Unitarian controversy.

[3] Park, "Review of H. B. Smith's *Faith and Philosophy*,"
Bibliotheca Sacra, XXXV, 137 (January, 1878), 201; see also
Elizabeth L. Smith, ed., *Henry Boynton Smith: His Life and
Work* (New York: A. C. Armstrong and Son, 1881), p. 144.

88

reconciliation. In a note appended to the published
version of his address, he recalled that he originally
"intended to avoid all trains of remark adverse to the
doctrinal views of any party or school belonging to the
Convention." But in retrospect he was aware that "some
clergymen of Massachusetts would not adopt as their own"
the ideas he had felt it necessary to express, and he
thus confided in "their proverbial charity."[1] Park's
biographer asserts, "There can be no doubt...that the
sermon was intended to be irenic."[2] But he also cites
the widening influence of the Abbot Professor at this time
and affirms that "there was already something in his mind
of the flush of anticipated victory and of the hope of
a general prevalence of this /Hopkinsian/ theology."[3]
Park's irenic tone was thus apparently based more upon
confidence in, rather than doubtful humility before, the
truth.

An indication of Park's widening influence can be
found in the unusually large crowd assembled at an annual
Convention that was admittedly "not a popular institution"
to hear an annual address (on a weekday) that was usually

[1]Park, "Intellect and Feelings," p. 533, n.2.

[2]Frank Hugh Foster, The Life of Edwards Amasa Park
(New York: Fleming H. Revell Company, 1936), p. 149; see
also Park, "Unity Amid Diversities of Belief Even on Imputed
and Involuntary Sin," Bibliotheca Sacra, VII, 31 (July,
1851), 647.

[3]Foster, Life, p. 148.

"formal and perfunctory."[1] The large congregation was
apparently not disappointed by what this renowned and
eloquent holder of the coveted Harvard D. D. had to say.
Despite, or perhaps because of, his confidence in his
own Edwardsean way of doing theology, Park felt free to
spread his theological net as wide as possible to take in
as many dissident factions as he could. F. H. Foster
speculates that

> He may have thought that he had an opportunity
> to show Unitarians that orthodoxy was not as
> blind to ethical truths as some of them may
> have thought.... And perhaps he thought
> that it might promote good feeling among
> the adherents of the old school of Calvinism,
> if they found that the new school acknowledged
> a certain truth in their distinctive doctrinal
> views....[2]

By what theological means could Park possibly hope
to bring about these feats of reconciliation? Bushnell
and Smith had not satisfied him in the sphere of religious
knowledge. He would distinguish truth known by the intellect
from that derived from the feelings, but in such a way as
not to undermine the former, as Bushnell in particular had
seemed to do. Truths suggested by the feelings can be
contradictory when one attempts to express them in
intellectual, or rational terms. But theological statements
based thereon still involve "the substance of truth"

---

[1] Ibid., p. 149. cf. comments about the crowd and
Park's effect upon them from The Boston Courier and from
an Andover student, J. W. Wellman, in Park, Memorial
Collection of Sermons compiled by Agnes Park (Boston: The
Pilgrim Press, 1902), p. 74.

[2] Foster, Life, p. 150.

according to "the wants of the well-trained heart."[1]
The theology of the feelings is not concerned with precise
definition and argument but with what pleases the sensibilities and the "healthy affections." It leans toward the
particular, the visible, the tangible, as opposed to the
general and the abstract. It may be vague and loose in
its statements but is always forceful. "It is too buoyant...
to compress itself into sharply-drawn angles."[2] It is
"elastic" rather than "comprehensive": "it brings out
into bold relief now one feature of a doctrine and then
a different feature, and assumes as great a variety of
shapes as the wants of the heart are various."[3]

*   *   *

In short, the theology of the feelings (the theology
of Bushnell and perhaps Smith?) would seem to be the
theology of reconciliation par excellence, having the
potential of infinite adaptability. But it would also
seem to be a form of theology which the serious seeker
of truth could not take very seriously--a theology that
is merely figurative, rhetorical, poetic; i.e., it would
seem to be a theology for the preacher rather than the

---

[1]Park, "Intellect and Feelings." p. 535.

[2]Ibid., p. 536.

[3]Ibid.

theologian. Since Park was interested in both vocations,
the problem of the relationship of theology and preaching
received a good deal of attention from him long before
1850 and helped to mold his understanding of the relation
of intellect and feeling. In his inaugural address as
Bartlet Professor of Sacred Rhetoric at Andover (1836),
Park asserted that "the preacher must feel that his success
in preaching depends not on his graces of delivery...so
much as on his enlarged and familiar acquaintance with the
principles of religion."[1] In other words, every preacher
must be a theologian of sorts.

Park gave a variety of reasons for this assertion,
most of them appealing to pragmatic or pious ends. For
example, theological study invigorated the mind and heart
of the preacher, gave him self-confidence, earned him the
respect of the congregation, etc. But Park also affirmed
that theological study was necessary for preaching not
only because it (the former) "discloses the precise truths
which are fitted to renovate the heart" but also because
it "discloses the essential truths which glorify God."[2]
Ultimately, it was the preacher's vocation to study and
declare the latter truths in the hope that they could be
both known and loved. Knowing pragmatically which truths

---

[1]Park, "Connection Between Theological Study and
Pulpit Eloquence," The American Biblical Repository, X,
27, s. 1 (July, 1837), 170.

[2]Ibid., pp. 182 and 187. For the reasoning based on
pragmatic piety, see pp. 170-182.

would renovate which heart and having the vigor, confidence,
and respect to drive these truths home was, in the final
analysis, secondary in importance to the task of glorifying
God by studying, knowing, declaring and loving the whole
Truth. Park was arguing for theological integrity in
pulpits that were yielding more and more to a mechanical,
result-oriented evangelism. The preacher must know what
he is talking about: "The Deity is not glorified by
conversions, but by conversions to the truth."[1]

But one may well ask if Park was not also arguing for
the primacy of what Jonathan Edwards would have called a
"notional" (i.e., rational, intellectual) knowledge of the
Truth. Was the preacher, in Park's view, merely called
upon to convey abstract theological propositions more
effectively to the common man? Park did indeed say that
"all sacred rhetoric is but a new arrangement of the
materials of theology."[2] He also (in another context)
identified systematic theology with "essential theology,"
and sacred rhetoric with "modal theology," calling the
former "the substance of divine truth," and the latter,
"this substance fitly arranged" for presentation.[3] Thus,
from the purely intellectual point of view, preaching was
on the periphery, and systematic theology was at the center

---

[1]Ibid., p. 188.

[2]Ibid., p. 191.

[3]Park, "The Mode of Exhibiting Theological Truth," The American Biblical Repository, X, 28, s. 1 (October, 1837), 436.

of things so far as apprehending the Truth was concerned.

This was not, however, the only point of view Park took. "To represent the Divine excellencies so that they shall be apprehended," he averred, "is the sacred eloquence of thought; so that they shall be loved is the sacred eloquence of feeling...."[1] Both kinds of eloquence were involved in preaching,[2] but the latter had a definite priority for Park. If it be true, Park asserted, "that to know God is to glorify him, then to make him known is to glorify him more extensively; and if to make him known be glorious to him, to make him loved is still more glorious."[3] This would not seem to mean merely that the preacher converted systematic theology into a rhetorically moving message.[4] Such a message could be nothing more than a hopeful

---

[1]cf. Park, "Theological Study and Pulpit Eloquence," p. 187.

[2]Ibid., pp. 171 and 188.

[3]Ibid., p. 187; see also p. 188.

[4]Park would appear to stand against both affective rhetoric for its own sake and the opposite extreme of entrapping the "convert" in theological logic. If Harriet Beecher Stowe is to be believed, the latter practice was rather common among New England ministers, especially those of the Edwardsean variety. In her novel Oldtown Folks (1869), the minister Mr. Avery (Lyman Beecher) is described as one who "believes that sinners can be converted by logic" and who has in fact "caught numbers of the shrewdest infidel foxes" in his neat little "logic-traps." cf. H. B. Stowe, Oldtown Folks, ed. Henry F. May (Cambridge, Massachusetts: Harvard University Press, 1966), p. 255. See also Charles H. Foster, The Rungless Ladder (Durham: Duke University Press, 1954), p. 175. Foster and May have done an excellent job of interpreting Mrs. Stowe's literary work as a sensitive barometer of the New England religious mind.

instrument of the Spirit, in any case.[1] Park seemed to
imply that preaching in some sense became a norm for
systematic theology just as systematic theology was both
source and norm for preaching. In Park's Bartlet Inaugural
the normative function of preaching was only implied and
basically negative. Whatever the Spirit and the "impulses
of man's moral nature" consistently ignored or opposed in
preaching was almost certainly bad theology.[2] Put another
way, theology which, when preached with the proper emphasis,
rhetoric, etc., failed to make God loved was almost
certainly untrue; for the final aim of the Christian
revelation, with which both theologian and preacher worked,
was not merely to make the Truth known but to make it loved.

Of course, the main thrust of Park's Bartlet Address
was that preaching without theological study is dead. But
as his career progressed, he more explicitly and positively
affirmed the reverse as well. Theology must meet the test
of a heart-oriented preaching. Known as well for homiletical
as for theological acumen, Park, in one sense, may be said
to have devoted his whole career to the search for a preachable theology. It was, after all, not systematic theology
that he saw fit to publish near the end of his life but
Discourses on Some Theological Doctrines as Related to the

---

[1]See Park, "Theological Study and Pulpit Eloquence,"
p. 189.

[2]Ibid., pp. 186 and 189.

<u>Religious Character</u>[1]--discourses that "were designed to
exhibit certain practical relations of certain theological
doctrines, to show that the doctrines were to be revered
for their use in religious experience as well as for their
harmony with sound reason and divine inspiration."[2]

Even if one grants, however, at least an implicit
reciprocal norming of theological study and preaching in
Park's earlier thought, what significance does this have
for the relationship between intellect and feeling which
he outlined in his 1850 Convention Address? It means that
the serious seeker of truth could (and should) take the
theology of the feelings seriously, even though this
particular figurative form of theology was dominant in
preaching, rather than in systematic theology. The preacher
was more than a popularizing and affective mouthpiece for
the "notional" religious knowledge of the intellect. He
appealed to the theological norm of the heart as at least
an implicit negative check upon that of the head.

The word "norm" here is important. The heart was
seldom a true theological "source" for Park. This was in
line with his basic understanding of "mental philosophy."
In his inaugural address as Abbot Professor at Andover
(1847), Park asserted, "The original law of our constitution
is that feeling shall follow perception; and in obedience

---

[1](Andover, Massachusetts: Warren F. Draper, 1885),
390pp.

[2]<u>Ibid.</u>, p. iii.

96

to this law the heart is often enlarged as the understanding
is expanded, and the moral nature contracts as the mental
range is limited."[1] Here again Park was emphasizing the
intellectual side of man's nature as the basic source of
truth. If preaching without theological study was dead
for the Bartlet Professor, so piety without intellectual
endeavor failed to measure up for the Abbot Professor.
"He who is able to take large views of divine truth," Park
affirmed, "is thereby capacitated for large measures of
love."[2] Park was not unmindful of the charge that the
intellect sometimes deadens the emotions. But he reasoned
as follows:

> The severe argumentation of a theologian often
> prepares his feelings for the influence of the
> doctrine which has absorbed his thoughts. The
> emotion is lighted up by the fires of the
> intellect.... Piety is an intellectual as well
> as a moral exercise, and often requires a
> vigorous coöperation of the understanding with
> the affections.[3]

*   *   *

Evident in Park's Abbot Inaugural was an implicit faith
in the harmony of intellect and feeling, but the latter was
not yet made an explicit norm for the truths derived from

---

[1]"The Religious Influence of Theological Seminaries,"
published as an "Introductory Essay" in the second edition
of Writings of Reverend William Bradford Homer, ed. E. A.
Park (Boston: T. R. Marvin, 1849), p. xiv.

[2]Ibid., p. xiv.

[3]Ibid., p. xv.

the former.   In the Convention Address of 1850 this situation
was changed.   Before his large and diverse Boston audience,
Park proposed his own version of the Vincentian Canon:

> Decidedly as we resist the pretension that the
> church is infallible, there is one sense in
> which this pretension is well founded.... She
> is not infallible in her bodies of divinity,
> nor her creeds, nor catechisms, nor any
> logical formulae; but underneath all her
> intellectual refinements lies a broad substance
> of doctrine, around which the feelings of all
> renewed men cling ever and everywhere, into
> which they penetrate and take root, and this
> substance must be right, for it is precisely
> adjusted to the soul, and the soul was made
> for it.[1]

This was as close as Park ever came to agreeing with Bushnell.
He then stated the normative role of the feelings explicitly
as follows:

> These universal feelings /"of all renewed men"7
> provide us with a test for our faith.   Whenever
> we find, my brethren /the Congregational ministers
> of Massachusetts7, that the words which we
> proclaim do not strike a responsive chord in
> the hearts of the choice men and women who
> look up to us for consolation, when they do
> not stir the depths of our own souls...; or
> when they make an abiding impression that the
> divine government is harsh,...devoid of sympathy
> with our most refined sentiments,...then we
> may infer that we have left out of our theology
> some element which we should have inserted, or
> have brought into it some element which we should
> have discarded.   Somewhere it must be wrong.[2]

The normative role of the feelings not only became
explicit in Park's Convention Address but also became more
positive and active than in most of his previous writings.

---

[1] Park, "Intellect and Feelings," p. 545.

[2] Ibid., emphasis Park's.

The heart was no longer simply a passive, negative check
upon the head, approving or disapproving whatever the
intellect proposed as true:

> Our sensitive nature is sometimes a kind
> of instinct which anticipates many truths,
> incites the mind to search for them,
> intimates the process of the investigation,
> and remains unsatisfied, restive, so long
> as it is held back from the object toward
> which it gropes its way....[1]

Nevertheless, it is important to remember that the heart,
for Park, was essentially blind in the search for truth.
Referring to the notion of Pascal that divine truths
"should enter from the heart into the mind" and not vice
versa, Park remarked:

> These words mean, not that the heart ever
> perceives, for the intellect only is per-
> cipient, but that holy feelings prompt the
> intellect to new discoveries, furnish it
> with new materials for examination and
> inference, and regulate it in its mode of
> combining and expressing what it has
> discerned.[2]

In sum, the feelings could "anticipate" and "intimate"
instinctively in the direction of the truth, but they
could only "grope" toward it. As an instinctive force,
the feelings provided motive power, raw empirical material,
and a kind of normative regulation for the work of the
intellect in doing theology.

But the suspicion lingers that the intellect could
just as well do without a "blind" heart in the comprehension

---

[1] Ibid.

[2] Ibid., p. 564, Note D.

and communication of religious knowledge. There are in
fact a number of statements and arguments in Park's Convention Sermon which imply as much. For example, in
defining the theology of the intellect, Park asserted,
"It is the theology of speculation, and therefore comprehends
the truth just as it is, unmodified by excitements of
feeling. It is received as accurate not in its spirit
only, but in its letter also."[1] Park went on to detail
the various characteristics of intellectual theology which
set it off from the theology of the feelings. It is based
on logical and empirical evidence. It is "general,"
"abstract," "literal" (as opposed to "figurative"),
"intelligible," "defensible," and "precise."[2] In short,
it would seem that the head is a good deal more trustworthy
than the heart in the search for religious truth.

This impression is strengthened by the following
analogy:

> But while the theology of reason derives
> aid from the impulses of emotion, it
> maintains its ascendancy over them....
> It may be roughly compared to the pilot
> of a ship, who intelligently directs and
> turns the rudder, although himself and
> the entire vessel are also turned by it.[3]

In one of the notes appended to the published version of

---

[1] Ibid., p. 534.

[2] Ibid., pp. 534-535.

[3] Ibid., pp. 545-546. In the very next sentence (p. 546),
Park also compared the intellect to a man's eyes, which
direct the movement of his hands and feet (representing
blind feelings) but cannot do without them.

the Convention Sermon, Park reinforced this analogy with
another: "As the head is placed above the heart in the
body, so the faith which is sustained by good argument
should control rather than be controlled by those emotions
which receive no approval from the judgment."[1]

Contrary to one's first impression, there is reason
to believe that the motive behind statements like these
was not truly rationalistic, in the sense of making the
intellect the fundamental judge of religious truth. The
chief motive seems to have been much less doctrinaire:
it was a compelling desire for reasonable clarity in
theological statements. That desire was coupled with an
underlying faith that such clarity would, in the end,
reconcile warring religious factions better than linguistic
relativism based upon romantic or evangelical appeals to
intuition. In addition, clearer, better theology might
also provide a more lasting religious renewal in New
England. In "The Theology of the Intellect and That of
the Feelings," Park was not really distinguishing two
forms of theology but rather two forms of language. True
theology actually had but one form for him, and that was
clear, rational discourse. When one understands this, one
understands why it was that Park, despite his deference
to the feelings, seemed to be continually elevating the
intellect above them in his Convention Address. The

---

[1] _Ibid._, p. 567, Note F.

feelings, and language based thereon, might illustrate and motivate; they might provide material for, limit the sphere of, and even test the validity of the theological enterprise. But they could not control that enterprise because it was nothing if it was not clear and understandable--understandable not only to the orthodox faithful but to the "cultured despisers" (including the Unitarians) as well. The obvious medium for such understandability was intellectual or scientific language.

When Park referred to intellectual theology as "the truth just as it is," accurate in "spirit" and "letter," etc., he was clearly using, with apologetic intent, the model of the discipline of science. Park and his age had a growing faith in the efficacy of scientific endeavor. But he did not believe that rational, scientific methods and propositions were, in the final analysis, the only way, or even the most fundamental way, of comprehending and communicating religious truth in its broadest sense. He admitted that "the literal doctrines of theology are too vast for complete expression by man...."[1] Their clearest and most authoritative expression was in rational or scientific terms, but such an expression was no guarantee of that felt comprehension, that love of the truth without which mere knowledge was dead. It was this felt comprehension which found stimulus and expression in the language (not the "theology") of the feelings. In short, theology without feeling

---

[1] Ibid., p. 549.

was dead. But did one have to know the truth intellectually before he could love it, or comprehend it inwardly?
What was the relationship between scientific theology and
the religious life?

In his apologetic desire for clarity and understandability, Park admittedly all too frequently appeared to
limit religious truth or knowledge to sets of rational propositions. His theological method, unlike that of Bushnell,
placed a great deal of faith in creedal statements. Ideally,
such statements should not be couched in the language of the
feelings: "Whenever a discrepancy exists between a creed and
an expression of devotional feeling..., the symbol of faith
ought to be in a style so prosaic and definite as to form
the decisive standard of appeal...."[1] Park believed that
the Scriptures and certain historic New England creedal
statements (especially cherished by the Old Calvinists) based
too literally thereon were filled with the language of the
feelings. Such language, when taken literally as the basis
for rational theological systems, created all sorts of misunderstanding and resultant divisiveness. Unless this language could be viewed in its true figurative sense, it presented logical absurdities and contradictions to the intellect.

Here lies the basis for Park's concern for theological
clarity. One should never confuse one kind of language
with another. The language of the intellect could not move

---

[1]Ibid., p. 567, Note F; see also p. 554.

the heart; the language of the heart appeared absurd to
the intellect. The theologian had to make careful use of
this linguistic distinction when he interpreted Scripture.
Park had selected two apparently contradictory Scripture
passages (I Samuel 15:29 and Genesis 6:6) as texts for his
Convention Sermon.[1]   In the course of the sermon he cited
numerous other such passages relating broadly to sinful
human nature and man's part in the salvation process. How
could such passages be reconciled? The obvious answer for
Park was to interpret them as couched in the language of
feeling. According to Park's somewhat dialectical theological method,

> The theology of the intellect explains that of
> feeling into an essential agreement with all the
> constitutional demands of the soul. It does this
> by collating the discordant representations which
> the heart allows, and eliciting the one self-
> consistent principle which underlies them....
> When this principle has been once detected and
> disengaged from its conflicting representations,
> it reacts upon them, explains, modifies, harmo-
> nizes their meaning. Thus are the mutually
> repellent forces set over against each other,
> so as to neutralize their opposition and to
> combine in producing one and the same movement.[2]

Park believed that when the intellect had examined the
"origin," "intent," and "influence" of the contradictory

---

[1]In essence, these passages posed the question "Does
God change his mind?" Genesis 6:6 (KJV) reads, "And it
repented the Lord that he had made man on the earth, and
it grieved him at his heart." I Samuel 15:29 (KJV) countered
with the assertion that "the Strength of Israel will not
lie nor repent: for he is not a man, that he should
repent."

[2]Park, "Intellect and Feelings," p. 546.

104

emotive biblical texts in question, it would educe the
following doctrinal "light" (or "self-consistent principle")
from their collision: "that the character of our race
needs an essential transformation by an interposed influence
from God."[1]

*   *   *

Almost two decades later (1869) Bushnell recalled this
venture of Park into synthetic biblical interpretation and
remarked concerning the doctrinal light purportedly educed:

> It does not appear to be observed, that this
> very sentence, which affirms the great, inev-
> itable, scientific truth of regeneration, is
> itself packed full of figures and images, and
> is, in fact, interpretable only with more
> difficulty and more ambiguity than any and all
> the figures proposed to be resolved by it.[2]

This was perhaps a fair criticism of the operation of Park's
theological method in this instance, but it was profoundly
unfair if directed at the method as a whole. It is of
dubious validity, in any age, to criticize those seeking
greater understandability and clarity in theological
language by crying, "Metaphor, metaphor, all is metaphor."[3]

---

[1] Ibid., p. 547.

[2] Horace Bushnell, "Our Gospel a Gift to the Imagination,"
in Building Eras in Religion (New York: Charles Scribner's
Sons, 1881), pp. 269-270. The essay was first published in
Hours at Home, Vol. VII (1869).

[3] Of more recent vintage but equally unfair is the
similar criticism made of Bultmannian theological interpretation that demythologizing is really remythologizing.

Some metaphors are, in fact, more illuminating than others;
and the intellect is crucial in distinguishing and interpreting these.

Bushnell apparently had nothing but relativistic
scorn for Park's attempts at greater theological precision.
To his own question as to whether there is "any hope for
theologic science left," Bushnell emphatically replied,
"None at all.... Human language is a gift to the imagination so essentially metaphoric...that it has no exact
blocks of meaning to build a science of."[1] Both Park and
Bushnell sought to reconcile divergent theological statements. But Bushnell saw all language, not just emotive
language, as figurative and thus as incapable of conveying
"any truth whole, or by literal embodiment." Any language
(abstract or concrete, scientific or poetic) could only
point figuratively to one side of the truth. "Hence a
great many shadows, or figures, are necessary to represent
every truth."[2]

Bushnell was willing to engage in theological dialogue
with the various figures and shadows representing one
truth on the assumption that if one could discover and
clarify the partial truth involved in each figure, one
could come to a more comprehensive understanding of the

---

[1] Bushnell, "Gospel, Gift to Imagination," p. 272.

[2] Bushnell, "Christian Comprehensiveness," The New
Englander, VI (1848), 84.

truth as a whole. Of course, if it was to have any
theological value, such a search for comprehensiveness
had, however tentatively, to rely upon other, more adequate
figures than those whose truths were to be comprehended.
How could one find and manipulate these other figures:
through the intellect, the heart, or some interrelation-
ship of the two? Was it enough simply to elevate spirit
over dogma and cry,

> Let Calvinism take in Arminianism, Arminianism
> Calvinism; let decrees take in contingency,
> contingency decrees; faith take in works, and
> works faith; the old take in the new, and the
> new the old--not doubting that we shall be as
> much wiser as we are more comprehensive, as
> much closer to unity as we have more of the
> truth?[1]

Park obviously felt such a theological method was
gravely deficient. Theology was more than intellectual
"shadowboxing" with truths which the heart knows immediately. The elevation of unformed truth (spirit) over
formed truth (dogma) might reconcile theological factions,
but it tended to an uncritical or vague theological
eclecticism which Park could not accept. Real theological
comprehensiveness and lasting theological reconciliation
had to take theological distinctions and refinements with
the utmost seriousness. It was through these distinctions
and refinements that the intellect, in its own right,
sought to comprehend truth. The heart (as a norm) aided

---

[1]Ibid., p. 111.

the intellect in the latter's search for truth through
theological refinement; but inward, unformed apprehension
of truth could not predetermine the shape or outcome of
such theological refinement. Enthusiasm or vague eclecticism
would tend to follow such a predetermination.

In the final analysis, however, one is left with
ambivalence and paradox when one focuses upon Park's
Convention Sermon of 1850 and tries to sort out the relations
of head and heart, of intellectual theology and the inward
faith of the religious life. There are statements in this
sermon which clearly imply an ultimate elevation of inward
over intellectual religious knowledge. "The true history
of doctrine," Park asserted near the end of the sermon, "is
to be studied not in the technics, but in the spirit of
the church."[1] This would seem to mean that one can get at
the spirit without the technics, or, in terms of the
problem raised earlier, that one can have an inward experience
or comprehension of religious truth without first knowing
it intellectually or propositionally. But it is difficult
to reconcile such assertions with the earlier analogy of
the ship's pilot.

In a sermon which was obviously designed to clarify
the relations of intellect and feeling in response to
Bushnell's (and, to a degree, Smith's) apparent undermining
of the former by the latter, such ambiguity is both

---

[1] Park, "Intellect and Feelings," p. 560.

frustrating and provocative. Park was apparently aiming at an as yet dimly conceived synthesis of two important modes of religious knowledge and expression. What he seemed to be saying was that intellect and feeling should not be elevated or emphasized one over the other, because they work from completely different, noncompetitive, but equally valid perspectives. Unfortunately, this tantalizingly adumbrated synthesis was never to reach full elaboration during his career.

Chapter V

CONFLICT WITH PRINCETON

The tone and emphasis of much of Park's theological
work up through the 1850's seem to indicate a conviction
that less rationalistic formulations were necessary if
New England theology and religious life were to be revi-
talized and delivered from arid polemical rigidity.[1] This
does not mean that the substance of Park's Edwardsean
theology changed radically during these years. He continued
to believe that his "scientifically" improved and vigorously preached version of Consistent Calvinism was the best
way to revive New England's religious fervor. But the
forms in which he presented his theology definitely came
to reflect serious attention and openness to theological
options or possibilities like those presented by W. G. T.

---

[1]cf. Edmund Kimball Alden, Notes on Park's Lectures
on Systematic Theology (1846-47; ms. in Oberlin College
Library), pp. 2 and 7, where Park speaks against party
spirit in theology and calls for the elevation of "spirit"
over "words" in biblical interpretation. Also see Park,
"The Duties of a Theologian," The American Biblical
Repository, II, 4, s. 2 (October, 1839), pp. 376-379; Park,
"Introductory Essay on the Dignity and Importance of the
Preacher's Work," in The Preacher and Pastor, ed. Park
(Andover: Allen, Morrill, and Wardwell, 1845), p. 18;
and finally, Park, "The Theology of the Intellect and That
of the Feelings," Bibliotheca Sacra, VII, 27 (July, 1850),
pp. 543-544.

Shedd and James Marsh.

The high point of such attention and openness obviously came in Park's Convention Sermon, where reconciliation of warring theological factions was plainly high on the agenda. Such a reconciliation was apparently to be accomplished by a greater emphasis upon the role of the feelings in theology and hermeneutics. Though the precise roles of intellect and feelings were not fully clarified in the sermon, there were clear signs of better things to come if Park had continued to follow up some of his lines of thought. Writing a few years after Park's death, no less a liberal theological voice than George A. Gordon was led to speculate upon the significance which Park's Convention Sermon might have had as an adumbration of theological change. Gordon declared that if Park

> had allowed his thought in that great discourse to control and shape his entire teaching, instead of being the last of the old order of theologians, he would have become the first of the new. If he had utilized his insight that the content of genuine Christian feeling is an eternal content while the theories of the intellect chase each other...like shadows over the summer grass; if he had turned the intellect upon the deposit of faith laid up in the Christian heart, stored in the Christian consciousness, treasured in the soul of Christ; if he had allowed the enlightened conscience to cleanse the Augean stable of the medieval understanding, Edwards A. Park would have stood for the dawn of a new day in America.[1]

---

[1]George A. Gordon, "The Achilles in Our Camp: An Acute and Inspiring Characterization of the Late Dr. Edwards A. Park," The Congregationalist, LXXXVIII, 24 (June 13, 1903), p. 840, col. 2.

Gordon's florid rhetoric perhaps exaggerated the liberal tendencies of Park's sermon; but other liberal spokesmen, writing closer to the event, also seemed to think Park was moving in their direction. The Christian Examiner was not terribly impressed with Park's restatement of "the well-known variance between truth as stated in disjointed sentences and hyperboles, and truth as drawn out in carefully worded phrases." But the editor thought he discerned "intimations of a more significant idea" beneath Park's "rich rhetoric." What that idea was he did not make clear, but his general attitude toward Park's sermon and its implications was definitely positive.[1] Another liberal organ compared Park to Bushnell, arguing that like Bushnell, he was attempting, in his Convention Sermon, "to suggest a method of interpretation whereby he /could/ reject certain of the old dogmas and still retain his adherence to the literal sense of the Scriptures as the rule of faith without having them constantly quoted against him."[2] But like the Examiner, this reviewer found Park's sermon more significant for what it implied than for what it said. Park seemed to "have caught a glimpse of a true idea," but his exposition thereof left much to be

[1]"Review of Park's Discourse on the Theology of the Intellect and That of the Feelings," Christian Examiner and Religious Miscellany, XLIX, Fourth series XIV, 2 (September, 1850), 296.

[2]William B. Hayden, "Professor Park's Discourse," The New Jerusalem Magazine, XXIV, 1 (January, 1851), 14.

112

desired.[1]

Given Park's later theological development, one may
be inclined to dismiss this basically positive liberal
response to his sermon as mere wishful thinking. After
all, Park's primary theological focus seemed to be on the
improvement and defense of Consistent Calvinism along the
lines of the Scottish Philosophy. Where then would he have
derived the necessary intellectual resources and inspiration
for the new theological direction, or perspective, which
seemed to be developing in his Convention Sermon? If Park
had spent all his time studying the works of men like Reid,
Hopkins, and Emmons, this question might be difficult to
answer. But Park did not let his interest in a particular
philosophical or theological perspective blind him to other
currents of thought that were sweeping the intellectual
landscape of his day. His personal library was well stocked
with the works of the British romantics and even included a
relatively large amount of Swedenborgian literature.[2] He
was not averse to the citation of Coleridge and Plotinus
alongside Locke and Stewart if he could prove or illustrate
a point thereby.[3] Thus, his emphasis upon the role of the

---

[1]Ibid.

[2]See the Catalogue of the Theological Library of the
Late Professor Edwards A. Park of Andover, Mass. (Boston:
C. F. Libbie and Company, 1903).

[3]cf. Park's sermon on "Conscience" in Discourses on
Some Theological Doctrines as Related to the Religious
Character (Andover: Warren F. Draper, 1885), p. 295f.

feelings in his Convention Sermon is not a totally unexpected turn in his theological development, for it was
not without foundation in his reading and thinking.

Once this foundation is recognized, the cautiously
positive liberal interpretations of the implications of
Park's sermon seem rather reasonable. But Park's "liberal
days" were numbered after the 1850's. The reasons for
this were varied, but an important one seemed to stem from
the controversy which Park's Convention Sermon provoked.
His qualified success in bringing the liberals under his
hermeneutical umbrella became a source of increasing alarm
to the more conservative spokesmen for Reformed orthodoxy.
His modest attempt at theological reconciliation had failed.
Given the theological situation of the day, this failure is
not terribly surprising. Bushnell's apparent anti-creedalism had greatly upset the orthodox community. And anyone
sounding remotely like him was likely to incur a certain
amount of the orthodox wrath, particularly if he received
praise from the wrong quarters. The most prolonged and
intense wrath which Park incurred came, not unexpectedly,
from Charles Hodge (1797-1878) of Princeton.

*   *   *

Since 1822, the year Park began his college work at
Brown, Hodge had occupied a professorship in the Presbyterian
seminary at Princeton. Few men have embodied a school or

114

a theological tradition as completely as did Hodge. His
association with Princeton, either as student or as professor, stretched over almost seven decades of the nineteenth century. Thousands of divinity students heard his
lectures, and thousands more undoubtedly read them in his
Systematic Theology (three volumes, 1871-73).[1] Following
in the intellectual footsteps of John Witherspoon and
Archibald Alexander, Hodge developed a rigidly confessional
exposition and defense of the Westminster tradition based
upon the self-evident truths of Scottish Common Sense and
the absolute verbal authority of the Scriptures. His work
gave decisive shape to that tradition known as the Princeton
Theology, a tradition which nourished "Old School" Presbyterians and other theological conservatives through many a
bout with the new ideas and "neologians" of the nineteenth
century.

Hodge was no anti-intellectual, however. He might
fear the intellectual creativity of a Jonathan Edwards or a
Friedrich Schleiermacher, he might decry the conclusions of
German biblical criticism, but the massive erudition and
impressive dialectical skill displayed in his theological
labors clearly revealed no disparagement of the life of
the mind at Princeton. Nor was the life of the heart
neglected in Hodge's scholastic-like defense of Westminster.

[1]cf. John Oliver Nelson, "Charles Hodge," in The
Lives of Eighteen from Princeton, ed. Willard Thorp
(Princeton: Princeton University Press, 1946), p. 192.

Revivalism was insubstantial in the eyes of Hodge; it
encouraged doctrinal laxity. But true orthodoxy was
linked inseparably with true inward piety. One simply
did not have one without the other.[1] For Hodge, this
union of a learned orthodoxy with a vital piety meant
that when one defended Westminster dogma, one was, in
effect, defending the Christian life itself. There was
thus a strong sense of mission in his career, particularly
in his intra-denominational sparrings with the New School
men and in his extensive polemical attention to various
non-Presbyterian heretics. Few deviations from the pure
Westminster tradition escaped notice in the influential
Princeton Review, for which Hodge did the lion's share of
the editorial labor. Since many of these deviations
originated in New England, it is not surprising that Hodge
and the Review were especially sensitive to the slightest

---

[1]Here Hodge was closely following his intellectual
hero Archibald Alexander, the first professor at Princeton
Seminary (founded 1812) and the actual founder of the
Princeton Theology. Alexander was given to a somewhat
romantic, intuitional inwardness, through which, strangely
enough, he found decisive support for strict Scriptural and
confessional authority. Hodge never emphasized intuitional
immediacy in the same manner as Alexander; but he nonetheless
maintained Alexander's linkage between piety and doctrine,
sometimes to the extent of sounding rather like a "New
School" man on such issues as the "internal testimony" of
the Spirit. Hodge was obviously not frightened by the
specter of subjectivism as much as some of his conservative
Princetonian successors were. See Bernard Ramm, Witness of
the Spirit (Grand Rapids: William B. Eerdmans Publishing
Company, 1959). For a good historical perspective on the
Princeton Theology (including the Hodge-Alexander relationship touched upon above), see John Oliver Nelson, "The Rise
of the Princeton Theology: A Genetic Study of American
Presbyterianism until 1850" (Yale University: unpublished
Ph.D. dissertation, 1935).

hint of heresy emanating from that veritable "West Point"
of Congregational orthodoxy in Andover.

When the hint came from so eminent a source as Andover's
Abbot Professor, and when it was contained in an address that
went through three printings in the space of a few months,
attracting the attention of everyone from conservative Congregationalists to Unitarians and Swedenborgians, it was
definitely time for Princeton's chief theologian to sound an
alarm. The alarm came in the form of an unsigned article in
the Princeton Review less than five months after the offend-
ing address. As might be expected, the basic issue upon
which Hodge focused in his initial critical response to
Park's Convention Sermon was that of the authority and
interpretation of Scripture. Agreeing with some of Park's
liberal sympathizers, Hodge accused Park of propounding an
interpretive theory that would allow the rejection of "certain
doctrines which stand out far too prominently in scripture
and are too deeply impressed on the heart of God's people to
allow of their being denied."[1]

---

[1]Charles Hodge, "Professor Park's Sermon," The Biblical
Repertory and Princeton Review, XXII, 4 (October, 1850),
646. The complete Hodge-Park controversy involved three
articles by Hodge, each followed by a rebuttal from Park.
Each was widely read and reprinted. Beginning with Park's
reply to the first Hodge article, cited above, they appeared
as follows:

(1) Park, "Remarks on the Biblical Repertory and Princeton
Review," Bibliotheca Sacra, VIII, 29 (January, 1851), 135-
180.

(2) Hodge, "Professor Park's Remarks on the Princeton
Review," The Biblical Repertory and Princeton Review, XXIII,

*   *   *

This was a serious charge, for Park shared with Hodge
a strong profession of faith in biblical authority. Their
conflict over Park's Convention Sermon cannot properly be
understood without first exploring precisely what each
meant by this profession. Park instructed his first class
in theology to "acquire a Scriptural Theology." But this
meant, for him, that one "should entertain no view contrary to the Bible," not that "no item of faith should be
received except from the Bible."[1] If student notes are
any indication, Park was an avid user of proof texts. But
he did not seem to regard them with great dogmatic seriousness, at least in his early career. His rationale for them
appeared to be pragmatic apologetics. Certain other semi-
narians and denominations were always ready with such texts,
so the Andover men must not be left wanting. "Our men have
the gold but not the small change," Park once told a class,

_____

2 (April, 1851), 306-347.

(3) Park, "Unity Amid Diversities of Belief, Even on Imputed
and Involuntary Sin," Bibliotheca Sacra, VIII, 31 (July,
1851), 594-647.

(4) Hodge, "Professor Park and the Princeton Review,"
The Biblical Repertory and Princeton Review, XXIII, 4
(October, 1851), 674-695.

(5) Park, "New England Theology," Bibliotheca Sacra, IX,
33 (January, 1852), 170-220.

[1] Alden, Lecture Notes (1846-47), p. 6.

with tongue in cheek.[1]

As one might infer from this, Park was definitely not a defender of verbal inspiration.[2] He might employ rationalistic arguments to defend Scriptural authority in general in relation to the truths of natural theology, but he was not concerned about the specific authority of the words of Scripture. He defined biblical inspiration in his Andover lectures as follows:

> such a divine influence upon the minds of the writers as caused them to teach in the best possible manner, whatever they intended to teach, and especially to communicate religious truth without any error either in religious doctrine or religious impression.[3]

On the surface, Hodge's definition of inspiration sounds very similar. Hodge spoke of "an influence of the Holy Spirit on the minds of certain select men, which rendered them the organs of God for the infallible communication of his mind and will."[4] But the key term here is "organs of God," for Hodge meant by this that what the biblical writers said, God said, and that they "were controlled by Him in the words which they used."[5] Hodge was very much aware of the

---

[1]Ibid., p. 7.

[2]This he made abundantly clear in his lectures: cf. George Park Fisher, Notes on Park's Lectures on Systematic Theology (1850-51; ms. in Yale University Library), pp. 120ff.

[3]Cited in Frank Hugh Foster, A Genetic History of the New England Theology (Chicago: The Univeristy of Chicago Press, 1907), p. 495.

[4]Charles Hodge, Systematic Theology, three volumes (New York: Charles Scribner's Sons, 1872), I, 154.

[5]Ibid., p. 164.

implications of this emphasis upon verbal inspiration, and he strove manfully to deal with them.

For example, he refused to allow the charge that his notion of inspiration involved a mechanical dehumanization of the biblical writers.[1] How then, one might ask, could they be the infallible organs of God? The answer came in the form of an ingenious distinction between "what the sacred writers themselves thought or believed, and what they teach."[2] The sacred writers, Hodge declared, "were not imbued with plenary knowledge," but with plenary inspiration. They were infallible only "for the special purpose for which they were employed," i.e., "only as teachers, and when acting as the spokesmen of God."[3] When not acting in that capacity, they shared the errors and imperfections common to their age and to humanity generally.

This noble attempt to preserve the humanity and historicity of the biblical writers might have succeeded had Hodge more carefully defined and delimited their special divine teaching function and the infallibility based thereon. His extension of the blanket of infallibility to cover not only "moral and religious truths" found in the Scriptures, but also biblical "statements of facts, whether scientific, historical, or geographical,"[4] brought him into conflict

---

[1] Ibid., pp. 156-157.

[2] Ibid., p. 170.

[3] Ibid., p. 165.

[4] Ibid., p. 163.

with the best science and criticism of his age and seemed
to contradict his own distinction between inspired teaching
and common human fallibility. At this point, his divergence
from Park on the question of biblical authority clearly
reveals itself. Hodge and Park shared a number of fears
about the intellectual milieu of the nineteenth century.
Both came away from their respective German tours with
considerable uneasiness about much of German philosophical
and theological speculation. But Park never developed
the fear of German biblical criticism which Hodge's
emphasis upon verbal inspiration made almost inevitable.

The key word in Park's definition of inspiration is
"religious." It was religious truth, not historical or
scientific fact, which was the focus of Park's understanding
of infallibility.[1] Park agreed with Hodge that the infallibility of the sacred writers extended only to the "special
purpose" which they served as divine spokesmen. But he did
not believe this purpose was served, in literal fashion,
with every word these men wrote. One must keep in mind the
paramount purpose of the biblical authors to communicate
religious truth and must look behind the words to their
fundamental sense or substance. Since the Scriptures were
filled with the often contradictory or inaccurate language
of feeling, a literal interpretation thereof was usually a
superficial and incorrect one in Park's view.

---

[1] cf. Foster, Genetic History, p. 494.

*   *   *

There was thus a fundamental cleavage between Hodge and Park on the question of biblical inspiration and interpretation, and it was this cleavage which stood at the heart of their polemics in regard to Park's Convention Sermon. One of the issues involved in this cleavage was plainly that of science and criticism versus Scripture, though this was not actually a key point of division between Hodge and Park in their polemical battles over Park's sermon. Their key points of contention lay rather in the two conflicting sets of doctrinal and confessional presuppositions which they used to interpret Scripture. But whether it was a question of relating Genesis to geology, to history, or to the doctrine of sin, the problem of the nature and extent of biblical inspiration and authority remained the overarching issue to be resolved if men like Hodge and Park were ever to see eye to eye.

The notion that significant contradictions and inaccuracies might occur in writings whose every word was felt to be inspired and infallible was anathema to Hodge. Equally anathema was the suggestion that such contradictions and inaccuracies could be explained only in terms of a non-literal language of the feelings. He railed against such ideas in his initial attack upon Park's Convention Sermon as follows:

> ...this theory /Park's distinction between intellect and feeling7 is destructive of the

>authority of the Bible, because it attributes
>to the sacred writers conflicting and irrec-
>oncilable representations.... In...uninspired
>men, there might be, on the hypothesis assumed,
>this conflict between feeling and knowledge,
>but to attribute such contradictions to the
>scriptures is to deny their inspiration. Besides
>this, the practical operation of a theory which
>supposes that so large a part of the Bible is
>to be set aside as inexact, because the language
>of passion, must be to subject its teachings to
>the opinion and prejudices of the reader.[1]

This last charge about reader prejudice carried a
particular barb; for Hodge was, in effect, accusing Park
of hedging about the "plain sense" of the Scriptures with
principles of interpretation designed to support Park's
version of Consistent Calvinism. This accusation was not
altogether unjustified. Park was not above using the
Scriptures as a mere buttress to his theological propositions, rather than as norm or source thereof. There is
a sense then in which his theology was, in fact, unbiblical,
as Hodge charged, despite his efforts and attestations to
the contrary.[2] But Hodge was certainly exaggerating and
distorting Park's theological manipulations of Scripture
when he described the interpretive principles of Park's
Convention Sermon thus:

>If an assertion of scripture commends itself
>to our reason, we refer it to the theology
>of the intellect, and admit its truth. If
>it clashes with any of our preconceived
>opinions, we can refer it to the theology
>of the feelings, and deny its truth for the

---

[1] Hodge, "Park's Sermon," p. 673.

[2] See F. H. Foster's good discussion of this matter
in his Genetic History, pp. 475-477.

> intellect. In this way, it is obvious any
> unpalatable doctrine may be got rid of, but
> no less obviously at the expense of the
> authority of the word of God.[1]

The unfairness of this description of Park's handling

of Scripture can plainly be seen when one recalls that Park,

as Hodge scornfully confirmed, clearly recognized, in his

Convention Sermon, the real inaccuracies and contradictions

in Scripture. Part of the thrust of that Convention Sermon

was an honest attempt to reconcile these inaccuracies and

contradictions with a notion of comprehensive biblical

authority which would satisfy Congregational orthodoxy and

yet avoid the sweeping rigidity of Princeton. It could be

argued that one who approached the Scriptures with the

"preconceived opinion" of verbal inspiration was more likely

to misread or manipulate them than one who recognized a

certain human fallibility in them. Hodge's attempts to

gloss over or explain away Scriptural contradictions were

no less manipulative of the inspired Word than Park's

alleged avoidance of "unpalatable doctrine" in the Scriptures

by consignment to the theology of feeling.[2] In short,

neither Hodge nor Park interpreted the Scriptures without

resort to "preconceived opinions." Hodge's attacks on

Park's Convention Sermon were often as much concerned with

threats to the authority of the Westminster confessional

---

[1] Hodge, "Park's Sermon," p. 646.

[2] See Hodge, Systematic Theology, I, 169ff.

tradition as with any alleged undermining of biblical
authority, though it is difficult to separate the two in
his thinking.

Hodge was on stronger ground when he concentrated his
attacks upon specific applications of Park's interpretive
principles instead of upon Park's prejudicial doctrinal
posture in general or upon his lack of concern for verbal
inspiration. In examining Park's examples of emotive, or
figurative, theological statements in the Scriptures,
Hodge observed, not without warrant, that Park was often
misinterpreting as figurative what were in fact "the formal
didactic assertions of the inspired writers."[1] Creedal
statements (e.g., Westminster) based upon such didactic
assertions, Hodge noted, were neither intended as figurative
in themselves nor meant to introduce "theory" or "philosophy"
into a supposedly metaphoric biblical context.[2] Thus far,
Hodge's critique showed some merit. But he insisted upon
seeing Park's attempts to read the Westminster doctrinal
standards figuratively as a Bushnellian subterfuge to
minimize significant differences of belief. A clever use
of the distinction between intellect and feeling, Hodge

---

[1]Hodge, "Park's Sermon," p. 656. This was particularly
true of Park's figurative interpretations of Pauline
passages on sin. One might, for example, legitimately debate
the precise "didactic" meaning of Romans 5:18, which relates
the "offence of one" (Adam) to the condemnation of all.
But to call this verse "figurative" is to verge on
exegetical irresponsibility. cf. Park, "Intellect and
Feelings," pp. 546-547.

[2]Ibid., pp. 648-649.

felt, would enable "a man to profess his faith in doctrines which he does not believe." In other words, such a distinction would "allow a man to assert contradictory propositions" through the aid of "that chemistry of thought which makes all creeds alike."[1]

This lesson in "creedal chemistry" was, of course, a rather extreme caricature of what was actually happening in Park's Convention Sermon. But it nonetheless contained, as many caricatures do, a kernel of truth. Park certainly did not believe that all creeds were alike; for he made it abundantly clear to his students and others that the New Divinity, or the Edwardsean theological tradition, with some minor improvements of his own, contained the best formulations of Christian truth yet to appear on the stage of Western history. But this confidence in his own theological position did not lead Park to separate himself from those who disagreed with him. Rather, he sought to demonstrate, especially in his Convention Sermon, that his version of Consistent Calvinism was capable of maintaining both a "substantial" identity with the Westminster tradition and a cautious openness to modern intellectual currents as well. That is, he sought to establish hermeneutical principles which would allow Old Calvinists, Consistent Calvinists, and even Unitarians to find at least a modicum of common theological ground to stand upon. Some of his

---

[1]Ibid., p. 646.

applications of these principles were strained enough
almost to justify Hodge's charges about creedal chemistry.
But the principles themselves were seriously developed
and honestly employed without resort to the kind of verbal
trickery Hodge professed to discern. In other words, Park
did not profess faith in doctrines he did not believe.

$$*\qquad\qquad*\qquad\qquad*$$

Nevertheless, Hodge did raise some legitimate questions
about the general validity of Park's interpretive principles
beyond their specific application. One of these questions
arose from Park's ambiguous and misleading terms in distinguishing the literal language of the intellect from the
figurative utterances of the feelings. Park often seemed
to say that what was true in one kind of language might be
false in the other. Hodge rightly denied that this could
be so in any absolute sense. Figurative language, he
averred, "when interpreted according to established usage...
is not only definite in its import, but it never expresses
what is false to the intellect."[1] Park's important interpretive distinction between intellect and feeling would
thus seem, in Hodge's eyes, to be false, or at best inconsequential. But despite his often ambiguous language, Park
really meant this distinction to be relative rather than

---

[1]Ibid., p. 652.

absolute. That is, both the intellect and the feelings ultimately apprehended the same truth, but in significantly
different modes.

Hodge's point would have been stronger had he pointed
out Park's own undermining of the intellect-feeling distinction through the all too frequent use of the intellect to
judge and censor the theology of the feelings. As his criticism stood, however, Hodge actually agreed with Park more
than he realized. His argument against Park's crucial interpretive distinction was based upon the assumption that the
intellect was the final arbiter of all truth, the interpreter
of the feelings according to "established usage." "No utter-
ance," Hodge declared, "is natural or effective as the language of emotion, which does not satisfy the understanding."[1]
Metaphors, in other words, must not be confused with falsehoods.[2]

Another related charge which Hodge made against Park's
intellect-feeling distinction was that it was based upon a
false psychology. "Both scripture and consciousness," asserted Hodge, "teach that the soul is an unit; that its
activity is one life."[3] But Park's Convention Sermon seemed
to deny this fundamental truth by assuming an "undue dis-
severing" of the "human faculties."[4] The Abbot Professor

---

[1] Ibid.

[2] Ibid., p. 665.

[3] Ibid., p. 661.

[4] Ibid.

appeared "to take for granted that there are two percipient principles in the soul"--the intellect and the feelings.[1] These principles, or faculties, were allegedly capable of perceiving contradictory truths.

This was probably Hodge's worst misunderstanding of what Park was about in his sermon. Park actually shared with him the notion that the intellect alone could fully perceive truth and that the feelings were essentially "blind" in this respect. Hodge may have exceeded Park's tendency toward a scholastic elevation of intellect over feelings in his notion that the "latter is but an attribute of the former, as much as form or colour is an attribute of bodies."[2] But, on the whole, the two men were in close agreement in the realm of "mental philosophy." And this agreement is scarcely surprising when one remembers their common adherence to the Scottish Philosophy.

Such an adherence on Hodge's part created special problems, for he had to reconcile the authority of consciousness, or "common sense," with that of inerrant Scriptures which contained "all the facts of theology."[3] He did this by a rather strained application of his fundamental exegetical tenet that "God cannot contradict himself."[4] It was this tenet which Hodge felt to be under

---

[1] Ibid., p. 660.

[2] Ibid., p. 661.

[3] Hodge, Systematic Theology, I, 15.

[4] Ibid.

attack in Park's Convention Sermon, where two often contradictory theologies, both supposedly scriptural, were apparently proposed; and where, in addition, important contradictions were openly alleged in God's very words. By
Hodge's lights, Park could not appeal to anything in
Scripture itself or in created nature, including consciousness, to guide or justify such a cavalier treatment of God's
Word. Nor could he appeal to the inward religious experience
(feelings) of the renewed heart, though Hodge certainly
recognized such experience in the form of the "internal
testimony" of the Spirit.[1]

These avenues of justificative or normative appeal
were closed to Park because, in Hodge's words, God "cannot
force us by the constitution of the nature which He has
given us to believe one thing, and in his Word commanded
us to believe the opposite." In other words, "all the
truths taught by the constitution of our nature or by
religious experience, are recognized and authenticated in
the Scriptures," plainly and literally interpreted.[2] God
is incapable of self-contradiction, whether within or without the Scriptures. Of course, Park was not, in reality,
attempting to set truths derived from consciousness or
religious experience over against biblical truth, any more
than Hodge was. His basic "heresy" in this regard seemed,

[1]See Hodge, "Park's Sermon," pp. 672-673.

[2]Hodge, Systematic Theology, I, 15.

from Hodge's polemics, to be his willingness to use consciousness and religious experience as norms or guides for non-
literal interpretations of Scripture. That is, he refused
to accept Hodge's forced harmonization of the inerrant,
literally construed words of Scripture with what man's
natural constitution, "common sense," and religious feelings
led him to believe.

Of course, this refusal often left him open, in
Hodge's eyes, to the not completely unwarranted charge that
he was exalting natural over revealed theology, or to the
less justified allegation that he placed subjective over
objective, revealed authority. But if he was guilty of
these charges any more than Hodge himself, his guilt stemmed,
ironically, from his attempted defense of the very tenet
Hodge accused him of undermining: that God cannot contradict himself either in nature or in revelation. Both Park
and Hodge regarded theology as an empirical, inductive,
scientific discipline. Park encouraged his students to
base their theological statements upon "evidence." But
what was the source of such evidence? For Hodge the answer
seemed obvious. "The Bible," he affirmed, "is to the
theologian what nature is to the man of science. It is his
store-house of facts."[1] These facts, or truths, the theologian is called upon "to collect, authenticate, arrange,
and exhibit in their internal relation to each other."[2]

---

[1]Ibid., p. 10.

[2]Ibid., p. 1.

Park's view of theological evidence seemed somewhat less mechanical or literalistic. The "facts" of Scripture often needed careful interpretation before they could be meaningfully collected, arranged, and harmonized with themselves and with other facts, such as those of natural and religious experience. And the means or principles of such interpretation were not always self-evident within the scriptural facts themselves. In other words, divine self-contradiction in the facts of Scripture and experience could, in Park's view, often be avoided only through the use of interpretive principles not solely derived from Scripture itself. Scripture was not always the best interpreter of Scripture for a theologian attempting a convincing empirical demonstration of the universal harmony of divine truth.

*   *   *

In sum, one might say that the crucial difference between Park and Hodge in terms of theological method was the manner in which they arranged and interpreted the scriptural "facts" which their scientific theologies purported to represent. But the issues which Hodge raised in his review of Park's sermon often obscured more than they clarified the precise nature of this central difference. The major issue in Hodge's debate with Park was not to be found in questions of psychology or of the "established

usage" by which one assures the separation of metaphor from
falsehood. And Hodge's charges about Park's scriptural and
creedal manipulations were so extreme that they seriously
distorted the crucial interpretive issue actually at stake
in the controversy.

For example, one might easily get the impression from
Hodge's comprehensive attack upon Park's intellect-feeling
distinction that such a distinction had no meaningful place
in Hodge's own hermeneutics. But in the less polemical
context of his theological lectures, Hodge described "the
inward teaching of the Spirit, or religious experience" as
"an invaluable guide in determining what the rule of faith
/the Bible/ teaches."[1] Then he went on to make the following
startling statement:

> So legitimate and powerful is this inward
> teaching of the Spirit, that it is no uncommon
> thing to find men having two theologies,--one
> of the intellect, and another of the heart. The
> one may find expression in creeds and systems of
> divinity, the other in their prayers and hymns.
> It would be safe for a man to resolve to admit
> into his theology nothing which is not sustained
> by the devotional writings of true Christians of
> every denomination.[2]

Here in a nutshell was a clear affirmation, from
supposedly hostile quarters, of the central distinction in
Park's Convention Sermon and of the emotive canon of
universality based thereon. Hodge carefully limited the

---

[1] Ibid., p. 16.

[2] Ibid., pp. 16-17.

scope of this affirmation lest anyone think him guilty of
Park's alleged sin of placing some sort of romantic intuition
above the authority of Scripture, creed, and "common sense."
He made it quite clear that Scripture was the final, objective theological norm, judging both the theology of the
intellect and that of the heart.[1] But Park, who claimed to
offer a scriptural theology, could scarcely dissent from
such a limitation. Thus, notwithstanding Hodge's attacks
thereon, the general validity of interpretive principles,
like the intellect-feeling distinction, was not really a
serious question in his dispute with Park. This is true
despite the fact that such principles were not wholly derived from Scripture but were at least partially defined
by appeals to consciousness and religious experience.

In other words, Hodge did not fully and consistently
apply his dictum that Scripture is its own best interpreter.
That Park seemed in practice to recognize no such dictum
could not, therefore, in itself, be consistently regarded
as evidence of a sinister intent to manipulate Scripture.
Hodge's sweeping charges in this regard were, in effect,
called into question by his own interpretive practice.
That same practice caused Hodge's extensive questions
about the psychological and linguistic soundness of the
intellect-feeling distinction to seem rather superficial
and beside the point. The real issue dividing the

---

[1]Ibid.

theological methods of Hodge and Park, as indicated in the beginning, was the issue of biblical inspiration.

Regardless of whether they agreed or disagreed on the validity of various interpretive principles, there was always one major, overriding presupposition which decisively separated them. This was the assumption on Hodge's part of a rigid doctrine of verbal inspiration in his understanding of biblical authority. Any hermeneutical principle Hodge accepted, including the distinction between intellect and feeling, had, in the end, to reinforce a literal interpretation of Scripture. Thus, when he qualified his acceptance of the intellect-feeling distinction by deferring to the final, objective norm of Scripture, he was really separating himself from Park more than at first appears. He meant by this qualification much more than the prohibition of significant contradictions between scriptural truth and the truths, or principles, of consciousness, nature, and religious experience. Such a prohibition Park could essentially accept. But Hodge wanted to limit all the truths, or "facts," of theology to a literally interpreted, comprehensively inerrant Scripture.

Park refused to accept this limitation. He believed that Scripture contained the most important, though not all, theological facts, or truths, and that these truths served as the decisive key to the understanding of nature and consciousness. But he could not accept the notion that nature, consciousness, and even religious experience could do no more than buttress or confirm literal scriptural truth. In other words, though Scripture was the central theological norm for Park, it was not always a clear, and certainly not a literally inerrant norm. Its interpretation could thus be significantly aided, not simply confirmed, by principles and facts from sources beyond itself.

*   *   *

As can be seen, the crucial issue of biblical inspiration was closely related, in the context of the Hodge-Park controversy, to the questions of natural versus revealed theology and of subjective versus objective (written) authority. Unfortunately, Hodge's initial review of Park's sermon created a distorted and misleading image of these central issues. And Park's rebuttal a few months afterward in the Bibliotheca Sacra, following Hodge's arguments much too closely and literally, did little to improve or clarify that image. Park devoted most of that rebuttal to lengthy and sometimes trivial corrections and clarifications of Hodge's misunderstandings of the distinction between intellect and feeling. It seems that Hodge had imposed upon Park's sermon a kind of radical theological dualism which the author had never intended. He did this by misconstruing the linguistic and psychological basis of the intellect-feeling distinction, as well as its interpretive and doctrinal implications. Employing almost sophist subtlety

on occasion, Park argued in detail against each of these
misconstructions. His aim was to demonstrate that, properly
understood, his sermon did not set up two radically different, often contradictory theologies or scriptural interpretations, "both equally correct."[1] Such a dualistic
notion was in fact completely foreign to the meaning and
purpose of the sermon.

It was not two essentially different "kinds," but two
basic "forms," or "representations," of Christian doctrine
that Park claimed to be describing in his Convention address.
In other words, the theology of the intellect was "precisely
the same with" the theology of the feelings "in its real
meaning, though not always in its form."[2] Park was particularly distressed about Hodge's accusations regarding his
lack of respect for biblical authority.[3] He flatly denied
Hodge's charge that he ascribed essential and irreconcilable
contradictions to the Scriptures. This could not be the
case, he declared, for he was in fundamental agreement with
Hodge "that the Bible teaches one and only one definite
system of doctrines."[4] Superficial contradictions might
appear in the various biblical forms of expression; but
when properly interpreted through the use of the intellect-

---

[1]Park, "Remarks on the Biblical Repertory and Princeton
Review," Bibliotheca Sacra, VIII, 29 (January, 1851), 142.

[2]Ibid., pp. 142, 149.

[3]Ibid., p. 172.

[4]Ibid., p. 149.

feeling distinction, all these forms, or figures, pointed
to the same substance of truth.

This exchange between Hodge and Park on scriptural
interpretation reminds one of two ships passing in the night,
each unrecognized by the other. In his haste to minimize
the essential differences between two "forms" of theology,
and the not unrelated divergence between himself and Hodge,
Park failed to recognize and speak to the basic issue or
assumption concerning Scripture which really divided the
two men. He simply restated, in essentially the same terms,
the very concept of figurative biblical interpretation whose
appearance in his Convention Sermon had drawn Hodge's bit-
terest attacks. He did not seem to understand that, for
a man who believed in verbal inspiration and strict, literal
interpretation of the Scriptures, an admission of contradictory statements by the sacred writers was tantamount to
the heresy of denying their role as the organs of God. It
was not enough to "interpret" these writers as agreeing "in
substance." They must agree in literal form as well.

In reality, neither Hodge nor Park really appreciated
the other's basic presuppositions on biblical authority and
interpretation. Hodge could see no need for, and much danger
in, Park's figurative reading of Scripture. The plain sense
of Scripture should satisfy any true Christian, he felt.
He thus accused Park, with some justice but with much
distortion and misunderstanding as well, of theological
dualism, or double talk, and of scriptural manipulation to

maintain such dualism. Park, in turn, set out merely to
correct the overt distortion and misunderstanding involved
in these accusations, without speaking to the underlying
but clearly recognizable issue of verbal inspiration.

            *   *   *

    Despite Park's failure really to engage Hodge on the
basic issue dividing them, and despite his tedious restate-
ments of positions and concepts already made abundantly
clear in his Convention Sermon, his rebuttal to Hodge's
review is not without value in gaining a clearer understanding of his theological method and its development.
Near the end of that rebuttal he set out to reply in detail
to a specific charge by Hodge which especially irritated
him. Hodge had argued in the concluding summary of his
review that Park's sermon provided "no adequate criteria...
for discriminating between the language of feeling and that
of the intellect."[1] In effect, Hodge was saying that it
was by arbitrary opinion or doctrinal prejudice that Park
determined the literal accuracy or error, truth or falsity,
of a scriptural or creedal statement.

    Park's reply to this charge took the form of a valuable
summary of the criteria of theological truth which he felt
had been operative in his Convention Sermon. Some of these

---

[1]Hodge, "Park's Sermon," p. 673.

criteria applied to the substance, rather than the language, of a doctrinal statement; others (the more intellectual), to its form. But all were important in determining the full truth of such a statement. It is perhaps significant that Park began his list of truth criteria with religious experience. A doctrine which did not agree with "right or Christian feeling" was automatically suspect.[1] This criterion was supplemented by two others, of a subjective nature, which owed much to Park's commitment to Common Sense philosophy. Underlying "pious feelings" were the "necessary impulses of the soul," or of man's "original constitution" (i.e., his divinely created nature), which were also acceptable norms of theological truth.[2] The Fall did not fully destroy such norms in Park's eyes. Nor did it destroy the normative power of man's moral feelings or sensibilities vis-à-vis scriptural or creedal statements. Such statements could be meaningfully evaluated according to their "moral tendencies."[3]

But moral tendencies and the "necessary impulses" of consciousness, or original constitution, did not have the last word in Park's list of truth criteria. Fourth on that list stood a strong reaffirmation of Park's "Vincentian Canon." The doctrinal substance (beneath changing forms)

---

[1] Park, "Remarks on the Princeton Review," p. 177.

[2] Ibid.

[3] Ibid., p. 178.

140

to which the feelings of all renewed men "ever and every-
where" have clung was a fundamental judge of present
theological adequacy.[1] In effect Park was bracketing the
consciousness and moral awareness of the natural man with
the present and past, individual and collective religious
experience of renewed, Christian men. Natural subjectivity
apparently required the normative aid of grace to be a
fully adequate criterion of theological truth.

The final two criteria of theological truth on Park's
list moved away from the predominantly inward or subjective[2]
focus of the first four toward a more objective, intellectual, or propositional emphasis. No doctrinal statement
or scriptural (or creedal) interpretation should ever
disagree with "other well known truths," or with "other
interpretations known to be right."[3] In other words,
theologians, insofar as they employed the language of
the intellect, must never contradict themselves or their
recognized authorities. A theological system containing
logical contradictions contained falsehoods as well. But
in addition to avoiding contradictions, the theologian,
according to Park's final criterion, had to make certain

[1]Ibid., pp. 178-179.

[2]The words "inward" and "subjective" are used here to
cover Park's rather rationalistic, Common-Sense, psychological
emphasis, and his somewhat romantic-sounding model of religious experience, both of which were intertwined in the first
four truth criteria, as they were in the Convention Sermon
itself.

[3]Park, "Remarks on the Princeton Review," pp. 179-180.

that his doctrinal formulations and interpretations rested
upon the solid foundation of "reason enlightened by
revelation," or of a "valid argument from the word or
works of God."[1] In connection with this last test of
theological truth, Park cited some of the more misleading
statements in his Convention Sermon relative to the
elevation of head over heart in the realm of religious
knowledge. But these citations were basically out of
keeping with the overall tone and emphasis of his summary
of theological criteria. On the whole, as his dispute
with Hodge began, Park seemed to be reaffirming and even
strengthening his vote of confidence in the normative
theological role of religious experience.

                *   *   *

     The controversy between Hodge and Park concerning
issues raised in the Convention Sermon was by no means
ended by Park's first rebuttal. In a second polemical
response to Park, Hodge concentrated on what he considered
the essential doctrinal differences between the two.
"From an early period in the history of the Church,"
declared the Princeton divine, "there have been two great
systems of doctrine in perpetual conflict. The one begins

---

[1]Ibid., p. 179.

with God, the other with man."[1] Speaking as a Reformed
doctrinal historian, Hodge labeled the former Augustinian-
ism, the latter Pelagianism.[2] Describing the distinctive
tenets of the latter, he noted that it began with "a theory
of free agency and of the nature of sin, to which all the
anthropological doctrines of the Bible must be made to
conform."[3] This theory affirmed that sin and moral character consisted of individual acts, always subject to a
"power to the contrary," and that "ability limits responsibility." There could thus be no "original sin," and
grace and regeneration were resistible. God governed the
world and made salvation possible, through the atonement,
by means of example and moral suasion.[4]

Completely antagonistic to this "Pelagian" system was
the Augustinian "vindication of the supremacy of God in
the whole work of man's salvation."[5] This supremacy was
absolutely necessary since fallen humanity was "utterly
ruined and helpless." Sin and righteousness were states
derived, respectively, from Adam and Christ, not from free
acts of personal responsibility. Grace and regeneration

----

[1]Hodge, "Professor Park's Remarks on the Princeton
Review," The Biblical Repertory and Princeton Review, XXIII,
2 (April, 1851), 308.

[2]Ibid., p. 326.

[3]Ibid., p. 309.

[4]Ibid., pp. 309-312.

[5]Ibid., p. 312.

were irresistible gifts of a divine sovereign. And that
sovereign governed and saved, not through benevolent influence, but according to an absolute justice, literal satisfaction of which was accomplished in the atonement.[1]

Hodge, of course, claimed adherence to this "Augustinian" system, which was "confessedly mysterious," rather
than "characteristically rational."[2] "It is an undeniable
historical fact," said he, "that this system underlies the
piety of the Church in all ages."[3] He called it (the
Augustinian system) a "great granitic formation," which
had "withstood all changes" and all challenges, including
those of "logic, indignation /and/ wit."[4] It was thus the
height of absurdity for Park to attempt to reconcile this
system, in any sense, with his Pelagian, or semi-Pelagian,
doctrines.

*   *   *

Yet this is exactly what Hodge believed his opponent
was doing with the intellect-feeling distinction. He
described Park's interpretive method as taking two contradictory doctrinal statements and supposedly "disclosing
the fundamental principle in which they agree for substance

[1]Ibid., pp. 312-317.

[2]Ibid., p. 317.

[3]Ibid., p. 319.

[4]Ibid., p. 319.

144

of doctrine."[1] For example, the statement that Adam's sin was imputed to his posterity found substantial agreement with its contrary in the "fundamental principle" that "the sin of Adam was the occasion of certain evils coming upon his race."[2] Hodge was particularly distressed that Park seemed to regard the "Augustinian" concept of original sin as "only an intense form of expressing this definite idea" (i.e., Adam's "occasioning" evil).[3]

To say, declared the Princeton divine, "that the corrupt nature which we derive from our first parents is really sinful, is a different doctrine from that which is expressed by saying, our nature though prone to sin is not itself sinful." These were, for Hodge, "irreconcilable assertions," not merely "different modes of stating the same truth."[4] Park responded to these Princetonian arguments by, in a sense, conceding their truth. In a long article entitled "Unity Amid Diversities of Belief, Even on Imputed and Involuntary Sin,"[5] he admitted that the "old theory of imputation," if taken literally, could not be harmonized with any notion of personal moral responsibility for sin. But, he averred, the "old writers," such as

---

[1]Ibid., p. 325.

[2]Ibid.

[3]Ibid.

[4]Ibid., p. 328.

[5]Bibliotheca Sacra, VIII, 31 (July, 1851), 594-647.

Turretin, whom Hodge frequently quoted in support of
Reformed orthodoxy, "in their better hours" were "wont
to give up their doctrines of a literally imputed sin."[1]
He was sure that such writers actually had "substantially,
at least in their practical meditations, the same general
faith" as that outlined in his Convention Sermon.[2]

Returning to his intellect-feeling distinction, the
Andover divine asserted that "while it is natural for a
good man to use these bold metaphors /regarding imputation/
sometimes in the enforcement of truth, he is unable to
persevere in uniformly employing them as literal phrases."[3]
In addition, Hodge's notion of original sin was against
"common sense": "As a theory," maintained the Abbot Professor, "it is too absurd to be retained in the mind without an unnatural effort, and such an effort must be inter-
mittent."[4] Park then began to list arguments demonstrating
the essential "unity amid diversities" of theological
opinion on original sin. Those who claimed to believe in
imputed or passive sin frequently denied the implications
of their own position, he asserted, by refusing to make God
the author of sin, or to allow one sin to be the punishment
for another, or even to allow individual men to feel

---

[1] Ibid., p. 626.

[2] Ibid., p. 615.

[3] Ibid., p. 618.

[4] Ibid., p. 619.

"either penitence or remorse" for Adam's sin.[1] These professed believers in literal imputation of a totally sinful nature to mankind also could not deny all the "amiable sentiments" belonging to that nature.[2]

Most significant of all, however, was the inability of the proponents of passive sin to attribute to it a definite moral character. To do so, Park averred, with lengthy supporting arguments, was to confuse human nature with human actions or choices, to identify the occasion of sin with the sin itself.[3] Not even the great Augustine made such an identification, he declared, except in metaphor. Referring to his Princeton opponent, Park queried, "Did he not know that Augustine often wrote in the language of feeling, and that after all his eloquent expressions in regard to passive sin, he declared them to be only figurative expressions?"[4]

*   *   *

This was more than Hodge could bear. In a final relatively brief reply to Park, he accused the Abbot

---

[1]Ibid., pp. 629-635.

[2]Ibid., p. 635.

[3]Ibid., pp. 635-643.

[4]Ibid., p. 643.

Professor of "evasions, and playing with words."[1] He
found "nothing new as to substance or form" in Park's
arguments, except that they were presented "with less
than common logical force and discrimination."[2] He also
objected strenuously to his Andover opponent's "manner of
conducting the discussions." Park represented his
(Hodge's) articles, he declared, "as little else than a
series of misstatements."[3] In truth, however, it was Park
who misunderstood and misstated at every turn:

> There is a large class of words to which Professor
> Park attaches a meaning different from that in
> which they are used by theologians of the Reformed
> Church, and he, therefore, unavoidably misunder-
> stands and misrepresents their doctrines. To this
> class of terms belong such words as imputation,
> guilt, punishment, condemnation, satisfaction,
> justification, nature, natural, moral, disposition,
> voluntary, etc.[4]

In a word, where orthodox Reformed doctrine was concerned, the Abbot Professor clearly did not know what he was
talking about; therefore, as Hodge saw it, there was no
further need to debate with him. Thus, after briefly
reiterating the differences between the "Augustinian" and
"Pelagian" systems in light of Park's misconceptions regarding original sin, the Princeton divine took his leave

---

[1]Hodge, "Professor Park and the Princeton Review," The
Biblical Repertory and Princeton Review, XXIII, 4 (October,
1851), 687.

[2]Ibid., p. 678.

[3]Ibid., p. 687; cf. also pp. 688-695.

[4]Ibid., p. 678.

of the controversy. He did, however, make a remark in the course of his article which drew a lengthy concluding rebuttal from his opponent. If Park hoped "to succeed in his present course," said Hodge, he had first "to answer Edwards on the Will, Edwards on the Affections, and Edwards on Original Sin."[1]

*   *   *

The Andover divine responded to this comment with his own exposition and defense of Edwardsean theology, which will not be detailed here.[2] It would seem, however, that these two great polemicists had again passed each other like ships in the night without really meeting on the central issues raised. Each largely occupied himself with restating his own position, making little attempt to comprehend and debate the fundamental philosophical and doctrinal presuppositions of the other. The controversy between them nonetheless had great significance for Park's theological method. Throughout his conflict with Hodge, he clung tenaciously to his distinction between intellect and feelings. Even though it was not the center of attention in the more specifically doctrinal phases of the polemics,

---

[1]Ibid., p. 686.

[2]Park, "New England Theology," Bibliotheca Sacra, IX, 33 (January, 1852), 170-220; see chap. VII.

it continued to play a not inconsequential role therein.
In fact, the awareness reflected in this distinction of the
importance of the feelings, or inward experience, to religion and theology continued to be a factor in Park's theological development for some time after the dispute with
Hodge had run its course.

Evidence of this continuity can be seen in an interesting address which Park delivered at the dedication of a new
library building at Amherst College. The address, given
almost two years after the last skirmish in the battle with
Hodge, was entitled "Taste and Religion Auxiliary to Each
Other" and was designed to demonstrate "the importance of
Aesthetic in connection with Religious and Moral Culture."[1]
It made more explicit a supportive continuity which Park
assumed and indirectly referred to in his Convention

---

[1]From an account of the library dedication in The
Hampshire and Franklin Express (Amherst, Massachusetts,
November 25, 1853), cited in Emily Dickinson's Home: Letters
of Edward Dickinson and His Family, ed. Millicent Todd
Bingham (New York: Harper and Brothers Publishers, 1955),
p. 319. A full "Report of Professor Park's Address" was
later printed in the weekly Express (December 2, 1853, 3,
cols. 3-4). Park was, of course, no stranger to Amherst,
having taught "mental and moral philosophy" there before
coming to Andover. Not surprisingly, given his reputation
as preacher and theologian, he was invited to preach before
students and townspeople alike on the Sunday preceding the
dedication ceremony (which took place on Tuedsay,
November 22). The poet Emily Dickinson heard him that
Sunday and could scarcely contain her emotion. To her
brother Austin, she wrote, "I never heard anything like
it, and dont expect to again, till we stand at the great
white throne...." (Emily to William Austin Dickinson,
November 21, 1853, printed in Bingham, p. 137) Unfortunately, no record of her impressions of Park's dedicatory
address seems to have survived (see Bingham, p. 319).

Sermon--a continuity between feelings related to aesthetic
and to religious experience. In effect, Park was continuing
at Amherst a theme expressed in a different manner several
years before at the ministerial convention in Boston.
Religion, morality, and theology were as much dependent
upon feelings and inward experience as were the arts.
Intellect without feeling, like prose without poetry, was
dead so far as "taste" and "religion" were concerned.

Even in the late 1860's, Park was still making
constructive use of the intellect-feeling distinction,
particularly in his sermons, to stress the normative
theological importance of religious feeling or experience.[1]
His refusal to yield to Hodge's attacks on that distinction
drew increasingly favorable press in such liberal organs
as the Christian Examiner. One writer for that journal,
after reviewing the entire dispute between Hodge and Park
blow by blow, had no doubts that Park had carried the day:
"A more complete and triumphant victory has not recently

---

[1]Park's sermon at the dedication of the North Andover
Congregational Church in May of 1866 illustrates this point.
Preaching on the text of Romans 1:16, he invoked a form of
his trusted distinction between intellect and feeling to
demonstrate the significance of the use of sensible images,
the most important being the facts of Christ's life, in
proclaiming the "power of the gospel." Such images were
not mere emotive functions or illustrations of abstract
(intellectual) theological truth, but standards and norms
of such truth. See Mrs. William Franklin Snow, "Notes of
Sermons Delivered by Edwards A. Park and Others in the
Andover Theological Seminary Chapel /and elsewhere/" (1862,
1866; ms. in Oberlin College Library), pp. 33-34.

been won on the field of controversy."[1] But Park might
well have been distressed by the "practical lesson" which
the admiring reviewer found in such a "triumphant victory":
"Creeds, as bonds of union, are useless. The terms in
which they are written are as ambiguous as the terms of
Scripture.... The terminology of theology is the apple of
discord."[2] Park was, of course, interested in clarifying
and "scientifically" improving, but not in totally dis-
carding, traditional Reformed creedal statements. A
clearly written creed, which did not confuse the language
of the intellect with that of the feelings, was far from
useless, in his mind, as a bond of union. By attributing
to Park an anti-creedal position which seemed to transform
significant theological differences into mere matters of
terminology, his liberal admirer had simply reinforced
Hodge's most extreme charges. Park's relatively cautious
emphasis upon the theological role of the feelings or
religious experience was beginning to place him in a
difficult situation.

That situation was certainly not improved when
another liberal spokesman implicitly identified Park,
along with Bushnell, as a "prime mover" in the "yet

---

[1] R. P. Stebbins, "The Andover and Princeton Theologies,"
Christian Examiner and Religious Miscellany, LII, fourth
series XVII, 3 (May, 1852), 335.

[2] Ibid.

undeveloped scheme of the New Theology."[1] In this context,
"new theology" meant certain "progressive" or "liberal"
deviations from strict Westminster doctrine, which the
writer discerned within still nominally orthodox Reformed
communions.[2] When this author cited none other than
Charles Hodge as the leading authority on the "new
theology," by virtue of Hodge's position as the "most
distinguished defender of the old," there could be little
doubt as to the proper classification for Park.[3] Park
could not help but be disturbed by the following conclusion
regarding the "new theologians" which his liberal interpreter came to on Hodge's authority:

> Can these earnest and able divines...be
> regarded as actually holding the sub-
> stance of the old doctrines? Certainly
> not, we answer.... So, too, answers
> Dr. Hodge.[4]

Here again the basis of Hodge's attacks upon Park was
given credence from unexpected quarters. Both Hodge and
the Unitarians seemed to agree that Park's distinction
between the theology of the intellect and that of the
feelings was a distinction in substance as well as form.

---

[1]George E. Ellis, "The New Theology," Christian
Examiner and Religious Miscellany, LXII, fourth series
XXVII, 3 (May, 1857), 357.

[2]Ibid., pp. 321-328.

[3]Ibid., p. 340.

[4]Ibid., p. 357.

In other words, Park did not really believe or accept,
in any sense (metaphoric or literal), the Old Calvinist
doctrines he ascribed to the inaccurate, but substantially
truthful, language of the feelings. His Convention Sermon
merely manipulated terms and distinctions to mask his
fundamental break with Reformed orthodoxy.

*   *   *

Such interpretations of the motives behind Park's
widely read sermon, coming as they did from both extremes
of the theological spectrum, were rapidly placing the
famed Abbot Professor in an untenable position. His
arguments that he was merely improving the form, not
altering the substance, of Westminster doctrines seemed
to fall on deaf ears. As a result, significant changes
of emphasis began to occur in Park's theological work
during the 1860's and 1870's. Though his sermons, in
some instances, continued to reflect a constructive
emphasis upon the interdependence of theology and religious
experience, intellect and feeling, his lectures indicated
an increasing tendency to transform the intellect-feeling
distinction into an empty polemical device. Thus, a
distinction whose initial aim had been reconciliation with
Old Calvinism, and cautious openness to new theological
trends as well, became a contrivance for retrenchment
behind old dogmatic barriers. Hodge's charge that Park

was using the feelings, not as a legitimate, constructive theological norm, but as a stratagem for dealing with unpalatable doctrines, assumed a belated truth. The theology of the feelings became little more than a pejorative term for the "irrational" theology of Park's opponents.

In sum, given the kind of response his Convention Sermon received and given his position at the "West Point" of New England Congregational Orthodoxy, Park apparently felt an increasing need to defend his own orthodoxy. Such a defense led him ultimately to position himself against the forces of theological change in nineteenth-century America. It also led to a decisive, normative triumph of intellect over feelings in his theological method.

Chapter VI

THE GREAT DISRUPTION

Park did not become embroiled in another controversy
of the magnitude of his battle with Hodge until the end
of his career. And when he entered the lists for the
last time, he was no longer on the side of doctrinal
freedom and innovation. He was, in effect, attempting
to thwart a theological revolution that was rapidly
engulfing not only Andover Seminary but the entire
Congregational communion as well. During the late 1860's
and particularly during the 1870's, Park found himself
increasingly isolated from the rest of the Andover faculty
on curricular and other matters. The course of this
progressive isolation is perhaps nowhere better traced
than in his annual reports to the Andover Trustees.[1]

Throughout the 1840's and 1850's these reports reveal
a man whose whole life was bound up in the affairs of
Andover and of Congregationalism, and whose influence in
those affairs was great indeed. There is thus a special
poignancy in the reports for 1861 and 1863, where Park

---

[1]See "Annual Reports to the Board of Trustees of
Andover Theological Seminary," 1838-81, in the Archives
of Phillips Academy. Such reports were required of
faculty members by the constitution of the seminary.

speaks of a decline in the quality and number of Andover
students, and in the prestige and influence of the seminary.
Andover's most celebrated professor obviously believed
something was wrong with the way in which the seminary
was being operated. But his true feelings in this matter
were reflected only indirectly when he called for more
funds and better facilities. Such appeals were almost
routine with him; pessimism about the fate of his beloved
seminary definitely was not.

The roots of such pessimism were implied in a special
section of his 1863 report (dated June 9) in which he
discussed preparations for his forthcoming European trip.
As he outlined the alternate lecture schedule by which
the seminary was expected to get through the year without
him, he began to lament not only the failing health which
had made his trip necessary, but the absence, through
death or retirement, of all his "old colleagues." Only
in Austin Phelps, his successor in the Bartlet Chair,
could he still find an old friend and kindred spirit on
a faculty which was steadily becoming alien to him.[1] It
is not without significance that the year 1863 marked the
inauguration of Egbert C. Smyth (1829-1904), who had just
returned from the fountains of German learning at Berlin
and Halle, to the Brown Professorship of Ecclesiastical

---

[1]cf. Frank Hugh Foster, The Life of Edwards Amasa
Park (New York: Fleming H. Revell Company, 1936), pp. 175
and 227.

History at Andover.

That particular professorship had created special
problems for Andover since its foundation. The seminary's
founders feared that awareness of the historical diversity
of Christian thought might undermine the true Westminster
faith in which all Andover students were supposed to be
carefully schooled. The study of church history was thus
relegated to a small portion of the senior year after the
correct interpretations of Scripture and creed had been
thoroughly learned.[1] Unfortunately, the first Brown
Professor had not learned these interpretations thoroughly
enough himself to prevent Andover's Trustees and Visitors
from dismissing him for serious doctrinal deviations.[2]
After his dismissal, the study of church history at Andover
lapsed into an innocuous quiescence until the appointment
of W. G. T. Shedd to the faculty in the early 1850's.
Shedd's idealistic and organic view of history, though
employed within thoroughly orthodox doctrinal channels,
seemed to disturb Park and others; and, as a result, he

_____

[1]cf. Leonard Woods, History of the Andover Theological
Seminary (Boston: James R. Osgood and Company, 1885),
p. 188.

[2]cf. Woods, History, pp. 172-173; also see Henry K.
Rowe, History of Andover Theological Seminary (Newton,
Massachusetts: For the Seminary, 1933), pp. 68-69. The
professor in question was James Murdock, a Yale-trained
scholar of no small erudition, who held the Brown Chair
from 1821 to 1828. He unsuccessfully appealed his dismissal from Andover all the way to the Massachusetts
Supreme Court, in a case that set important precedents
for future litigation surrounding the seminary.

eventually accepted an appointment to the faculty of Union
Seminary in New York.[1]

But Shedd had begun a mild revolution in the church
history department, and the appointment of Egbert Smyth
as his successor was to bring that revolution to its
fruition. Smyth's German studies had increasingly attracted
him to the concept of historical development. In a lecture
to Andover's senior class of 1874 extolling "The Value of
the Study of Church History," he asserted that no Christian
doctrine could be properly comprehended apart from its
history. "Theology," he boldly declared, "is essentially
a growth, and should be studied as a growth."[2] Furthermore, Smyth averred, the history of the Church and of
Christian doctrine could not be legitimately separated
from the general history of mankind. Such notions as this
could scarcely have been more distressing to the venerable
Abbot and Bartlet professors.

This distress was multiplied when Smyth and some of
the other younger faculty members proposed the so-called
"Parallel Course." The traditional plan of instruction
at Andover assigned the first year to the study of Sacred
Literature, the second to Christian Theology, and the third

---

[1] On Park's attitude toward Shedd, see Foster, Life,
p. 233. See also Park to Bela Bates Edwards, October 2,
1847, C. R. Park Family Papers.

[2] Egbert C. Smyth, The Value of the Study of Church
History in Ministerial Education (Andover, 1874), p. 14.

to Sacred Rhetoric and Ecclesiastical History.[1] This plan
allowed Park the undivided attention of the Middle Class;
and he took full advantage of his "monopoly year," lecturing six days a week from eleven o'clock in the morning
until noon, and frequently until half past noon. These
lectures attracted numerous "wandering scholars," who,
following the custom of the day, traveled from school to
school to hear various "name" professors. Park was understandably reluctant to accept the proposed new course
plan, which called for the simultaneous or parallel teaching of the various disciplines throughout the three years
of instruction. He saw such a plan as a threat to his
position of influence and to the integrity of his discipline
as well. It forced him to divide his time among the
various classes and destroyed the unity and effectiveness
of his lectures. He also saw it as a device to reduce or
mask student boredom with the instruction in Sacred
Literature and Church History, by mixing with that
instruction his own more stimulating theological teaching.[2]

But most important of all, Andover's leading professor
came to see the Parallel Course as a threat to the historic
theological position of the seminary, which he felt
obligated to defend. Smyth's lectures and methods raised

---

[1] cf. Woods, History, p. 186.

[2] See Park's "Reports to the Andover Trustees,"
1866-68; 1877; 1880. Phillips Academy Archives.

the strong possibility that the New England Theology
might be superseded. In Park's eyes, the raising of such
a possibility was tantamount to heresy. It is thus
scarcely surprising that he vigorously opposed the position-
ing of Smyth's teaching alongside his own in the Andover
curriculum. In addition, the teaching of two other
younger professors, Charles M. Mead and Joseph H. Thayer,
reinforced Park's opposition to the Parallel Course.
Coming to Andover shortly after Smyth, these two biblical
scholars were well versed in German critical-historical
methods and continued with rigorous honesty the trends in
biblical study begun by Moses Stuart. But unlike Stuart,
they were not capable of combining an orthodox evangelical
faith with their critical methodology.[1] Since Park was
unable to accept the latter without the former, he came
to regard the work of Mead and Thayer as at best uninspired
pedantry, and at worst outright heresy.[2] If Stuart had
taught him to respect important aspects and assumptions of
German critical scholarship, Mead and Thayer caused him to

---

[1]Stuart himself had his difficulties on this point, at
least so far as his students were concerned. In 1825 his
use of German critical works in his teaching was investi-
gated by a committee appointed by the Andover Trustees.
The committee concluded that though such works provided
valuable knowledge about the Scriptures, their indiscrim-
inate use threatened "to chill the ardor of piety" and to
induce "universal skepticism." They therefore recommended
more professorial discretion and guidance in such matters.
How much heed Stuart paid to this admonition is uncertain.
See Woods, History, pp. 173-178.

[2]See Foster, Life, pp. 234-235.

ignore and even despise such scholarship.

Despite Park's heated objections, the Parallel Course was established in the late 1860's, and he ceased attending faculty meetings. In response to an inquiry from the Trustees, he listed four reasons for his action: (1) he had done more than his share of administrative work for Andover already; (2) his health was failing; (3) he strongly dissented from the direction the new faculty were taking; and (4) he felt the need to devote full time to his teaching.[1] Of these four, only the second and third had any real importance, and Park actually saw them as interrelated. He declared:

> I do not agree with the members of the Faculty in reference to the mode of conducting the Seminary. I do not feel able to bear any responsibility for their methods of administration since I disapprove of many of them. I have not sufficient health for engaging in discussions with regard to the changes which have been made. The most that can be expected of me is to make no active opposition to measures which I privately think have been injurious to the institution, and to measures which I foresee will be injurious.[2]

The health problem alluded to here was no mere ruse or rationalized excuse. It tended to isolate Park from the affairs of Andover almost as much as his dispute with the new faculty. During the 1870's, he was forced to give up one by one the various activities which had created and

---

[1] Park to the Andover Trustees, April 11, 1871. Phillips Academy Archives.

[2] Ibid.

ensured his pervasive influence over the life of the
seminary. His regular chapel preaching came to an end,
as did his many "recruiting" sermons for Andover at
surrounding colleges.[1] Likewise terminated were his
evening Gesellschaften, his long walks, and his after-
class debates with students. But worst of all, his
failing eyesight forced him to reduce his regular classroom lectures and to rely increasingly upon student
assistants who could read their notes to the class.[2]
In the academic year of 1874-75, he was unable to lecture
at all and was forced to accompany his old friend Phelps
to a sanatorium.

Throughout these years of declining health and
influence, Park's reports to the seminary trustees were
filled with lamentations over Andover's general state and
particularly over the heterodoxy and often the poor moral
character of his students.[3] More extended and persistent

[1]See Park, "Report to the Andover Trustees," July 1,
1873. Phillips Academy Archives. Also see Andover
Trustees to Park, June 29, 1875, C. R. Park Family Papers.

[2]Ibid., 1874 and 1878. Apparently the students'
notes were more systematic and complete (and certainly
more readable!) than Park's own. In the report to the
trustees of June 24, 1871, he even mentioned lecturing
himself from the notes of his own students. But in the
reports for 1880 and 1881 (his final years before retirement), he expressed considerable skepticism about the
accuracy and effectiveness of student notes and student
readers. The necessity of almost total reliance upon
them during these years may well have hastened his decision
to retire.

[3]cf. Park, "Reports to the Andover Trustees," 1871,
1872, 1874, 1876.

than his complaints of the early 1860's, these later jere-
miads left no doubt as to the cause of the problem. It was
the Parallel Course and the increasing influence of the new
faculty.[1] When it became evident, however, that the new
curricular arrangement was there to stay, Park grudgingly
accommodated himself to it.[2] Noting that his complaints to
the trustees had had no effect, he resumed attendance at
faculty meetings in the late 1870's to make his voice heard,
despite his poor health.[3] But the gulf between him and the
rest of the faculty continued to widen, and his efforts to
regain his former influence were to no avail. A new intellectual world was in the making, and the responses of Park
and of his younger colleagues to that world were radically
different.

*   *   *

One of the most important elements in that new world

---

[1] Ibid., 1877. It should perhaps be noted that that influence was not always decisive in curricular or other matters. Though the Parallel Course remained substantially in-
tact, Park and Phelps occasionally won the Trustees' approval
for modifications in it, often over the strong protests of
their younger colleagues. For the conclusion of one such
exchange, see Andover Trustees to Professors Smyth, Thayer,
and Mead, September 3, 1877, copy in C. R. Park Family Papers.

[2] Ibid., 1874. Park saw to it that the lecture hours
assigned to him were strictly observed. If any of the junior
faculty encroached upon these hours, immediate reparation was
usually demanded and made: cf. letter of Egbert C. Smyth to
E. A. Park, November 7, 1877, in C. R. Park Family Papers.

[3] Ibid., 1876.

164

was Darwinism. In the years following the Civil War, when
the theory of evolution was just beginning to have an
appreciable impact on the American mind, Andover received
a number of generous endowments, bringing in new lecture
series, new professors, and new ideas at an accelerated
pace. One of the new chairs, the Stone Professorship, was
significantly titled "The Relation of Christianity to the
Secular Sciences." Its first occupant John P. Gulliver
assumed his duties in 1879. His inaugural address on
"Christianity and Science" focused apologetic attention
not so much upon Darwin himself, whose significance he
greatly understated, but upon the materialistic philosophy
of men like Herbert Spencer. It was this philosophy, not
science or evolution as such, which formed the worst threat
to Christianity, according to Gulliver.[1] His modest efforts
to defend the faith through a reasoned refutation of
Spencer and others represented the first open and systematic
attempt by an Andover professor to deal with the problems
posed by the methods, assumptions, and discoveries of the
new science.

Throughout his career, Park remained largely silent on
the issues Gulliver raised.[2] In his report to the trustees
of 1871, he noted that "some branches of Natural Theology

---

[1]cf. John P. Gulliver, Christianity and Science
(Andover, 1879).

[2]See Frank Hugh Foster, A Genetic History of the New
England Theology (Chicago: The University of Chicago Press,
1907), p. 475.

connected with the speculations of Darwin and Huxley have rendered it necessary to change the order and proportion of my lectures."[1] But the key words here are "speculations" and "order and proportion." Park, to the end of his life, regarded Darwin's work as presenting no more than an interesting hypothesis. As such, it might engage the speculative powers of the theologian, at odd moments. But until it received a more conclusive demonstration, he should not seriously trouble himself with it or substantively modify his theology to meet its challenges.

This is not to imply that Park felt the Christian faith could not be harmonized with evolution. He was not prepared bluntly to identify evolutionary theory with atheism, as did his old enemy Charles Hodge in a publication entitled What Is Darwinism? (1874). He had admired the rigorous intellectual honesty with which Moses Stuart met the problems raised by Sir Charles Lyell's Principles of Geology (1830) vis-à-vis Genesis. And he could see no reason, in principle, why this same sort of dialogue between science and religion should not be continued in the case of Darwinism. Theology was, after all, scientific, in Park's view; and, as such, it could never lose sight of empirical evidence. But theology and science had distinct spheres of truth and evidence to which their methods were applied.

----

[1]Park, "Report to the Andover Trustees," June 24, 1871; pp. 6-7.

And one had always to keep this in mind when interpreting
Scripture or creed. The Bible, as Stuart had made clear,
was not a book of science. Park accepted this assumption
and entertained the fundamental belief that, in the final
analysis, scientific and religious truth were not in
conflict.

To demonstrate this belief, he encouraged his friend
George Frederick Wright to publish a series of articles
on Darwinian theory and its relation to Calvinism. Wright,
an Oberlin-trained Congregational minister in Andover with
an interest in geology, was singularly well-qualified for
this task. He presented a widely hailed geological paper
before the Boston Society of Natural History in 1876 and
enjoyed the friendship of such scientific luminaries as
Harvard botanist Asa Gray. With the aid of Gray, he submitted five articles to Park for the Bibliotheca Sacra from
1875 to 1880, "stating the arguments for and against Darwinism, and showing the bearing of that theory upon the doctrine of design in nature and upon theological opinions in
general."[1] These essays reflected a grasp of evolutionary
theory which drew praise from Darwin himself.[2] Wright concluded that "Calvinism and Darwinism had so many points in

---

[1]G. F. Wright, The Story of My Life and Work (Oberlin,
Ohio: The Bibliotheca Sacra Company, 1916), p. 137. See
also Michael McGiffert, "Christian Darwinism: The Partnership of Asa Gray and George Frederick Wright, 1874-1881"
(Yale University: unpublished Ph.D. dissertation, 1958).

[2]Ibid., p. 138.

common that theologians could not consistently cast stones at the men of science favoring a scheme in which 'predestination and foreordination' were salient features." He went on to observe that "from a philosophical point of view, Darwinism has all the unlovely characteristics of hyper-Calvinism without any of the redeeming remedial features inherent in the Calvinistic system. Pure Darwinism leaves no place for the gospel."[1]

*   *   *

Park was undoubtedly pleased with Wright's work, but he still refused to accept the theory of evolution. And he persisted in viewing efforts to harmonize Darwinism and Calvinism as primarily avocational activity on the part of the theologian. Such speculative activity was interesting and legitimate to be sure; but it required, for the time being, no substantive re-thinking of the New England Theology. Park took a similar attitude toward those speculations of Jonathan Edwards which did not harmonize with his own theological position. He was not about to allow the liberal new faculty members at Andover and their intellectual kin to claim the Edwardsean mantle. But this they seemed on the verge of doing when, in the fall of 1880,

---

[1]Ibid. See also Wright's "Science and Religion. Some Analogies Between Calvinism and Darwinism," _Bibliotheca Sacra_, XXXVII (January, 1880), 48-76.

just prior to Park's retirement, his colleague Egbert Smyth published what purported to be a long suppressed Edwards manuscript on the Trinity.

The manuscript, entitled Observations concerning the Scripture Oeconomy of the Trinity and Covenant of Redemption, had presumably been suppressed because of its heterodoxy. Its publication came in the wake of the public hue and cry aroused when Oliver Wendell Holmes charged Edwards' literary custodians with misrepresentation and outright censorship.[1] This accusation was scarcely new. As early as 1831, questions had been raised privately concerning the suppression of Edwards manuscripts. Twenty years later such questions had become public when Horace Bushnell in his preface to Christ in Theology accused the Dwight heirs of withholding from him an Edwards manuscript on the Trinity.[2] Strangely enough, however, Bushnell's allegation produced little more than a flurry of correspondence among the Edwards descendants, and it was left to Holmes to rekindle the fire.[3] As it turned out, only at Andover could that fire be quenched; for it was there that practically all the significant literary remains of Jonathan Edwards were housed.

---

[1]The charge occurred in an article on Edwards in the International Review, IX (July, 1880), 25.

[2]cf. Horace Bushnell, Christ in Theology (Hartford, 1851), p. vi.

[3]cf. Richard D. Pierce, "A Suppressed Edwards Manuscript on the Trinity," The Crane Review, I, 2 (Winter, 1959), 68-70, 73-75.

Smyth and Park, whose wives were Edwards descendants, had gained possession of the two major collections of these remains in 1865 and 1870, respectively. Their estrangement on matters of doctrine and academic policy[1] prevented what could have been a profitable editorial collaboration; for each contemplated, but never realized, extensive publication of his papers. Preparatory to such publication, each gave thorough study to his own collection of documents; and it was in the course of this study that Smyth became interested in the "case of the suppressed manuscript." Inquiries addressed to various Edwards descendants and to Park convinced Smyth that he possessed a copy of the treatise withheld from Bushnell.[2] His publication of that treatise, however, failed to quiet the controversy sparked by Holmes. For the document was in fact doctrinally innocuous enough to arouse suspicion that another more heterodox manuscript was still being suppressed.

It was to allay such suspicion that Park published his last major article in the Bibliotheca Sacra: a two-part discussion of the "Remarks of Jonathan Edwards on the Trinity," buttressed by extensive quotations.[3] The article

---

[1]There was, as might be expected, a certain amount of family bickering and bitterness among the descendants of Edwards relative to the appropriate custody of his papers. Some of this no doubt colored the relationship of Smyth and Park.

[2]cf. Pierce, pp. 75-78.

[3]Bibliotheca Sacra, XXXVIII, 149 and 150 (January and April, 1881), 147-187; 333-369.

indicated that Park possessed an original Edwards manuscript on the Trinity, which he had, unfortunately, mislaid.[1] His discussion of the supposed anti-trinitarian heterodoxy of this document was thus based upon other "writings of Edwards and memoranda of my own," with particular attention to selections from Edwards' unpublished "Treatise on Grace."[2] This treatise, Park maintained, contained "substantially" the ideas expressed in the lost manuscript. But he devoted about as much space to belittling the importance of Edwards' writings about the Trinity in general as to expounding their specific content.

Edwards' speculations upon the Trinity were said to have derived from "a few leisure hours" of "incidental studies" not directly connected with "his main work."[3] They were mere "tentative" hints of his thought on the subject, not intended as final conclusions for public consumption.[4] His editors had admittedly suppressed such hints when they "did not coincide with the known course of his thought" or were "unworthy of him."[5] But they felt justified in so doing "by the ancient rumor that the President was in the habit of writing down his thoughts as they occurred

---

[1]The interesting manner in which Park came to possess this ms. is discussed in Pierce, pp. 75-77.

[2]See Park, "Remarks on Edwards on the Trinity," p. 187n.

[3]Ibid., p. 149.

[4]Ibid., pp. 147-155.

[5]Ibid., p. 157.

to him, whether he sanctioned them or not."[1] At any rate, these "unsanctioned" jottings were relatively few, Park argued, when compared with the great mass of "approved" Edwards writings on the Trinity and other subjects.[2]

Remarkably, the public seemed to accept Park's general apology for the "orthodox" Edwards. His failure to refer to Smyth's publication would seem to indicate that Edwards produced at least two extended manuscript discussions of the Trinity, one in Park's possession and one (a copy) in Smyth's. Which one was withheld from Bushnell is not at all certain, but it is clear that Edwards gave more "special attention" to the Trinity than Park's article implied.[3] Nevertheless, public suspicion regarding Edwards' orthodoxy and the censorship of his papers tended to subside after Park's explanations. And this was just as well, for Holmes had really created a stir about nothing. When the manuscript Park had lost was finally discovered and published after his death, it proved to be little more heterodox than the Smyth document.[4] Its suppression apparently stemmed from Edwards' espousal of the Nicene doctrine of the Son's eternal generation: a doctrine rejected by later New England theologians.

---

[1] Ibid.

[2] Ibid.

[3] Ibid., p. 149.

[4] cf. George Park Fisher, An Unpublished Essay of Edwards on the Trinity (New York, 1903).

*   *   *

No sooner had Park successfully ended the controversy
over the Edwards manuscripts than he found himself embroiled
in a much larger conflict whose outcome would determine the
very future of Andover. The lines for this conflict were
drawn when he resigned from the Abbot Professorship in
1881. Like Leonard Woods before him, he expected to exercise
a decisive influence in the choice of his successor. His
candidate for that position was Frank Hugh Foster, a favorite
student of his in the mid-1870's and a frequent contributor
to the Bibliotheca Sacra, who, at Park's insistence, was
doing doctoral work at Leipzig when the search for a new
Abbot Professor began. Foster's scholarly credentials as
well as his intimate knowledge of and presumed commitment[1]
to the New England Theology made him an ideal choice, in
Park's view, for the key theological post at Andover. But
Park's estrangement from the rest of the Andover faculty
made any protégé of his automatically suspect.

His nominee was thus rejected in favor of Egbert Smyth's
younger brother Newman, who was then serving a Presbyterian
pastorate in Quincy, Illinois. The younger Smyth seemed to

---

[1]This commitment did not prove as firm or lasting as
Park may have hoped; for even as Foster wrote his definitive
Genetic History of the New England Theology (1907), his
theological allegiance was undergoing an obvious and decisive
change. His disenchantment with "Consistent Calvinism"
and volte-face toward theological liberalism were decisively
revealed in his Modern Movement in American Theology (New
York: Fleming H. Revell Company, 1939).

be perfectly in tune with the program of theological
modernization which the new Andover faculty had in mind.
Like most of his prospective colleagues, he had once
attended Park's lectures and had been influenced, to some
extent, by Scottish Common Sense rationalism. But later
thinking and experience led him to adopt a more organic,
subjective, developmental base for doing theology, as
reflected in his works on The Religious Feeling (1877) and
Old Faiths in New Light (1879). He was convinced that
Darwin, Spencer, and historical-critical methodology
necessitated a new apologetic theology. Paley, Butler,
the Scottish Philosophers, and Park no longer met the needs
of the age, though Smyth had obviously learned a great deal
from all of them.

Basic to his new theology was a concern for the
dynamics of faith in the context of the physiological and
psychological growth of the human personality. Faith, in
Smyth's view, was an act of the whole person, not just an
intellectual exercise. Following the christocentric
mediating theology of I. A. Dorner, he affirmed that one
came to faith only through a personal relation to the
"historical Christ." Since this emphasis upon an historical
figure might cast doubt upon the universality of Christianity and hence the justice of eternal divine retribution,
Smyth made a fateful suggestion before a "club of unbelievers"
in the area of his parish. In an address boldly entitled
The Orthodox Theology of Today (1881), he put forward the

hypothesis that those who had had no opportunity to know Christ in this life would be granted such an opportunity in the next.[1]

This hypothesis, which was labeled "future," or "second" probation by its detractors, became a rallying cry for the opponents of Smyth's election to the Andover faculty. When that election had been approved by both faculty and trustees, it was submitted for ratification in March, 1882, to the Board of Visitors, the three-member, self-perpetuating tribunal set up to protect the interests of Andover's Hopkinsian constituency. At this point the opposition forces swung into full public action with an editorial in the Congregationalist, a Boston weekly newspaper to which Park had close ties. Entitled "Professor Park's Successor," the editorial argued against the confirmation of Smyth's faculty appointment on the grounds that his theory of "second probation" was contrary to the Scriptural teaching of the universal decisiveness of this life.[2]

Smyth and his supporters regarded this eschatological issue of future probation as peripheral to the basic work of theological reconstruction which they hoped to accomplish at Andover. They felt that the Congregationalist had deceptively

---

[1]The hypothesis actually first appeared in a series of sermons entitled "Negative and Positive Elements in the Conception of the Future Life" which Smyth preached to his congregation in early 1881.

[2]"Professor Park's Successor," Congregationalist, XXXIV, 10 (March 8, 1882), 82, col. 2.

raised the issue more for its emotional impact in uniting
the anti-Smyth forces than for its substantive theological
importance.[1] But however overblown the "probation debate"
may have become, the Congregationalist, which became the
chief organ of opposition to the new faculty and the "New
Departure" at Andover, obviously felt that it was waging
a battle to preserve the historic doctrinal foundation of
Andover and of Congregationalism generally. The notion of
future probation was an accurate and effective signpost
pointing to the heretical heart of the "new theology" at
Andover. Its acceptance would most surely "cut the nerve
of missions."[2] And no one holding such a theory, in the
eyes of Park and the editors of the Congregationalist, could
legitimately subscribe to Andover's Associate Creed.

With this latter assertion the opponents of the New
Departure placed a serious legal and doctrinal obstacle in
the way of Smyth's appointment. For all Andover professors
were required to pledge public adherence to the Creed every
five years.[3] Of course, the specific theory of future

---

[1] See William Jewett Tucker, My Generation (Boston:
Houghton, Mifflin Company, 1919), pp. 108-109.

[2] The phrase is Park's (cf. Foster, Life, p. 239); but
this was a cry taken up by a number of missionary officials,
including an early student and old friend of Park's, E. K.
Alden, who was then home secretary of the American Board of
Commissioners for Foreign Missions and an outspoken opponent
of Smyth's election to the Andover faculty. Park and Alden
continued to use their influence to oppose the sending abroad
of missionaries favoring the "New Departure."

[3] The complex legal status of Andover is well treated in
Richard D. Pierce, "Legal Aspects of the Andover Creed,"
Church History, XV, 1 (March, 1946), 28-47.

probation was not mentioned in the Creed. But Park and
his supporters were convinced that Andover's Hopkinsian
Associate Founders, who were responsible for the Creed
and the subscription requirement, would have repudiated
any such notion as plainly inconsistent with the doctrinal
position they hoped to protect. The pro-Smyth forces on
the faculty vigorously denounced this charge of "constructive
heresy" in a letter released to the press in mid-April, 1882.
And the letter seemed to have some effect upon the vacillat-
ing Board of Visitors, who were still deliberating over the
Smyth appointment; for they missed no private or public
opportunity to make clear their feeling that Smyth's
theological views were in full conformity with the Creed.

But, in the end, the numerous personal appeals and
letters which the Visitors received in opposition to Smyth's
appointment proved decisive. By a vote of two to one, he
was rejected. The official reason given was his tendency
"to use language more as expression of his feelings than of
his thoughts, and to conceive of truth sentimentally and poet-
ically rather than speculatively and philosophically. This
tendency, it was noted, might "interfere with his precision
as a teacher."[1] Such lame excuses really satisfied no one
and served only to worsen an already difficult situation.

---

[1] See Tucker, My Generation, pp. 115-116. One is
inevitably reminded here of Park's own distinction between
intellect and feelings, and of his increasing use of that
distinction to discredit rather than to find common ground
with his theological opponents.

The Andover Trustees attempted to circumvent the Visitors'
authority by offering Smyth a professorship not subject
to the Visitorial veto. But he refused, arguing that
such a move would only produce a lengthy legal contest
and would fail to settle the crucial theological issues
raised by his proposed faculty appointment.

Almost immediately he accepted a call to New Haven's
important Center Church, from whose pulpit he would
propagate his "poetic" theology for some twenty-five
years to come. Once removed from vocational uncertainty
and from the immediate arena of the developing Andover
controversy, Smyth set about to answer the theological
critics who had thwarted his seminary career. Within
a month after his rejection by the Visitors, he published
a careful critique of what he saw as the proof-text-
oriented, creed-bound "orthodox rationalism" of Park
and his followers.[1] Evidently looking to Edwards'
Religious Affections as inspiration, he called, in effect,
for a "new" New England Theology which would speak to
both head and heart in a dynamic, ethical, and scientific
manner. Informed by what Smyth would later label
"scientific spirituality," this new theology was to be
both orthodox and "progressive."

---

[1] Newman Smyth, "Orthodox Rationalism," Princeton
Review, LVIII, 4 (May, 1882), 294-312.

*   *   *

Park failed to give an immediate, direct response to the broader theological issues which Smyth raised in this critique, but continued instead to hammer away at the theory of future probation. In an installation sermon preached in October, 1882, he offered his most systematic refutation of the theory.[1] Basing his argument upon the universal awareness and validity of the divine law, he maintained that anyone who honestly desired to know (through conscience) and do his duty actually had saving "essential" faith, though not necessarily a "formal" historical faith in Christ. Such an essential faith was open to all in this life, regardless of their knowledge of the historical Christ. There was thus no need for a future probation for those who remained ignorant of a particular historical figure until death. If they died in sin, the law left them without excuse. Death was no accident in a predestined universe; for it formed the portal through which men passed to their just and eternal reward, based upon their actions, their "probation," in this life. Since the law was a hard taskmaster, the missionary spreading of the gospel was essential.

The question of future probation, as Park raised it

---

[1] See "A Sermon Preached by Professor E. A. Park at North Andover, October 11, 1882, at the Installation of Rev. H. H. Leavitt," Congregationalist, XXXIV, 43 (October 25, 1882), 361-362.

in this sermon, seemed indeed to point to a central
theological difference between him and his opponents at
Andover. The latter focused upon the goodness, mercy
and grace of God rather than his wrath or justice vis-à-vis
sin. The stubborn reality of the "law of sin and death"
did not seem to concern them as much as it did Park, for
whom divine goodness and grace were meaningless without
such a concern. Their anthropology thus tended to be more
optimistic than Park's. But Newman Smyth's critique of
"orthodox rationalism" went far beyond differing views of
sin, grace, and anthropology. It was, in effect, a call
for intellectual and theological freedom relative to
traditional doctrinal standards.

Such a call was somewhat anticipated when William J.
Tucker, an early proponent of the Social Gospel, replaced
Park's old friend Austin Phelps as Bartlet Professor of
Scared Rhetoric in 1880. Tucker prefaced his subscription
to the Associate Creed with the following statement:

> The creed which I am about to read and to which
> I subscribe, I fully accept as setting forth
> the truth against the errors which it was
> designed to meet. No confession so elaborate
> and with such intent may assume to be the final
> expression of the truth or an expression equally
> fitted in language or tone to all times.[1]

Two years later, in the aftermath of the probation debate
and Newman Smyth's rejection, the two biblical professors
Mead and Thayer resigned in protest against the five-year

---

[1]See Rowe, History, p. 19.

repetition of their creedal affirmation.[1] It began to
look as though Andover's doctrinal "strait jacket" would
destroy the seminary. Daniel Taggart Fiske, who was
serving as an interim lecturer in systematic theology
until the Abbot Chair could be filled and who was soon to
be chosen President of the Andover Trustees, published
what he hoped would be a relieving interpretation. In
The Creed of Andover Theological Seminary,[2] he argued
that this doctrinal standard was never intended as a
barrier to theological progress. Its Hopkinsian authors
favored a "New Divinity," a more "Consistent Calvinism"
than the Westminster orthodoxy to which Andover's original
"Old Calvinist" founders adhered. Such men could scarcely
have begrudged further theological improvements as time
and circumstance demanded. In addition, since the Creed
had to be accepted by both the Hopkinsian and the Old
Calvinist founders of Andover, it was written with a
"studied latitude" of expression, typical of compromise
documents. Omitted or muted were the more extreme
Hopkinsian "improvements" (e.g., sin as necessary to the
greatest good) upon the Westminster Shorter Catechism,
the exclusive doctrinal standard of Andover's original

---

[1]Mead went abroad (to Germany and England) for several
years and then returned to teach at Hartford Seminary.
Thayer joined the faculty of Harvard Divinity School.

[2]Daniel Taggart Fiske, The Creed of Andover Theological
Seminary (Newburyport, Massachusetts: Moses H. Sargent,
1882).

founders.[1]   As a result, a minute, literalistic subscription
to such a confession was never expected, either by the
seminary's associate or its original founders. The
personal judgment and interpretations of the professors
were to be respected as much as possible.

With ideas such as this on public display, Park
could restrain himself no longer. In May of 1883, he
brought out his own carefully argued interpretation of
The Associate Creed of Andover Theological Seminary.[2]
He began his analysis with a listing of four "doctrines
essential to the integrity of the Andover Creed," together
with corresponding deviations from these doctrines proposed
by the "new theology."[3]   Naturally, one of these essential
doctrines was the decisiveness of the present life in
determining one's eternal destiny. But his indictment
of the Andover heresy had now expanded beyond future
probation to include three additional errors: (1) the
questioning of biblical authority in favor of "Christian
consciousness"; (2) doubts cast upon the universal sinfulness

---

[1]The key points upon which the Creed tended toward a
more Hopkinsian than Westminster position were the imputation
of Adam's sin and Christ's righteousness, and the inability
of man to keep the divine law. The Catechism accepted both
these doctrines; the Creed modified both in favor of a more
individualistic understanding of sin and righteousness based
upon acts of personal responsibility. For the text of the
Creed, see the "Second Associate Statute" of Andover in
Woods, History, pp. 257-260.

[2]Park, The Associate Creed of Andover Theological
Seminary (Boston: Franklin Press, 1883).

[3]Ibid., Chapter I.

182

of unconverted men and the justice of divine retribution
against such men; and (3) a rejection of the governmental
theory of the atonement, with its emphasis upon Christ's
representative sacrificial vindication of the divine law,
in favor of an emphasis upon the incarnation and the
personal, moral example of Christ.

Having established the discrepancy between the new
theology and the Creed, Park went on to discuss the legal
implications of such a discrepancy. He exhaustively
examined the peculiar historical circumstances of Andover's
founding, including the expressed intentions of the two
sets of founders, many of whom Park knew and whose private
papers he had perused.[1] He likewise analyzed the complex
constitution and statutes of the seminary. It was his
conclusion that there was only one legal way to become an
Andover professor: a literal and complete subscription
to the Creed. No reservations or "escape clauses," such as
"on the whole" or "for substance of doctrine," could be
allowed.[2] Nor could any changes be made in this carefully
drafted confession. It was intended as a permanent legal
standard to protect the basic character of the seminary
and to prevent the misuse of its financial endowment.

One by one Park answered the opposing arguments of
Fiske and others. There was indeed reason for saying that

---

[1] Ibid., p. 2.

[2] Ibid., p. 92.

Andover's Hopkinsian founders were "progressive" and
"independent" thinkers, "but they regarded themselves
as having already excogitated the truth...." Their only
allowable progress was thus toward new illustrations,
"proofs," and defenses of that one final truth.[1] True,
that truth was somewhat compromised and inadequately
expressed by the Andover Creed. But this was no reason
for further compromises and "loose constructions" on the
part of individual faculty members. The Creed was
unmistakably clear as to the four essential doctrines
Park had singled out at the beginning of his discussion.
There was little doubt that its authors intended it as a
minimal doctrinal standard, the construction of which had
necessitated so much adjustment and dilution that no
further changes or qualifications could possibly be
tolerated.[2]

Park gave his primary attention in this work on the
Creed to the legal status of Andover's new theologians
rather than to the truth of their doctrines or to the
wisdom of creedal subscription. "The question here," he
argued, "is not whether they /the doctrines of the Creed/
are true, but whether the founders of the Seminary have
prescribed that they be taught."[3] But, of course, he

---

[1] Ibid., p. 94.

[2] Ibid., p. 90.

[3] Ibid., p. 95.

himself took the affirmative on both points and was
convinced that he had been unwaveringly true to his
pledge to teach the Creed. In addition, he was quite
sure that "nearly all the friends of Andover" were in
agreement with him and were far from regarding creedal
subscription as an antiquated requirement threatening the
seminary's continued existence. He maintained that "the
majority of Calvinistic ministers in New England at the
present day would not hesitate to subscribe the Associate
Creed." And even if they did hesitate, Andover could
always call on the Presbyterian Church in America or
Scotland for its faculty![1]

*   *   *

In Park's view the new faculty at Andover represented
a conspiratorial minority who were attempting to use the
seminary to promote their own heretical doctrinal views
within Congregationalism at large. His pamphlet on the
Creed was his most open and extended attack upon this
minority, and was clearly intended to unite the majority
of Andover's "friends" against them. But its effect was
not nearly as decisive or unitive as intended. It drew
as much critical as favorable reaction and tended to

---

[1]Ibid., p. 97. The Andover Constitution provided that
the faculty be of Congregational or Presbyterian affiliation.
It is somewhat ironic that Park, a staunch Congregationalist
who had often objected to Presbyterian rigidity in polity
and doctrine, now seemed to be relying upon that very

create intense polarization within the seminary's
constituency.[1] Meanwhile, the Andover faculty and trustees
had selected five new professors to be inaugurated in the
summer of 1883. Two of these new men were to occupy newly
endowed chairs of Biblical Theology and Biblical History
and Archeology. Two others were to replace Mead and
Thayer in Old and New Testament studies. And the fifth
man was to take over the much disputed Abbot Professorship.
All were suspect in the eyes of Park and his ministerial
supporters.

But the man who drew the most attention from the
defenders of the Creed was George Harris, a former student
of Park's who had been called from his Congregational
pastorate in Providence, Rhode Island, to replace the master
in the Abbot Chair. When questioned by the Visitors
concerning his view of future probation, Harris equivocated.
He "had not reached a definite opinion" on the matter, but
he saw no incompatibility between acceptance of such a
theory and subscription to the Creed.[2] Not wishing to
provoke further controversy, the Visitors claimed to be
satisfied with Harris' answer and confirmed his

rigidity to preserve his beloved seminary from error.
cf. Foster, Life, p. 239.

[1]cf. H. K. Rowe, History, p. 173.
[2]cf. Tucker, My Generation, p. 121.

appointment.[1] Park and his sympathizers were not so
easily satisfied. Convinced that the future of their
seminary was at stake, they were determined that no new
faculty should be appointed at Andover without an outright
repudiation of any "New Departure" from the Creed.

Toward this end they aggressively sought to influence
the religious press in their favor.[2] And as the week for
Andover's Anniversary (Commencement) and faculty inaugural
exercises drew near, they busied themselves with letters,
memorials, and petitions addressed to the Visitors,
influential alumni, and anyone else who might be sympathetic
to their cause. Strategy conferences were held at Saratoga
and elsewhere to find more acceptable nominees for the
posts to be filled by the professors-elect and to plan
an "open demonstration in opposition to the new departure...

---

[1]It should be recalled at this point that the "official"
Visitorial objections to Newman Smyth did not, in fact,
include his theory of future probation. The way was thus
left open for the approval of someone else who might also
accept the theory. The Board was understandably reluctant,
despite its own beliefs and the pressures exerted upon it,
openly to assume the role of heresy-hunter.

[2]One editor who came under particular fire from Park
for his supposedly "liberal" views on the Andover Creed was
William Hayes Ward of the New York Independent. The paper's
official position on this matter was apparently open to
more than one interpretation. For Ward's editorial associate
Kinsley Twining assured Park that he had misunderstood the
articles in question and that the Independent found "no
real trouble" with the Andover Creed, believing it should
be "taken substantially" as Park interpreted it. cf. Kinsley
Twining to E. A. Park, June 11, 1883, C. R. Park Family
Papers.

at the Alumni Meeting" during Anniversary Week.[1] Three

days before he was to deliver his inaugural address,

Harris received a letter, approved by Park and others,

urging him to defer his acceptance of the Abbot Chair

unless or until he was willing "explicitly to disavow"

any sympathy with the New Departure.[2]

Clearly no stone was being left unturned. The letter

to Harris, carefully avoiding theological issues and

direct accusations, argued that Congregational and public

opinion was turning against the New Departure and would

turn against Andover as well if its professors failed to

repudiate that heresy.[3] Admittedly, they said, there were

local congregations and ministerial councils who "tolerated"

the preaching of new theology in their midst, but the vast

majority utterly dissociated themselves from it. This

may well have been true, but there was an underlying tone

of hopeless desperation, ill-becoming a majority movement,

---

[1]See A. H. Plumb to E. A. Park, Boston, undated
(probably late May, 1883), C. R. Park Family Papers. Plumb,
a Congregational minister in Roxbury, Massachusetts, had
been a student of Park's in the late 1850's and had remained
committed to his teacher's basic theological positions.
He took an active role in opposing the new faculty at
Andover.

[2]A. H. Plumb to George Harris, June 10, 1883, copy in
C. R. Park Family Papers. Similar but briefer letters
went to the other professors-elect.

[3]This approach was taken because Harris had responded
to previous letters questioning his beliefs by vague
assurances that those who were "conservative in theology"
had nothing to fear in regard to his own views. cf. Plumb
to Park, Boston, Monday evening, June 11, 1883. C. R. Park
Family Papers.

in much of the correspondence of those who opposed the
new faculty. They vowed to "do what we can" but feared
they would "fail in saving the Seminary" because the new
professors were "very determined and very crafty."[1] It
is noteworthy that this very image of a "determined and
crafty" minority was also applied to Park and his sympathizers
by the new faculty.[2] Both groups apparently felt they
represented the best interests and the majority of their
denomination and were engaged in a worthy crusade on
behalf of those majority interests.

Unlike their opponents, however, the professors-elect
were the epitome of self-confidence. They knew they were
on the side of progress and would ultimately prevail. And
this confidence seemed justified by the failure of all
efforts to block or defer their inauguration. In his
inaugural address, entitled "The Rational and Spiritual
Verification of Christian Doctrine," Harris actually made
no absolute break with Park's theological teaching.[3] Like
Park, he argued that Christian beliefs must be put on a
rational and scientific basis. For example, unintelligible
relationships (e.g., imputation) between Adam's sin and

---

[1]cf. Plumb to Park, Boston, May ?, 1883. C. R. Park
Family Papers.

[2]cf. Tucker, My Generation, p. 108.

[3]The address was printed in full, with editorial comment
calling for an end to the Andover conflict, in the Christian
Union (June 14, 1883), pp. 469-473.

present sin could not be accepted. But unlike Park, Harris defined sin in a social context and saw original sin, not as the remote occasion of personal acts, but as the inheritance of social injustice. He tended, much more than Park, to stress the possibilities rather than the corruption of the individual man. In addition, though both Harris and Park had rather moralistic conceptions of sin and the atonement, Harris went far beyond his former teacher in stressing Christ's saving moral example, as opposed to the objective effect of his sacrifice.

Still, much of Harris' optimistic emphasis upon the moral and the reasonable seems to be on a continuum with Park's own theological assumptions. But there were some radical differences between the two men as well. Harris believed that no theology which failed to take Darwinism and its developmental implications seriously could properly claim to be scientific. Nor could one construct a scientific creed valid in all times and places. One might seek a broad doctrinal agreement on certain "fundamentals" spiritually verified by Christian, or better, "religious" consciousness. But such an agreement could never be bound by rational propositions or biblical proof texts. Notions of this sort were unacceptable and, in many respects, incomprehensible to Park.

*   *   *

Incomprehensible or not, however, they became Andover's
common theological coinage as the new faculty consolidated
its position. An important part of this consolidation was
the founding of the monthly Andover Review in January, 1884,
to serve as the seminary's new house organ. The way was
prepared for the new Review by the removal of the Bibliotheca
Sacra to the more hospitable environs of Oberlin where
Park's old friend George F. Wright became its editor.[1]
Designed to "advocate the principles and represent the
method and spirit of progressive Orthodoxy," Andover's new
scholarly journal was not long in provoking serious controversy.[2]

The controversy came primarily from a series of
editorials giving the position of the new faculty on such
central Christian doctrines as the authority of Scripture,
the Incarnation, the work of the Spirit, and the Atonement,
particularly as related to the eschatological issue of
future probation. First appearing mainly during the year
1885, these editorials were expanded and collected into

---

[1]Wright had gone to Oberlin as Professor of New Testament
Literature in 1881. A decade later he became, appropriately
enough, Oberlin's Professor of the "Harmony of Science and
Religion." His editorship of the Bibliotheca Sacra extended
from 1884 until his death in 1921. While Park was alive, the
two friends corresponded regularly regarding editorial poli-
cies and procedures. cf., e.g., Wright to Park, October 12,
1888 (C. R. Park Papers), on the subject of "increasing
circulation."

[2]The Review's prospectus, from which the quoted words

book form the following year under the supposedly irenic
title Progressive Orthodoxy. The polemic surrounding this
book seemed to derive as much from the theological method
espoused by the new faculty as from their specific
"departures" from the Andover Creed. That method
rejected the assumption that one could discover and state
the "eternal" truths of the gospel, in favor of a concept
of theology as a process of continuous critical inquiry into
the meaning of the Christian faith. Since the inquiry was
never finished, any formal, systematic statements produced
by it were regarded as tentative and incomplete references
to a complex truth.[1]

For this reason, the fact that much of the theology
found in Progressive Orthodoxy was (rightly) characterized
by its opponents as inconsistent and vague did not greatly
perturb its authors. What did perturb them was the more
fundamental charge that what they were doing had nothing
to do with orthodox Reformed theology and perhaps with
Christianity as well. In introducing the first issue of
the Andover Review, Egbert Smyth, one of the editors, had

were taken, is reproduced and interpreted in Tucker, My
Generation, pp. 136-137.

[1]cf. Daniel Day Williams, The Andover Liberals (New
York: Kings Crown Press, 1941), p. 64. It was this method
or attitude of progressive, tentative inquiry, rather than
any particular doctrinal system, that Williams called "the
one certain basis on which this school /the new Andover
faculty/ can be called liberalism."

argued that "every reader of these pages is now holding some belief as a part of his Christian faith...which Christian men of later generations will reject."[1] Such a statement seemed to the strict constructionists of the Andover Creed to open the floodgates of progressive theological speculation without reference to any definable norm. But the proponents of "progressive orthodoxy" argued that their norm was the spiritual awareness of the Incarnation. They claimed not to decline creedal tests of orthodoxy where applicable, and indeed they often retained much of the basic terminology of such tests. But the old terms tended to assume new meanings, at least in the eyes of their opponents. And since new theological questions were constantly arising, which, in their view, the old creeds could not answer, they found that "the question of orthodoxy happily merges in the more profitable question of truth."[2]

Such a merger was not so happily accepted by the "friends of Andover" opposing the new faculty. Led by such former students and old friends of Park as Joshua Wellman, a retired minister and an Andover trustee, and Henry Martyn

---

[1]Egbert C. Smyth, "The Theological Purpose of the Review," Andover Review, I (January, 1884), 6.

[2]See Tucker, My Generation, p. 142. Also see the editorial "The Accountability of the Ultra-Conservatives," Andover Review, I (June, 1884), 653-658, in which a distinction is drawn between an irresponsible "ultra-conservatism" of phraseology and a "true conservatism" which guides progress "along the solid highways of truth."

Dexter, the respected editor, scholar, and leader of
Congregationalism, these friends filed a lengthy "Complaint"
with the Board of Visitors against the Andover Review's
five editors.[1] Based primarily upon statements in Progressive Orthodoxy, the "Complaint," which was filed in the
fall of 1886, clearly reflected the hand of Park in its
composition.[2] The heresies cited were mainly elaborations
upon those mentioned three years before in his pamphlet
on the Associate Creed. The Review editors were accused,
for example, of undermining biblical authority, failing
to take sin and the divine law seriously enough, rejecting
a sacrificial atonement, and overemphasizing knowledge of
the "historic Christ" in salvation, the latter error
leading to the false theory of future probation.[3]

The hearings on these charges before the Visitors
in Boston in the fall and winter of 1886-87 were marked
by lengthy legal and doctrinal arguments which it is

---

[1]These editors were Egbert Smyth, William J. Tucker,
George Harris, J. W. Churchill (Jones Professor of Elocution
at Andover since 1869), and Edward Y. Hincks, a German-
trained scholar appointed to the new Chair of Biblical
Theology in 1883.

[2]See letter of Henry Martyn Dexter to E. A. Park,
July 18, 1885 (C. R. Park Family Papers), in which Park
was assured that the Visitors basically agreed with his
interpretation of the Andover Creed and would probably
welcome charges against the new faculty if only he would
study their Review and help to prepare such charges.
Dexter was convinced that the Review was a gift of
providence allowing its heretical editors publicly to
"hang themselves."

[3]See The Andover Case (Boston: Stanley and Usher,
1887), pp. xiv-xv.

unnecessary to detail here.[1] Finally in the summer of
1887 a divided Board reached a compromise verdict. Of
the five accused professors, only Egbert Smyth was found
guilty of any of the heresies named in the Complaint,
even though all five were responsible for the editorials
in Progressive Orthodoxy. Smyth appealed this unequal
verdict to the Massachusetts Supreme Court, which heard
the case in the fall of 1890 and ruled in his favor the
following year. The basic issue before the Court was not
heresy but the relative legal authority of the Visitors
vis-à-vis the Andover Trustees. The latter body found no
fault with Smyth or his colleagues and supported him
before the Court. The Court ruled that the Visitors
indeed had the authority to try and dismiss heretical
professors from the faculty, but not without consulting with
the Trustees.

This ruling opened the way for a new hearing before
the Visitors in 1892, this time with Trustee representation.
But the Visitorial membership had meanwhile changed; and
the case was prudently dismissed, thus ending six years

---

[1]See, among other sources, The Andover Case (cited
above), which contains "a careful summary of the arguments
of the respondent professors; and the full text of the
arguments of the complainants and their counsel, together
with the decision of the Board of Visitors." See also
The Andover Defence (Boston: Cupples, Upham, and Company,
1887), which contains the statements of the accused
professors and the arguments of their counsel.

of litigation.[1] The victory of the proponents of "pro-

gressive orthodoxy" at Andover was a severe psychological

blow to Park. Though his public role among the opposition

forces had become increasingly less active as the contro-

versy progressed and his age advanced, he continued to

provide advice and encouragement to those forces until

all hope was lost in 1892. He clearly recognized that

Andover's doctrinal direction would decisively affect

Congregationalism as a whole.

*　　　　　　　*　　　　　　　*

In fact, even as Park battled heresy at Andover,

a broader denominational conflict based upon similar issues

was rapidly taking shape. This conflict really began with

the so-called "Burial Hill Declaration" of 1865. Adopted

by the National Congregational Council assembled on Plymouth's

historic Burial Hill, the Declaration vaguely reaffirmed

----

[1] Unfortunately, this was not to be the end of
litigation relative to Andover. During the years 1908-26,
the seminary attempted an ill-fated affiliation with Harvard
Divinity School. Again, the Board of Visitors went to
court and, on this occasion, found themselves on the winning
side; for they successfully terminated the arrangement with
Harvard. Again, the primary issue was faculty adherence
to the Associate Creed. The end result of this later
institutional controversy was an affiliation of Andover in
1931 with the theologically more hospitable Newton Theological
Institution, a Baptist seminary. Of course, Park was not
involved, except proleptically, in these later difficulties
plaguing his beloved seminary; and they will therefore not
be discussed in detail here. A good treatment of them can
be found in George Huntston Williams (ed.), The Harvard
Divinity School: Its Place in Harvard University and in
American Culture (Boston: Beacon Press, 1954), pp. 185-210.

the denomination's seventeenth-century doctrinal symbols.
But it also emphasized the unity of Congregationalism with
other branches of Christianity on the basis of those
"fundamental truths" which all Christians accept.[1] The
term "Calvinism" was purposely omitted from this highly
generalized statement of Congregational faith; and that
omission drew strong protests from Park and others.
These protests continued and intensified over the next
decade as the National Council moved, under repeated
urging, to authorize a more explicit declaration of faith.
Such a move, the protesters felt, was designed to diminish
the allegiance of "modern Congregationalism" to the creeds
of the past.

Nevertheless, in the fall of 1880, the Council arranged
for the selection of twenty-five representative "commissioners" who were to prepare an updated Congregational
confession. Three years later the new "Commission Creed"
was ready for the press.[2] Coming little more than six
months after Park's "defense" of the Associate Creed and
his unsuccessful campaign to halt the inauguration of George
Harris and other New Departure men at Andover, this new
Creed received his most careful scrutiny. Three of the
twenty-five commissioners had refused to sign it, primarily,
it seems, on the grounds that it did not contain a

---

[1]cf. Williston Walker, The Creeds and Platforms of
Congregationalism (New York: Charles Scribner's Sons,
1893), pp. 553-565.

[2]Ibid., pp. 577-582.

"Scriptural eschatology."[1] This meant that the "Omission
Creed," as its opponents dubbed it, failed to make a clear
repudiation of "future probation." To Park and his
supporters, such an omission, given the polemics of the
day, could not be tolerated.

The general acceptance of this creed among Congregationalists, Park argued publicly, would be a "calamity."[2] His
old friend Austin Phelps saw in the new creed "an amiable
desire to harmonize numbers and to make room for varieties
rather than a stern purpose to vindicate truth and to
resist falsehood."[3] Since, according to Congregational
custom, the Commission Creed was not binding upon local
churches unless each so voted it, Park decided to draft a
counter-creed as a platform for those churches which
supported his views. Initially requested and adopted by
the Pilgrim Congregational Church of Worcester, Massachusetts,
and hence often called the "Worcester Creed," this twelve-
article platform was first published anonymously in 1884
under the simple title A Declaration of Faith.[4] When

---

[1] cf. Williston Walker, A History of the Congregational
Churches in the United States (Boston: The Pilgrim Press,
1894), p. 414. Also see Joseph Cook, "Professor Park and
His Pupils," in volume of same title, ed. D. L. Furber,
et al. (Boston: Samuel Usher, 1899), p. 139.

[2] See Park's "Criticism of the Commission Creed of
1883," in Joseph Cook, Current Religious Perils (Boston:
Houghton, Mifflin and Company, 1888), p. 401. See also
Cook, "Park and Pupils," p. 139.

[3] Cook, "Park and Pupils," p. 139.

[4] Boston: Thomas Todd, 1884, 6p.

Park's name finally became officially identified with the
Declaration fourteen years later, it had gone through a
number of other printings and acquired an impressive list
of over seventy "accordant signatures."[1]

Closely resembling the "Associate Creed" at many
points, but avoiding technical Hopkinsian terminology,
the Worcester Creed was, in effect, Park's mature personal
credo. It explicitly rejected the doctrinal errors of
the Andover faculty which he had spelled out in 1883,
devoting an entire article to the question of future
probation. True to the polemical heritage of Andover,
the creed was clearly predicated on the assumption that
the best way to state truth is to refute error. The
deleterious effects of this assumption became especially
apparent in Park's later writing and other activities
after his retirement. He became obsessed with the heresies
of the day and missed no opportunity, public or private,
to list and attack them.

One such opportunity came in the form of a symposium
on "Current Religious Perils" conducted in 1887 by the
popular Boston "Monday Lecturer," Joseph Cook. Cook, a
former student and close friend of Park's, applied an
"orthodox evangelical" perspective to a wide range of
contemporary issues and topics, including the Andover

---

[1]See "A Request and a Commendation" in Professor
Park and His Pupils, pp. 111-112.

controversy, as he spoke before the noonday throngs in
Tremont Temple. As the litigation involving the Andover
faculty entered its last stages and the Commission Creed
competed with the Worcester Creed for Congregational
allegiance, Cook, who supported the latter confession,
solicited publishable statements from various denominational
leaders, including Park, on the most pressing religious
"perils" of the age.

As expected, Park used this forum to recite his by
then all too familiar litany of theological evils associated
with future probation and "progressive orthodoxy": loss
of respect for the divine law and justice vis-à-vis sin,
for the sacrificial atonement, for biblical authority, and
so on.[1] The problem with such repeated litanies of evil
was that their actual effect was far from that desired.
They seriously interfered with two important projected
publications which should have formed the capstones of
Park's career: (1) a major exposition of the life and
thought of Jonathan Edwards, based upon the papers in
Park's possession and designed as an essential complement
to his works on Hopkins and Emmons; and (2) a definitive
presentation of his theological system as contained in .
his seminary lectures.

Together, these two works could have placed Park's
theological viewpoint before the public much more

See Joseph Cook, <u>Current Religious Perils</u>, pp. 212-215.

constructively and effectively than heresy-hunting. As
it turned out, however, neither ever made it to the press.
And this fact in itself became a minor source of dispute
during the Andover controversy, further weakening Park's
position. The seminary trustees had raised a fund to
provide for the publication of his lectures. And when
Park seemed to be using that fund to publish and lobby
against his theological opponents at Andover and within
Congregationalism at large, the trustees and the fund's
subscribers began to protest. Part of the problem was
actually his perfectionism and the overly ambitious goals
he set for his retirement work.[1] But when nothing seemed
to come of two years of retired labor except a controversial
pamphlet on the Associate Creed, the trustees demanded
and received a detailed explanation.[2]

Park argued that he had stated from the outset the
necessity of at least two years of preliminary study before

---

[1] He told the trustees from the beginning that at his
age he did not expect to be able to publish his theological
system "in a manner satisfactory to myself." He declared
that his work on it was begun "not with the buoyancy of
hope, but with the restlessness of despair." See letter
of Park to the Andover Trustees, June 13, 1881, Phillips
Academy Archives.

[2] See Park to the Andover Trustees, June 11, 1883,
Phillips Academy Archives. Park also made a special
introductory (and unconvincing) statement in his work on
the Creed, defending it as an integral step in the preparation of his lectures for the press: cf. Associate
Creed, p. 2. To his friends, who shared the trustees'
concern, he wrote countless letters of explanation and
reassurance, cf. Park to Mrs. Bela Bates Edwards, June 3,
1884, C. R. Park Family Papers.

substantive work on the text of his theological system
could begin. His major difficulty appeared to be the
selection of a proper "plan" for presenting that system.
He had initially used the Associate Creed as such a plan,
but the controversy over its authority had caused him to
consider a topical series of essays on disputed doctrines
(e.g., "future punishment"). Clearly, he was not about to
publish his lectures as his students had recorded them
without major restructuring to take account of the new
Andover heresies. And this fact so distressed some of the
contributors to his publication fund that they eventually
withdrew their financial backing.[1] When the trustees again
protested his delay in producing a manuscript for the press,
the year was 1889, the Andover controversy was almost over,
and Park felt he must make a different sort of reply.

The disorganized and incomplete state of his lecture
notes was proving more of a problem than he anticipated.
Chronic eye problems and a desire to adapt his lectures
to "the special needs of each particular class" had led
him to adopt a "free, and in a large measure extemporaneous
method" of communicating his thoughts in the classroom. He

---

[1]cf. William H. Willcox to Edward Taylor /treasurer of
the Park fund/, March 21, 1885, Phillips Academy Archives:
"If Professor Park would devote less time to assailing the
new theology and more to practising a new morality, I
think it would be a great improvement in both directions."
Willcox, in effect, accused Park of dishonestly using the
funds he had pledged.

202

was thus compelled, in preparing these thoughts for the
press, to make extensive use of student notes, despite
their discrepancies and inaccuracies. Sadly he wrote:

> I am still persevering in examining the relations
> of different parts of my theological system to
> each other; in examining and verifying the
> references to inspired and uninspired authors
> as these references were made in various notes
> of my lectures; and in collating the numerous
> hints which are noted down in my memorandum
> books as important for the lectures, if they
> ever should be published. How soon I shall be
> able to complete the work on which I am now
> engaged it is impossible to foretell.[1]

Ten years later he was still performing the tasks here
described. At his death he left trackless masses of notes
but not even the rudiments of a coherent book-length
manuscript.

Clearly, many factors contributed to this failure
to publish. But Park's aggressive involvement in the
Andover controversy during the early, and potentially
most productive, years of his retirement must finally
be given a major share of the blame. Unfortunately,
the adverse consequences of that involvement extended
far beyond his study. The uncompromising determination
of Park and his supporters to root out heresy not only
at Andover but within Congregationalism as a whole
hardened lines of conflict and created wounds which proved

---

[1]Park to the Andover Trustees, June 24, 1889,
Phillips Academy Archives.

203

difficult to heal.[1] Nowhere was this more apparent
than in the long battle for control of the American
Board of Commissioners for Foreign Missions in the
1880's and 1890's. Founded as an interdenominational
self-perpetuating corporation, the Board was particularly
vulnerable to partisan domination. Throughout the 1880's,
the Park forces actually did dominate it, and missionary
candidates favoring the Andover heresies (especially
future probation) were summarily rejected.

Needless to say, this policy brought the Board
into open and bitter conflict not only with the Andover
faculty but with many local churches and ministerial
councils as well. The Board was accused of imposing
upon missionaries doctrinal standards which the majority
of Congregationalists did not accept. Its adamant
refusal to modify its position created more alienation
than support. And it became a favorite target of
biting editorials in the Andover Review, whose editors
saw themselves as waging a "holy war" for theological
progress and intellectual freedom wherever they were

---

[1]It should be noted in passing that Park's struggle
against heresy was not limited exclusively to Congregationalism. To his Baptist friends, for example, he
constantly bewailed the spread of "New Departure" doctrines
within their denomination and especially at his old
alma mater, Brown University. cf. letters of Park to
Heman Lincoln, "Prof., Theol. Inst., Newton Center,
Mass.," February 4, and May 25, 1885, Brown University
Archives.

threatened.[1]   Gradually, beginning in the early 1890's,

the Board was "democratized," under pressure from the

National Congregational Council, and made more directly

representative of the churches who supported it.[2]   But

strong animosities continued to plague its operation

years after Park and his supporters had lost effective

control of it.   And similar lingering hostility afflicted

Andover and Congregationalism generally as a result of

the prolonged conflict which appropriately came to be

known as the "Great Disruption."

But as the sounds of battle gradually faded away,

it was clear that the forces of "progressive orthodoxy"

had won a lasting victory and that a theologically

transformed Congregationalism was entering the twentieth

century.   Though Park vigorously opposed that transformation,

it was his own interpretation of the New England Theology

---

[1]See Tucker, My Generation, pp. 144-145; 152-158.
See also Cyrus Hamlin, "The Andover Attack on the American
Board," Our Day, IX (1892), 709-720.

[2]cf. Walker, History, pp. 416-422.   See also Earl
Ronald MacCormac, "The Transition from Voluntary
Missionary Society to the Church as a Missionary
Organization among the American Congregationalists,
Presbyterians, and Methodists" (Yale University:
unpublished Ph.D. dissertation, 1960).

which, in many ways, made it possible.[1] It is upon that
interpretation and the historical understanding in which
it was grounded that the final two chapters will focus.

---

[1]This relationship received ironic recognition
from Archibald Alexander Hodge, the son of Park's old
Princeton opponent, in a review of Park's Discourses on
Some Theological Doctrines As Related to the Religious
Character (1885), a collection of sermons from his
active career, which proved to be the only book he
published in retirement. Now that Park's theology
had spawned "far more radical departures from the
traditional orthodoxy of the Reformed Churches than
his own polemic Hopkinsianism," Hodge believed the
former Abbot Professor was moving in Princeton's direction:
"We hail him with affection as a valuable ally in all
irruptions upon the 'New Departure' and defences of
the old Calvinism that his convictions, or the fortunes
of war, dispose him to undertake." cf. The Presbyterian
Review, VI, 23 (July, 1885), 561-562.

Chapter VII

THE NEW ENGLAND THEOLOGY INTERPRETED: EXERCISES IN HISTORICAL VINDICATION

Throughout his life Park proudly identified himself with the New England Theology. And this identification was not uninformed. His "Memoirs" of Hopkins and Emmons and his articles on Edwardsean theology and theologians in the Schaff-Herzog Encyclopaedia earned him a reputation as the foremost authority on the New Divinity tradition in the latter half of the nineteenth century. He was, in effect, both an Edwardsean theologian and a self-conscious Edwardsean historian. The two roles were closely intertwined in his career, and both were controversial. For example, one of his more important historical expositions of the New England Theology grew out of his theological battle with Charles Hodge. In his final contribution to that polemic, Hodge charged that Park's key doctrines on the will and sin placed him in conflict not only with Princeton but with Jonathan Edwards himself.[1]

---

[1] cf. Charles Hodge, "Professor Park and the Princeton Review," Biblical Repertory and Princeton Review, XXIII, 4 (October, 1851), 685-686.

Few charges could have incensed Park more.[1] Determined
not to let his opponent have the last word in this matter,
he published a detailed historical vindication of his
theological position. Conceding that Edwards and his
disciples "did not harmonize on every theme," he yet
argued that they agreed on the following "three radical
principles": "that sin consists in choice, that our
natural power equals, and that it also limits, our duty."[2]
These principles were at the heart of Park's own theological system; and he was convinced, despite Hodge's arguments, that they were, in fact, the very essence of the
New England Theology, as distinct from "Geneva" Calvinism.
They were, in Park's view, the fundamental "improvements"
which made Consistent Calvinism "consistent."

Park believed Hodge had misunderstood Edwards and
his disciples at two crucial points: on the meaning of
"natural ability" and on the proper definition of sin.
Hodge, Park asserted, interpreted the former as "nothing
more than the natural capacities of soul and body,"
exclusive of "an adequate power to use those capacities
as they should be used."[3] Piling up a long set of

---

[1]In the same article (Ibid., p. 695), Hodge declared
that Park was simply not well enough versed in "Old School"
theology to be worthy of further polemic attention from
Princeton. But Hodge himself, who was certainly no devotee
of Edwards, seemed to have no hesitation in questioning
Park's competence as an Edwardsean interpreter.

[2]Park, "New England Theology," Bibliotheca Sacra, IX,
9 (January, 1852), 175.

[3]Ibid., p. 178.

supporting quotations from Edwards, Bellamy, Hopkins, and others, the Andover divine argued that such an interpretation totally distorted the Edwardsean distinction between natural and moral ability. Properly understood, that distinction gave man the natural power "to choose or to refuse the same thing."[1] To rob man of this power after the Fall, as Hodge proposed, would be to make Adam the only free man in the universe. It would make man's natural ability a meaningless "incapable capacity." And this was clearly contrary to the teaching of Edwards, who argued that man's natural power and freedom had remained constant since creation.[2]

Without such constancy, one was unavoidably led, Park believed, to the notion of sin as a natural necessity. And that notion in turn made the divine law meaningless since powerlessness and necessity are "incompatible with obligation."[3] Such dire consequences could be avoided only by the ingenious Edwardsean distinction between certainty, or inevitability, and necessity. Given the motives and inclinations governing the human will, it was morally certain, but not naturally necessary, that man would sin.[4] Sinful humanity had the natural power of

---

[1]Ibid., p. 181.

[2]Ibid., p. 182.

[3]Ibid.

[4]Ibid., p. 185.

contrary choice but would not choose to use it. Herein lay the second point at which Hodge had misconstrued Edwards: the meaning of sin.

In a word, sin was sinning, according to Park's interpretation of Edwards. Only man's own moral choices and acts were truly sinful. Passive states, inclinations, or "tastes" often formed the "occasion" of sinful acts but were not in themselves sinful. At this point, however, Edwards' "enigmatical Treatise on Original Sin" began to cause Park difficulty.[1] Hodge found that treatise in fundamental agreement with his own concept of sin as primarily a native human state rather than individual acts. And his Andover opponent was forced to concede at least some superficial evidence favoring that point of view. Nevertheless, Park believed it was "the leading doctrine of that treatise that all sin is an act, committed in our own persons, or else in the person of him /Adam/ who infolded us within himself."[2]

The "or else" clause is extremely important here; for it was Park's view that Edwards postulated the "idea of our literal oneness with Adam" primarily to personalize the guilt of original sin rather than to provide speculative reinforcement for the doctrine of imputation. No man,

---

[1] The Great Christian Doctrine of Original Sin Defended (1758).

[2] "New England Theology," p. 204.

according to Park's reading of Edwards, could share Adam's guilt until, through sinful acts of his own, he willingly participated in Adam's rebellion. Edwards' metaphysical explanation of that participation Park, nonetheless, regarded as a "great error," an "astonishing theory," and a "strange phenomenon in mental history." The fundamental intention behind it was good; but some of the conclusions drawn from it were "alien from the spirit of New England divinity" and "incongruous" with Edwards' own "prevailing" doctrines.[1]

The problem was how to explain such blatant incongruities in the thought of so brilliant a theologian. A reasonable interpreter could scarcely argue, as in the case of Edwards' thought on the Trinity, that he was confronted with roughhewn speculations not intended for publication. Or so it would seem. And yet Park undertook to "excuse" Edwards' Treatise on Original Sin in a very similar vein. The work bore "signs of hurried composition," he declared, and was published prematurely due to its author's untimely death. "Indian wars," the "embarrassing influences" of a frontier parish, and a "constitution shattered by the fever and ague" doubtless prevented adequate revision, qualification, or explanation at several important points in the treatise. Given more time and fewer distractions, Edwards surely would have clarified himself so as not to

---

[1]Ibid., pp. 204-205.

212

be identified with the "error that sin lies in something
beside moral agency--an error hostile to the whole spirit
of his creed."[1]

*   *   *

Though these "excuses" for Edwards' work on Original
Sin received no reply from Princeton, they did not go
unanswered among Park's more conservative theological
opponents in New England. Edward Alexander Lawrence,
professor of ecclesiastical history at the Theological
Institute of Connecticut (later Hartford Seminary), found
much to ridicule in Park's circumstantial arguments ad
hominem.[2] And Nathan Lord, president of Dartmouth, held
up the Abbot Professor's misconceptions to public scorn
in a lengthy open letter to Andover's most dogmatic Old
Calvinist trustee Daniel Dana.[3] Park had allowed his
speculative imagination to run away with him, both averred,
not only in interpreting Edwards on sin but in expounding
the fundamental theology of the entire "Edwardsean School."
It was Park's own "favorite ideas" and "images," not those

---

[1]Ibid., p. 208.

[2]cf. E. A. Lawrence, "New England Theology: the
Edwardean Period," American Theological Review, III, 1
(January, 1861), 66-67.

[3]Nathan Lord, A Letter to the Rev. Daniel Dana, D.D.,
on Professor Park's Theology of New England (Boston:
Crocker and Brewster, 1852).

of Edwards and his immediate disciples, that the critics
found throughout the Andover divine's analysis of "The
New England Theology."

But these "favorite ideas and images" received little
specific attention in Lord's letter. He found too obvious
for elaboration the general recognition that Park deviated
from and often misunderstood his New Divinity heritage.
It was the dialectical nature of that heritage and of
Park's method of interpreting it that most concerned his
Dartmouth critic. For example, Lord sarcastically inquired,
at one point, whether Park's "three radical principles"
of the New England Theology (regarding sin and natural
ability) were to be taken "literally" or "spiritually,"
i.e., according to the intellect or the feelings.[1] Did
Edwards and his disciples literally subscribe to these
principles as creedal tenets, or were they merely an
"interpreting genius and spirit"? It really made little
difference how one answered this question, Lord declared;
for Edwardsean theology "said yes, today, and no, tomorrow;
at one time, hypothetically, you can if you will, at
another, absolutely, you cannot because you will not."[2]

Park's three principles would thus, at most, seem to
be but one facet of a complex speculative dialectic. In
Lord's view, one could as easily prove their rejection as

[1]Ibid., pp. 12-13.

[2]Ibid., p. 13.

214

he could their acceptance by the New Divinity men. The
members of that school were often as inconsistent and
changeable as "cameleons" in their speculations.[1] Nevertheless, "down to the time of Emmons," they did not allow
changeable reason to triumph over unchanging revelation.
They realized that the Bible, the Catechism, and Christian
experience gave the only true "practical" and "historical"
account of sin and human ability. Though that account
contained many mysteries conducive to speculation, no
amount of abstract explanation could ultimately replace
the revealed word.[2]

Interpreting Edwards and his early disciples by the
"lurid ray" of Emmons, Park gave some of their tentative
and changeable philosophizing (summarized in his three
principles) an absolute quality it was never intended to
have. In Lord's words, he "made them sacrifice the facts
of the Bible which they believed..., to an image with which
they sometimes played."[3] This was considerably overstating
the case, but the Dartmouth divine was touching upon an
important element in Park's understanding of theology and
history: i.e., his faith in rational propositions based
upon the self-evident principles of "common sense." From
that faith came the dynamic polarity which Park set up

---

[1]Ibid., p. 14.

[2]Ibid., pp. 17-19.

[3]Ibid., p. 19.

between intellect and feeling. And upon that polarity
hinged the fundamental interpretive method that he applied
not only to Scripture and the Westminster symbols but to
his own Edwardsean theological heritage as well.

Park saw the speculations of the New England Theology
not as tentative "images" to be trifled with but as serious
attempts to interpret the Bible so "as to make sensible
men confide in it."[1] The "practical and historical facts,"
to use Lord's words, of Scripture, Catechism, and Christian
experience were acceptable to the heart but often not to the
head. Not wishing to reject Lord's "facts" as absolutely
untrue, Park attempted to establish a fundamental continuity
between them and the more "precise" formulations of the
Edwardseans. Viewed comprehensively, for example, Edwardsean
theology and Westminster were really saying the same thing
in different modes. Any superficial rational inconsistencies
between them could be dealt with quite adequately through
the mediating dialectic of intellect and feeling. That is,
whenever one encountered a doctrinal statement in conflict
with "common sense," one relegated it to the realm of feeling.

$$*\qquad\qquad*\qquad\qquad*$$

In sum, Park maintained that the formulations of the
Westminster divines and of the New Divinity men differed,

---

[1]Park, "New England Theology," p. 210.

216

particularly in regard to sin and human ability, because the former had transformed the "intense expressions" of inspired Scripture into "the exact phrases of a metaphysical creed."[1] Thus far, he was simply reiterating a central point in his Convention Sermon of 1850. But what happened when the Edwardseans themselves seemed to stray from the path of common sense (i.e., from Park's "three radical principles")? From Lord's point of view, this would create no problem. The members of that school were, after all, theological "cameleons" who played with tentative and often inconsistent speculative images. A partisan like Park, however, could scarcely accept such an interpretation.

The New England Theology was, by definition, an improved and more "consistent" Calvinism. Like any other bold scientific experiment, it was an ongoing project, always open to new light. But its fundamental touchstone was the rational confidence of "sensible men." It was that touchstone which made Edwards' Treatise on Original Sin so difficult to explain. Certainly its careful metaphysical formulations could not reasonably be regarded as couched in imprecise figurative or emotive language. But it hardly seemed possible that the great Edwards could make the mistake of lesser divines in reading the "intense expressions" of Scripture regarding sin as literal, scientific truth. Park was thus left with a considerable interpretive dilemma,

---

[1]Ibid., p. 187.

which he clumsily attempted to resolve through doubtful circumstantial explanations.

As a rule, however, he was not driven to such lengths in reconciling the "missionary of Stockbridge" with common sense. When, for example, he was unable to find in Edwards a clear-cut distinction between man's will and his "constitutional sensibilities," he placed the blame upon "the want of a precise nomenclature."[1] Like Emmons, Park was disturbed by any apparent attribution of moral character to man's "heart" or "affections" except as they were shaped by the choices of his free will. Any reasonable theology presupposed, in his view, a reasonable faculty psychology, which, among other things, demanded that choice and motive be kept separate.[2] He was convinced that Edwards indeed intended to keep them so but sometimes used "nomenclature," such as "temper" and "affections," in a manner that seemed to confuse voluntary moral "exercises" with involuntary "natural feelings."

Here the subtlety of Edwards' thought and the flexible

---

[1] Park, "New England Theology," in Philip Schaff (ed.), A Religious Encyclopaedia; or, Dictionary of Biblical, Historical, Doctrinal, and Practical Theology (New York: Funk and Wagnalls, 1891, third edition), III, 1635. Hereinafter cited as Schaff-Herzog Encyclopaedia.

[2] On this point, cf. F. H. Foster, A Genetic History of the New England Theology (Chicago: University of Chicago Press, 1907), pp. 64-65 and passim. Foster's obsession in this work with a "threefold division of the mind" (will, understanding, and emotion), as opposed to a twofold one that confused will and emotion, owed much to Park.

variety of his language, which so disturbed Lord, came to
Park's rescue. They provided him a relatively simple
means of solving his interpretive difficulty without
resort to the intellect-feeling distinction. When Edwards
spoke of "moral character as inhering in the heart," he
must have been referring, Park thought, to an active,
voluntary faculty. This interpretation seemed plausible
because when Edwards wanted to speak of man's constitutional
or involuntary emotions, he usually used terms such as
"animal affections" or "natural feelings," and these terms
were explicitly divorced from any moral significance.[1]

Thus did Park marshal Edwards to his support in
defending the notion that all moral judgment rested upon
man's free will. To have placed it elsewhere, he believed,
would have been to deny a key tenet of the New England
Theology that "our natural power equals, and that it also
limits, our duty."[2] Many of his critics insisted, however,
that there was no truly free will in Edwards. The treatise
on the Freedom of the Will, they argued, maintained a
"literal inability of the soul to act otherwise than it
does act." This meant that fallen man had "wholly lost
all ability of will to any spiritual good accompanying

---

[1]Park, "New England Theology," in Schaff-Herzog
Encyclopaedia, III, 1635.

[2]cf. Park,"New England Theology," Bibliotheca
Sacra, IX, 175.

salvation."[1] To counter this argument, Park felt it
necessary to employ a form of his trusted intellect-
feeling distinction.

Edwards bound the will, he averred, only with a
"moral inability." It was "an inability improperly so
called" because it referred to a profound, intensely
expressed truth of Scripture and experience rather than
to a scientific or metaphysical dictum. That truth, in
brief, was the certainty of human sin. Like the Westminster
divines, Edwards was capable of using figurative language
to refer to this truth even in the most carefully reasoned
context. But he never confused moral certainty with
literal natural necessity. Sin might be certain or
inevitable, but human liberty was equally certain. And
that liberty was no less than "the power of electing
either of two or more objects."[2] Thus, when confronted
with Edwards' apparent acceptance of the notion that
fallen man had no real power to will or do good, Park had
a familiar response. He construed Edwards "as denying
this proposition in its literal, and affirming it only in
its figurative sense,...believing that since the Fall,
man has all the freedom or liberty which he ever had,

[1]Park, "Jonathan Edwards," in John McClintock and
James Strong (eds.), Cyclopaedia of Biblical, Theological,
and Ecclesiastical Literature (New York: Harper and
Brothers, 1894), III, 66. Hereinafter cited as McClintock
and Strong.

[2]Ibid.

or can be imagined to have."[1]

*   *   *

The problem of human freedom and moral responsibility presented itself not only in Park's interpretation of Edwards but in his reading of the eminent Edwardsean disciple Samuel Hopkins as well. Within months after his defense of himself and the New England Theology against the aspersions and misconstructions of Charles Hodge, he published his thorough, carefully researched "Memoir of the Life and Character of Samuel Hopkins."[2] Appearing as part of a new edition of Hopkins' works, the "Memoir" in itself received limited critical notice. But it was an important product of Park's efforts as theologian and historian to come to terms with his tradition, and it remains to this day an invaluable historical resource. Perhaps the most damning criticism of the work came from a review in the Christian Examiner.

The reviewer, George E. Ellis, praised Park's "great fidelity in representing the character and course of Hopkins." But Ellis' own assessment of that "character and course" bore little resemblance to the image Park had

---

[1]Ibid.

[2]First published in The Works of Samuel Hopkins (Boston: Doctrinal Tract and Book Society, 1852), I, v-viii, 1-164; printed separately by the Society in 1854.

attempted to convey. He (Ellis) described Hopkins as
"blunt, rigid, inflexible, and uncompromising." Worse than
that, he found nothing in that great divine's "doctrinal
writings" which could "bear the test of Scripture or reason."[1]
It was precisely that dual test upon which Park's "Memoir"
concentrated most forcefully. There was no doubt in his
mind that the substance of his subject's theology was both
reasonable and scriptural, in the best tradition of
"Consistent" Calvinism.

Nevertheless, like Edwards, Hopkins could sometimes
sound rather "inconsistent" on the subjects of human freedom,
sin, and moral responsibility. For example, Park found
numerous passages in his works declaring "that the children
of Adam are not answerable for his sin" except "by approving
of what he did, and joining with him in rebellion." In
other words, original sin "cannot be distinguished from
actual sin."[2] But Hopkins also tended to favor and employ
some of the more "unfortunate expressions" regarding
identity with Adam found in Edwards' treatise on original
sin. Park attributed this seeming incongruity to nothing
more than an "affectionate attachment" to a revered theological teacher. Hopkins was understandably reluctant
specifically to declare "his dissent from Edwards' philosophy

[1] George E. Ellis, "Prof. Park's Memoir of Hopkins,"
Christian Examiner and Religious Miscellany, LIV, fourth
series XIX, 1 (January, 1853), 128.

[2] Park, "Memoir of Hopkins," in Works, I, 216.

on this theme."[1]

Other noticeable deviations of Hopkins from "common-sense reasonableness" received, in varying form and scope, the useful intellect-feeling explanation. The notion that sin was necessary to the greatest good of the universe came, Park averred, not from "the influence of a merely metaphysical theory, but from the impulses of a heart panting for solace from the afflictions which result from sin."[2] A similar interpretation justified the much-maligned doctrine of "Disinterested Submission," which seemed to make "willingness to be damned for the glory of God" a condition of all true Christian discipleship. "There is a striking resemblance," declared Park, "between the feelings of Dr. Hopkins and the feelings of Fenelon, Madame Guion, and many other mystics, with regard to the endurance of pain for the divine glory."[3] In other words, Hopkins' "harsh doctrine" was not primarily a precise logical deduction of the intellect but a mystical impulse of the feelings. This interesting observation marks one of the few indications in Park's works of his awareness of the place of the New England Theology within the overall history of Christian doctrine and piety.

In sum, Park found that many of the rough edges, or

---

[1]Ibid., p. 217.

[2]Ibid., p. 189.

[3]Ibid., p. 211.

extreme positions, in Hopkins' theology could be smoothed over by attributing them to the heart rather than to the head. Or, viewed from another angle, they should be seen as nothing more than an elevation of inspiration over logic. Contrary to the judgment of the Christian Examiner, Park maintained that Hopkins frequently relied all too strictly on the Scriptures in formulating his doctrines. For one who took literally the Pauline declaration, "And whom he will, he hardeneth," speculations about the necessity of sin in the universe and of absolute submission to an inscrutable divine will could scarcely seem too severe.[1] And yet Park also described Hopkins as a champion of free, rational inquiry. Divine truth was boundless in his eyes, and he left no means of penetrating it untried.[2] Far from being "inflexible and uncompromising," he enjoyed a "comprehensiveness of mind" which admitted into his theological system sources and doctrines often thought to be incompatible. Stubborn antinomies like reason and revelation, human freedom and divine decrees yielded to the skillful Hopkinsian dialectic.[3]

How was such a masterful reconciliation achieved? In general, Park believed the answer lay in the fundamentally "practical and benevolent" aim of Hopkins' theology. That

---

[1] Ibid., p. 181.

[2] Ibid., p. 184.

[3] Ibid., pp. 185-187.

theology was not designed merely to satisfy abstract
speculative interests. Nor was it intended to make the
demands of the Reformed faith any more severe than they
already were. Its "prevailing" purpose was to prove

> that God ought to be a Sovereign, and, there-
> fore, is one; that his decrees are amiable, and
> therefore, we ought to acquiesce in them,
> whatever they may be; that his law is level
> to our natural power, and, therefore, ought
> to be obeyed forthwith.[1]

In short, by definition, there could be no true conflict
between the benign divine government revealed in Scripture,
and the freedom and moral responsibility assigned its human
subjects by the logic of sensible men.

*   *   *

The detailed resolution of this conflict in Hopkins
involved a number of important presuppositions. Among these
Park was pleased to find what he called the "germ of Emmonism."
Of those who followed in the intellectual train of Edwards
and Hopkins, Nathanael Emmons was perhaps the most daring.
His speculations pushed Hopkinsian tenets to, and in some
cases beyond, their logical limits. Widely thought to fall
into the latter category was his important "Exercise Scheme,"
which seemed to deny the existence of "any nature or state
back of the will."[2] Since that Scheme could play a

------

[1]_Ibid._, p. 172.

[2]_Ibid._, p. 200.

significant role in the historical vindication Park was
seeking for his theology, he was eager to demonstrate
that it was not strictly an invention or aberration of
Emmons.

Hopkins, he argued, was as intent as Emmons upon
maintaining "the moral innocence of all states preceding
choice." Like Emmons, he found it "difficult, and perhaps
impossible" to conceive of a "passive" nature behind man's
moral volitions. Some of Hopkins' contemporaries actually
interpreted him, correctly Park believed, to be at least
partially sympathetic to the notion that no "spiritual
substance" whatsoever supported man's choices or "exercises."[1]
Thus "Emmonism," even in its most radical form, was perhaps
not as far removed as it might at first appear from
Hopkins' own speculative efforts to protect human freedom
and responsibility against deterministic presuppositions.

As Nathan Lord had correctly perceived, Emmons was a
central figure in Park's interpretation of the Edwardsean
tradition. He was, in Park's eyes, the exponent par
excellence of the essential principles of the New England
Theology that sin is act and that man's natural ability
equals and limits his moral obligations. For this reason
the Andover professor's exhaustive Memoir of Nathanael
Emmons, published in 1861, and still an indispensable
biographical source, represented a major personal achievement

---

[1]Ibid., pp. 220-201.

in historical self-understanding.[1] Almost twice as long as his work on Hopkins, the new _Memoir_ attracted much wider critical attention. And this is not surprising, for Emmons was not an easy man to explain to the sensible minds of the nineteenth century. Though he lived well into that century, many found his ideas and his severe logic as anachronistic as his three-cornered hat, knee britches, and shoe buckles.

Anachronistic or not, however, he certainly occupied a radical position within his own New Divinity tradition. And that position proved both a great asset and a serious liability to the interpretive picture Park was attempting to paint. It was Emmons' grand design to "joint," in his words, the free human moral volitions of his "Exercise Scheme" onto a thoroughgoing system of direct divine efficiency. This design tended to fill his theology with seemingly irreconcilable contradictions.[2] For example, one

---

[1]Park, _Memoir_ of _Nathanael_ Emmons; with Sketches of His Friends and _Pupils_ (Boston: Congregational Board of Publication, 1861).

[2]It should be noted that Emmons actually produced no written "system" of theology as such. His thought was shaped by the pragmatic purposes of preaching and was preserved exclusively in sermons. He "had a profound horror of ontology"; and this fear led him to state boldly what he considered the "facts" or "truths" of experience, such as those relative to divine efficiency and human freedom, without attempting a detailed metaphysical reconciliation of their contradictions. His failure to deal adequately with these contradictions made Park's biographical task exceedingly difficult. "Had Emmons followed Hopkins' example and written out his theology in systematic form," observed Park's biographer, "he would probably have given expression in due form to his thoughts on psychology and philosophy, and

could definitely find abundant support in his writings for
Park's cardinal principle that ability must always equal
and limit obligation. He gave "a preëminence," Park asserted, "to those energies forming the natural power of men to
fulfil their moral obligations; for unless he did so, he
could not exhibit the honesty and honorableness of the
Lawgiver."[1]   But Park had to concede that his subject also
made God "the only efficient cause in the universe" and
affirmed "that man is not the efficient cause of his own
choices."[2]

Did not this extreme appeal to divine sovereignty,
in effect, make a mockery of any "natural power" man might
have to obey God's law? Park was convinced it did not and
founded his conviction upon the meaning of the word
"efficient." When Emmons, like Edwards, denied the human
will efficient causation, he meant, explained Park, that
"man does not begin his moral action by choosing to choose."
Only God could control the ultimate antecedents to choice.
It was God, as the "great First Cause," who made "the first
eternal choice" upon which all other choices "absolutely
depend." In other words, Emmons was using the term
"efficient" to mean that God was the only "independent"

---

himself cleared up certain difficulties which he left for
/Park/ to resolve." See F. H. Foster, Genetic History,
pp. 340ff.; and Foster's Life of Edwards Amasa Park (New
York: Fleming H. Revell Company, 1936), pp. 206-207.

[1]Park, Memoir of Emmons, p. 386.

[2]Ibid., p. 387.

cause in the universe. He was not, Park declared, seeking
to eliminate intervention of "second causes" between divine
and human activity.[1] He was merely "jealous of many remarks
on the forces of the material world, lest men should forget
their dependence on Him who created, sustains, and governs
all the forces of matter and mind."[2]

One might well imagine what Emmons, not to mention
Aristotle, would have thought of this explanation. Apparently Park himself was not completely satisfied with it, for
he rounded out his discussion of the matter by calling upon
his dependable intellect-feeling distinction. Emmons'
language regarding divine efficiency, he averred, was
actually "more intense than plain..., more emphatic than
exact." It was best understood "by considering the general
scope of his theology," which, in Park's view, left no
doubt as to man's natural abilities.[3] Further protection
for those abilities came from Park's interpretive distinction
between "mode" and "fact." "Emmons," he argued, "had such
an intense desire to represent the Providence of God as
coextensive and coincident with the Decrees of God, that
he overlooked all theories with regard to the mode of
conducting this Providence."[4] In other words, Emmons'

[1] Ibid., pp. 385-387.

[2] Ibid., p. 386.

[3] Ibid., p. 387.

[4] Ibid., p. 417.

emphatic language about divine agency was designed to
defend the good Reformed concern for the sovereignty of
God, not to specify the precise operation of that sovereignty. It was the fact that God's will ultimately prevailed, not the means to that end, which Emmons, perhaps
overzealously at times, wished to stress.

Here Park was, in essence, attempting to minimize the
role of what he called emotive or figurative language in
Emmons' theology. Viewed as a whole, that theology was
eminently practical and reasonable. Where it appeared
otherwise, as on the subject of divine causation, one had
only to look at its "general scope" and to consider the
reasonable intent behind the sometimes unreasonable (or
figurative) language. Nonetheless, there were instances
of "unreasonable language" in Emmons which severely
strained this interpretive framework. For example, implied
in the Hopkinsian notion of the necessity of sin to the
greatest good was a harsh conclusion which Emmons did not
hesitate to draw, namely, that God was the author of sin.

His repeated and seemingly unambiguous statements on
this matter received a variety of explanations from Park.
In the case of Adam's sin, for instance, when Emmons
appealed to the "immediate interposition of the Deity" and
excluded "the instrumentality of second causes," Park
interpreted him to mean "an interposition of new influences,
or a change of the former influences" through the "attendant

and governing agency of God."[1] In other words, "immediate,"
in Park's lexicon, somehow came to signify an indirect
agency or influence. But Emmons' remarks about the sin of
Adam's posterity seemed, if anything, even more forceful
in pointing to direct divine agency. In consequence of
Adam's disobedience, Emmons maintained, his descendants
were divinely determined to "begin to sin before they
should begin to be holy." God was said to execute this
determination "by directly operating on the hearts of
children, when they first become moral agents."[2]

To assertions such as these, Park attributed a generalized reference. Emmons was indeed saying that God acted
to "secure the occurrence of sin." But the precise manner
of that action, whether direct or indirect, he did not
intend to specify. In effect, Park was again equating
Emmons' emphatic statements about divine causation with a
general Reformed understanding of divine providence.
"There is no more objection to the doctrine of divine
efficiency securing the occurrence of all things, than to
the doctrine of divine purposes securing the certainty of
all things."[3] Thus did Park seek to rationalize Emmons'
"hard sayings" on the origin of sin.

There were cases, however, in which even this sort of

---

[1] Ibid., p. 405.

[2] Ibid., p. 407.

[3] Ibid.

broad rationalization did not seem appropriate. When
confronted with these, Park appealed to the strict biblical
literalness which he found in Emmons as well as Hopkins.
A case in point was Emmons' famous "Pharaoh Sermon," which
presented, in stark relief, some of the worst implications
of a divine causation defined in comprehensive and immediate
terms. Referring to God's intervention in the Old Testament conflict between Moses and Pharaoh, the sermon indicated what was necessary to fit the Egyptian ruler "for
destruction." It was not enough "barely to leave him to
himself," for "God knew that no external means and motives
would be sufficient of themselves to form his moral character."
The divine will "determined, therefore, to operate on his
heart itself, and cause him to put forth certain evil
exercises...." Repeatedly punctuating the sermon's catalogue of Pharaoh's evil deeds were the words "God stood
by him and moved him."[1]

But what placed this closely reasoned homily beyond
the pale of a generalized rationalization were statements
like the following: "He /God/ continually hardened
/Pharaoh's/ heart, and governed all the exercises of his
mind, from the day of his birth to the day of his death....
This was absolutely necessary to prepare him for this
final state," that is "for destruction."[2] This was

---

[1]Ibid., pp. 409-410.

[2]Ibid., p. 410.

double predestination with a vengeance. Divine authorship
of sin had been logically extended into divine authorship
of damnation. And however palatable one might make the
former with sweeping references to an indirect providence,
the latter was simply unthinkable to "sensible men." To
make matters worse, Pharaoh clearly formed no special
exegetical case in Emmons' preaching and theology. Though
not equally forceful on this point, his other sermons
seemed repeatedly to affirm direct divine responsibility,
according to an eternal plan, for each individual human
destiny, without distinction as to its good or evil character.

How was Park to interpret such a doctrine in a theologian whom he was attempting to picture as eminently
practical and reasonable? He decided to let Emmons explain
himself in an imaginative commentary the preacher might
have added to his own sermon:

> Do you shrink from saying: "God prepared Pharaoh
> /for destruction7"?...Do you shrink from these
> inspired words? I stand where the Bible stands.
> I say what the Bible says. If the Bible sanctions
> Hebrew idioms /or hyperboles7, they are good
> enough for my sermons.[1]

In other words, when it came to divine causation, Emmons'
extreme reverence for the inspired Word and "words" often
heavily outweighed his regard for practical reasonableness.
Taking the emotive metaphors of Scripture at face value, he
did not "shrink from" their harshest logical implications.
The substance of his resultant "theology of the feelings"

---

[1] Ibid.

regarding God's immediate earthly agency was correct, in Park's view; but it was much too figurative and exaggerated at many points to satisfy the intellect.

The major doctrinal emphasis in Emmons, as Park read him, was, however, perfectly satisfactory to the intellect. This was Emmons' concern for human freedom and natural ability. Protecting this concern was his definition of sin and righteousness exclusively in terms of choice or act. No passive state back of man's choices or exercises could limit or determine their voluntary moral character. In fact, as Park put it, he was "so eager to make men believe in the activity, by which he meant the voluntariness, of all moral character, that he used terms which seemed to represent activity as the very essence of the soul."[1] But such a representation, though appearing to maximize personal freedom and moral responsibility, could, Park realized, do precisely the opposite if carried to its logical extreme. For if the soul were nothing but acts or exercises, where was the actor or agent involved?

Emmons' doctrine of divine efficiency would seem to make the answer to this question self-evident. He saw no problem in saying that "God creates within us free moral exercises." But his confidence that such an arrangement, without qualification, placed man under "an absolute necessity of acting freely" was apparently not shared by his

---

[1] Ibid., p. 412.

biographer. For Park's sympathies, at this point, tended
to lie with those critics of Emmons who declared "that an
exercise which is not self-originated cannot be voluntary,
and if it is made free, it is not free."[1] The retention
of the soul as an effective "second cause" in Emmons was
therefore essential to the historical vindication Park
sought from that divine.

The prime spokesman for the doctrines of human freedom
and moral responsibility which formed the essence of the
New England Theology surely realized that "the soul is not
a mere series of exercises, but possesses powers, and is
a substance."[2] The emphatic language of Emmons' "Exercise
Scheme" was actually intended, Park believed, not to deny
that the soul existed but to stress that its nature flowed
from and was solely defined by choices and actions, rather
than vice versa.[3] Emphatic or not, however, Emmons' extreme
references to the activity of the soul seemed, to many
observers, to be integrally related to his strong support
of free moral agency, which Park so admired. This meant
that Emmonsian theology was, at best, a double-edged
weapon in the historical defense of Park's three "radical
principles" regarding sin, ability, and obligation.

----

[1]Ibid., p. 406.

[2]Ibid., p. 412.

[3]Ibid., p. 413.

*   *   *

Making this duality especially clear was a review
essay written in response to Park's Memoir Of Emmons by
Henry Boynton Smith.[1] Smith readily admitted that Emmons
"made very sweeping statements about /natural/ ability,"
even allowing mankind a "natural power to frustrate those
divine decrees which they are appointed to fulfill."[2]
But given the Hopkinsian divine's forceful advocacy of
divine efficiency and his difficulty in conceiving of a
substantial soul, the reviewer could, in reality, find
little more than an "abstract possibility of a different
/human/ volition from the one actually created" by God.[3]
"His natural ability," Smith maintained, "had in fact no
hold, or substance, no background to support it." In other
words, it lacked "a real will and a real soul."[4]

In effect, Smith was saying that Emmons' attempts to
hold together doctrines of radical human freedom and even
more radical human dependence were fundamentally unsuccessful. This meant that the interpretive assumptions of Park's
Memoir were at best half-truths. In Smith's terms, Park

---

[1]Henry Boynton Smith, "The Theological System of
Emmons," in Faith and Philosophy (New York: Scribner,
Armstrong, and Company, 1877), pp. 215-263. Initially
published in American Theological Review for January, 1862.

[2]Ibid., pp. 244-245.

[3]Ibid., p. 244.

[4]Ibid., p. 247.

had retained Emmonsian "phraseology" but altered "its
sense." He had kept "the exercises and denied the efficiency that produces them."[1] Stated another way, Park's
Emmons "held to exercises definitely, and to divine
efficiency indefinitely."[2] The former belonged to the
theology of the intellect; the latter, to that of the
feelings. But, Smith argued, if Emmons' theology was
anything, it was precise and logical throughout. Thus, if
one explained away his extreme doctrine of divine causation,
one unavoidably explained away his doctrine of free human
agency as well. As Smith put it, "Emmons himself is explained away."[3]

In what he called an "emasculating process," the
reviewer saw Park as reducing Emmons' "distinct and distinctive propositions...to the terms of a less severe system."[4]
Emmonsian deviations from Park's three "radical principles"
involved more than superficial differences of language and
emphasis. The "rough edges" of Hopkins' theology might be
smoothed over by appeals to such differences, but Emmons'
"rugged mountains" were not so easily leveled.[5] As Park
himself had conceded years before the publication of his

---

[1] Ibid., p. 248.

[2] Ibid., p. 261.

[3] Ibid., p. 216.

[4] Ibid.

[5] Ibid., pp. 215-216.

biographical masterpiece, "If he /i.e., Emmons7 erred in
his speculations, it was, generally, at his starting points,
not in the way from them to his conclusions; in his premises
rather than his reasonings."[1] In other words, Emmons was
not a man to be dealt with on less than fundamental terms.
iie took great care in arriving at his formulations. If one
disagreed with his language or emphasis, one almost certainly
disagreed with his basic premises or "starting points" as
well.

It was this characteristic integrity which Park, in
Smith's view, was less than candid in recognizing in the
Emmons Memoir. No amount of exegetical manipulation, argued
the reviewer, could disguise the fact that Park's theological
starting point was man, while Emmons' was God. The thought
of the latter rested "ultimately upon a theological basis";
that of the former, "upon certain assumed ethical maxims."[2]
The dichotomy described here was perhaps too sharp, but
another reviewer of the Emmons Memoir tended to confirm it.

George Park Fisher, who had assumed the chair of
ecclesiastical history at Yale Divinity School in 1861,
was struck by the similarity between Park's interpretation
of Emmons and the theology of Nathaniel Taylor.[3] With its

---

[1]From Park's letter of June 1, 1848, on "Nathanael
Emmons" in William B. Sprague, ed., Annals of the American
Pulpit (New York: Robert Carter and Brothers, 1859), I, 699.

[2]H. B. Smith, "The Theological System of Emmons,"
p. 238.

[3]George Park Fisher, "Professor Park's Memoir of Dr.
Emmons," New Englander, XIX, 75 (July, 1861), 720. Fisher,

238

emphasis upon a free human will whose choices possessed
moral character only by virtue of a "power to the contrary,"
that theology did in fact seem fundamentally concerned
with certain "assumed ethical maxims" of the "common sense"
variety. And since this concern appeared unavoidably to
abridge divine sovereignty, Fisher could not understand
how the theocentric Emmons could be read as a Taylorite.
A man who sought "to graft human activity, including every
particular choice, upon a positive divine energy as its
cause" was not likely to approve a vague formula balancing
the "certainty" or "inevitability" of such activity against
a "contrary power."[1] "We had been under the impression
always," said Fisher, "that Dr. Emmons and his followers
looked upon Dr. Taylor's formula as insufficient and
Arminian in its tendency." But given Park's contention
that his subject "merely taught the previous certainty of
every moral act, transgression included," how, wondered
the reviewer, did Emmons differ from the New Haven position?[2]
"Dr. Taylor went as far as this," declared Fisher; and he
accused the Abbot Professor of "cutting off the claws...of

---

a Brown alumnus and a student of Park's in the early 1850's,
first became professionally associated with Yale as professor and college pastor in 1854. He taught church
history there until 1901. His numerous publications,
ranging over such topics as "future probation," original
sin, and the theology of Nathaniel Taylor, perceptively
placed New England religious thought within the broader
context of the history of Christian doctrine.

[1]Ibid.

[2]Ibid.

the author he has taken in hand."[1]

It should be said that in regard to Park's interpretation of the Emmonsian doctrines of sin and free will, the criticisms of Smith and Fisher had considerable validity. The biographer did often seem to be "emasculating" or "de-clawing" his subject. But at least one area of Emmons' thought appeared to lend itself rather well to a reading through Taylorite glasses. This was his doctrine of the atonement. A man like Emmons, who defined sin, righteousness, and even the soul itself in terms of voluntary individual acts, was not likely to apply a fundamentally different perspective to salvation or damnation. It was not Adam or Christ but each soul's moral exercises that played the decisive role here. Emmons conceded that man obtained "pardon" through the atonement, but he grounded salvation in "holy obedience."

For Emmons, as for Taylor, the objective impact of the atonement was greatly diminished, or at least redirected. It lacked substitutionary or imputed redemptive value for sinful humanity. Both saw such value as undermining the moral system within which mankind was supposed to live.

---

[1]Ibid., pp. 720-721. In an interesting letter addressed to Park not long after he had assumed the Bartlet Chair of Rhetoric at Andover, the aged Emmons, responding to a query from his young friend, remarked, "I do indeed go about halfway with the Taylorites, and then stop and turn against them with all my might." (Emmons to Park, August 7, 1838, ms. in Yale University Library) Apparently Park forgot the last half of this reply, in Fisher's eyes at least.

In Taylor's view, the atonement was fundamentally a cosmic demonstration to vindicate the divine moral government and to provide motives to salvation. Uppermost in Emmons' mind was the governmental aspect, directed primarily to God, rather than to man or the universe. He regarded Christ's death as no more than the "occasion" of divine favor and forgiveness toward humanity, as merely the removal of a preliminary obstacle to salvation. It was actually the Emmonsian concern for divine sovereignty which took precedence here. The atonement was a necessary part of the plan of salvation revealed in Scripture. But it did not obligate God to save any or all. The ultimate reason why some were saved and others damned still lay with the sovereign divine will.

There would seem, however, to be a conflict between God's sovereign will and man's "holy obedience" in Emmons' view of the salvation process. Carefully avoiding any federal or covenant-oriented resolution of that conflict, Emmons placed his trust in direct divine efficiency. It was, after all, God, not man, who controlled the moral exercises involved in holy obedience. Taylor could not accept such a radical definition of the God-man relationship in salvation. He approved the Emmonsian emphasis upon moral exercises but rejected any immediate intervention of divine efficiency. But whether one looked to Taylor's voluntary moral acts or to Emmons' inscrutable divine will as finally decisive in the saving process, the role of the atonement remained basically constant. It was an event with cosmic but very limited personal dimensions, carefully removed from the immediate arena of divine-human interaction in redemption.[1]

*   *   *

In a work published just prior to his Emmons biography, Park identified Emmons as an important contributor to the development of the so-called "Edwardean theory of the atonement."[2] Also known as the "New England" or "Governmental" theory, this understanding of the atonement found its

_____

[1]For a good, succinct discussion of Emmons and Taylor on the atonement, see Foster, Genetic History, pp. 210ff.

[2]cf. Park, "The Rise of the Edwardean Theory of the Atonement," in The Atonement: Discourses and Treatises, ed. Park (Boston: Congregational Board of Publication, 1859), p. lxxix. See also the two Emmons sermons reprinted in this volume as an editorial indication of what Park considered his subject's clearest statement of views on the atonement.

The nature and development of the doctrine of the atonement in Edwardsean or New England Theology has been a much-researched, much-reviewed subject. Some of the better studies and reviews after Park's include the following: George Park Fisher, History of Christian Doctrine (Edinburgh: T. and T. Clark, 1949, second edition), pp. 409-444; George Nye Boardman, A History of New England Theology (New York: A. D. F. Randolph Company, 1899), pp. 221-248; Frank Hugh Foster, "The Benevolence Theory of the Atonement," Bibliotheca Sacra, XLVII, 188 (October, 1890), 567-588 and XLVIII, 189 (January, 1891), 104-127; Joseph Haroutunian, Piety Versus Moralism: The Passing of the New England Theology (New York: Harper and Row, 1970), Chap. VII; and Dorus Paul Rudisill, "The Doctrine of the Atonement in Jonathan Edwards and His Successors" (Duke University: unpublished Ph.D. dissertation, 1945).

definitive expression in Jonathan Edwards, Jr.[1] Though
Emmons and the younger Edwards were by no means in full
theological agreement, they shared, as Park realized, some
of the same fundamental presuppositions that Emmons and
Taylor had in common in regard to the saving value of the
atonement. The most important of these Park summarized by
the "general proposition that the atonement was equal, in
the meaning and the spirit of it, to the payment of our
debts, but it was not literally the payment of either our
debt of obedience or our debt of punishment, or any other
debt which we owed to law or distributive justice."[2]

Behind this proposition lay Park's important distinction
between feeling ("the meaning and the spirit of it") and
intellect ("not literally").[3] But unlike a number of other
contexts in which that distinction produced rather strained
support for his interpretation of New England's theological
history, the result in this instance was a suggestive piece
of historical insight. In discussing the development of
the "New England" theory of the atonement, the Abbot
Professor looked back of Emmons and the younger Edwards to
the senior Edwards himself. The latter, like Emmons,

[1]cf. J. Robert Livingston Ferm, "Jonathan Edwards the
Younger and the American Reformed Tradition" (Yale University: unpublished Ph.D. dissertation, 1958), Chap. X.

[2]Park, "Edwardean Atonement," p. x.

[3]cf. Park, "The Theology of the Intellect and That of
the Feelings," Bibliotheca Sacra, VII, 27 (July, 1850),
pp. 535 and 563, note A.

recognized a literal substitutionary atonement as a threat to divine sovereignty, Park averred, and tended to move away from such a doctrine of redemption in his later writings.[1]

Focusing particularly upon Edwards' _Miscellaneous Observations on Important Doctrines_, the Andover divine found certain key definitions and distinctions which seemed to reflect an awareness of figurative versus literal meanings of the atonement.[2] One such definition involved Edwards' use of the term "merit." In a literal substitutionary understanding of the atonement, Christ's merit, as a moral or legal state, was imputed to the believer. But Park saw Edwards as moving increasingly toward a non-literal concept of saving merit as a "general recommendation, or a general means of securing favor." The relationship between Christ and the believer would then be comparable to a patron-client situation in which "the influence which recommends the patron prevails in recommending the client."[3] By defining merit in terms of influence rather than objective transference of character, Edwards was able, in Park's view, to

---

[1]Park, "Edwardean Atonement," pp. xii-xv; lxiv. For a concise modern discussion of the elder Edwards' doctrine of the atonement, see Conrad Cherry, _The Theology of Jonathan Edwards_ (New York: Doubleday and Company, 1966), pp. 93-96.

[2]The sections of Edwards' work which most interested Park were the observations "Concerning God's Moral Government" and "Concerning the Divine Decree in General and Election in Particular." Also receiving attention in this regard was Edwards' _Dissertation Concerning the End for Which God Created the World_.

[3]Park, "Edwardean Atonement," pp. xxiv-xxv.

distinguish between Christ's atoning "pain suffered in view of sin for the sake of upholding the authority of law, and pain suffered as punishment for sin, as the literal execution of the legal threat."[1]

Given definitions and distinctions of this sort, Park was not surprised to find that Edwards gave "a previously unwonted prominence to the element of love in the atonement."[2] Founded upon the Edwardsean concept of virtue as the expression of love to being as such, that prominence manifested itself, Park believed, in two basic ways. First of all, love, not retributive sacrifice, formed the primary motive force behind the atonement. But secondly, and more to the point, "sympathetic love" was a "principal means of the Redeemer's suffering, after he had undertaken the work of redeeming us."[3] In other words, Christ's suffering, in Park's reading of Edwards, was sympathetic rather than substitutionary. It was metaphorically rather than literally "in our stead."

Park, of course, acknowledged that what Edwards had to say about the atonement was never fully or consistently "governmental" in nature. Most of the father's expressed thoughts on that subject were far from those of his son. But the Andover professor was convinced that the fundamental

---

[1]Ibid., p. xxix.

[2]Ibid., p. xxxviii.

[3]Ibid., p. xxxix.

thrust of the father's later thinking was in the direction taken by the son and other Edwardsean disciples.[1] And that conviction was grounded in some of Park's most careful exegetical work. Not only the elder Edwards, however, but his two closest followers as well, Hopkins and Joseph Bellamy, received painstaking scrutiny for evidence of the early parentage of the "New England" view of the atonement.

Bellamy was particularly crucial in this historical investigation since he was not only the student and friend of the elder Edwards but the teacher of the younger Edwards as well. Again, Park conceded his subject's failure to develop a recognizably "modern" (i.e., "governmental") atonement theory. But, like the elder Edwards, Bellamy tended to shrink from the "logical results" of a strict substitutionary atonement when those results seemed to abridge divine sovereignty. Park found it especially significant that the younger Edwards' teacher was "careful to represent the atonement not as obligating God in justice to save us, but as 'opening a door for him to save us,' 'removing a bar to our salvation,'" and the like.[2] Such language, in Park's view, moved Bellamy toward fundamental agreement with his friend Hopkins' more distinctly governmental affirmations to the effect that in the atonement

---

[1]cf. Ferm, pp. 246-247, 260.

[2]Park, "Edwardean Atonement," pp. xlii-xliii; also cf. pp. xlvii-xlix.

"God executes the threatening of his law in the true meaning and spirit of it" but not in such a sense as to "alter the character of the sinner" or to "mitigate our demerit in the slightest degree."[1]

In other words, Bellamy and Hopkins, as their Andover interpreter read them, were well on the way to saying that Christ's death opened up the possibility (not the necessity) of **sal**vation for all while at the same time preserving the integrity of God's moral government. Such an understanding of the atonement threatened neither divine sovereignty and justice nor human freedom and moral responsibility. That Park was able to find evidence of it in the very "founder" of the New England Theology, not to mention the two earliest disciples of that "New Divinity," was a major coup in his efforts at historical vindication. A governmental concept of the atonement assumed increasing importance in later Edwardsean theology and played a decisive role in the Abbot Professor's own formulations. It blended in perfectly with his "three radical principles" of the New England Theology regarding sin, natural ability, and moral responsibility. If Edwards and his early disciples sometimes made statements relative to original sin, free will, and divine efficiency which seemed to undermine these three principles, their Andover interpreter could always appeal to their incipient "modern" theory of the atonement to set the record

---

[1] cf. Ibid., pp. 1-liii.

straight.

In sum, it could be argued that the central place which the atonement came to occupy in the development of Park's own theology was due primarily to his historical insight into his Edwardsean heritage. However much some of his doctrinal positions (e.g., on natural ability and free will) may have distorted that heritage to meet the apologetic exigencies of the last century, as he perceived them, his concept of the atonement appeared to have roots in the very fountainhead of the New Divinity tradition. It enjoyed the telling advantages of both appropriateness to that tradition and understandability, or adaptability, within the Scottish Common Sense milieu of Park's thinking. The manner in which he exploited these advantages by developing his "modern" theory of the atonement in tandem with his "modern" doctrines of sin and free will forms the subject of the concluding chapter.

Chapter VIII

THE NEW ENGLAND THEOLOGY "MODERNIZED":
REASON AND MORALITY TRIUMPHANT

Anyone who claimed even carefully qualified adherence
to orthodox Reformed doctrine, as did Park, assumed a
tremendous apologetic burden in nineteenth-century America.
The pervasive atmosphere of optimistic democratic humanitarianism tended to be rather inhospitable to the theocentric, paradoxical gospel of Augustine, Calvin, and
Edwards. Thoroughly committed to evangelical preaching,
missionary, and reform activity as the most effective
means of meeting the spiritual and social needs of the
age, Park was certain that such endeavors were best fur-
thered on the strong foundation of the New England Theology.
But that foundation was threatened, he believed, by two
forms of theology which seemed more at home in the intellectual milieu of the times: Unitarianism and Universalism.
Each of these in its own way underestimated the seriousness
of sin and left no room for a true atonement, as Park
understood it.

Paramount in the Unitarian understanding of sin and
salvation was the requirement that nothing in the God-man
relationship be exempt from the commonly accepted laws of

reason, science, and morality. The application of this
requirement to the atonement produced a Christ whose chief
saving value lay not in substitution for sinners but in
instruction and moral example. The Universalists were
somewhat less rationalistic and moralistic in their view
of the atonement. They simply followed the literal
Reformed satisfaction, or substitutionary, doctrine of
Christ's saving work to its logical evangelical conclusion.
That is, if Christ literally satisfied the penalty of the
law for the sin of any man, he did so for all mankind, and
thereby provided for the salvation of all. But whether
one rejected any literal satisfaction in Christ's work, as
did the Unitarians, or simply universalized that satisfaction,
as did the Universalists, the traditional Reformed notion
of a limited atonement was totally unacceptable.

Park confronted this challenge head-on by declaring
that his own "Consistent Calvinist" theory of the atonement
rejected limits as well. It was to Edward Dorr Griffin
(1770-1837), the great evangelical preacher who became
Andover's first Bartlet Professor, that he turned for
guidance in defending a general atonement within an
orthodox Reformed theological framework. A disciple of
of the younger Edwards, Griffin, as Park read him, applied
the benefits of the atonement to all men without surrender-
ing the concept of election as such.[1] If any man could

---

[1]cf. Park, "Dr. Griffin's Theory of the Atonement,"
Bibliotheca Sacra, XV, 57 (January, 1858), 132-178.

say that the atonement was not intended for him, Griffin averred, then the evangelical message of the pulpit was undermined. Since sin and the need for salvation were universal, a limited atonement was contrary to divine benevolence and justice. But a distinction had to be made between a general atonement and universal salvation.

The latter, Griffin and Park believed, unduly abridged divine sovereignty and reflected dishonor on the divine law. The atonement, therefore, had to be seen as a conditional benefit. It did not obligate God unconditionally to save all mankind. It was, after all, an offer of forgiveness and new life to all who would accept it. No one, in the eyes of Griffin and Park, could say he lacked the "natural" ability to effect such an acceptance. But what all men "could" do and what they "would" do were distinct propositions. Employing a trusted Edwardsean distinction, Griffin and Park concluded that a general atonement made universal salvation a natural but not a "moral" possibility.[1] This distinction, the two New Divinity men believed, preserved a non-causative doctrine of election as divine foresight regarding who would and who would not exercise the faith offered to all through the atonement.[2]

---

[1] Ibid., p. 158.

[2] cf. George Park Fisher, Notes on Park's Lectures on Systematic Theology (1850-51; ms. in Yale University Library), pp. 163 and 330-331.

252

Given this understanding of election, Park boldly
declared his belief that only a "verbal difference" existed
between the doctrines of limited and general atonement.[1]
Both doctrines, he felt, allowed for an atonement which was
sufficient for all but efficient only for some. Primary
reasons for this arrangement might vary from divine glory
to the general good of the universe, but both concepts of
the atonement definitely accepted some limitations on its
saving efficiency.[2] For Park, an atonement which was universal in intent but particular in application offered a
perfect means of reconciling divine mercy with divine
justice. Following his Edwardsean tradition, he saw love
as the fundamental divine characteristic, comprehending all
other attributes of God. The atonement was a necessary
expression of God's love for all mankind, but it included both
mercy and justice within itself. That is, God necessarily
saved some, through the atonement, because he needed to show
mercy; but he could not save all because he also needed to
manifest his justice. Mercy and justice, for Park, were both
equal revelations of divine love; and both, like all divine
attributes, were necessarily expressed.[3]

[1]Ibid., p. 338.

[2]cf. F. H. Foster, A Genetic History of the New England
Theology (Chicago: University of Chicago Press, 1907),
pp. 264-269.

[3]cf. Park, "All the Moral Attributes of God Are Com-
prehended in His Love," in Discourses on Some Theological
Doctrines as Related to the Religious Character (Andover:
Warren F. Draper, 1885), pp. 155-180.

In giving God's justice an important position in the expression of his love, Park felt he had decisively distinguished himself from both the Universalists' and the Unitarians' theological posture. Both these groups failed to take the divine law and the sin of mankind against that law seriously enough, in the mind of the Abbot Professor. Against the Universalists, he argued that the obedience, suffering, and death of one man could never literally satisfy the demands of the law for all. But this did not mean that one could simply ignore these demands and concentrate upon Christ's instruction and moral example, as the Unitarians seemed to do.[1] Something had to be done to clear up any possible misunderstanding of God's justice and of his attitude toward sin. That something was the atonement.[2] In his earlier theological lectures (ca. 1846-50), Park defined it as Christ's

> offering himself and being divinely accepted as a sacrifice and substitute for sinners, so as by his sufferings and death to render it consistent for God to pardon sin and bestow blessings on men who had committed it.[3]

Lest one mistake this definition for a literal substitutionary atonement theory, it should be noted that the important

---

[1] cf. Francis Duncan Kelsey, Notes on Park's Lectures on Systematic Theology (1871-72; ms. in Oberlin College Library), II, 238-250.

[2] See Park, "The Revelation of God in His Works," in Discourses (cited above), pp. 88-89.

[3] Edmund Kimball Alden, Notes on Park's Lectures on Systematic Theology (1846-47; ms. in Oberlin College Library), p. 256.

words here are not "sacrifice and substitute" but "to
render it consistent." The focus of the definition, in
other words, is not upon human sin or Christ's work as
such, but upon the needs of God's moral government.

Those needs were best served, Park believed, by
viewing Christ's death as figuratively equivalent to sinful
humanity's just punishment.[1] The emphasis here is, in
the final analysis, eminently practical. The atonement
flowed out of God's grace and love, not primarily to
satisfy an abstract law or to placate an affronted Deity,
but to protect the general welfare of the universe.[2] To
pardon obvious sinners without at least a token demonstration of due punishment would be to jeopardize the moral
system through which that general welfare was preserved.
Without abrogating man's individual responsibility under
the law, the atonement provided just enough figurative
legal satisfaction to render undeserved pardon "consistent"
(i.e., possible rather than necessary) with the divine
moral government of the universe.[3] As Park's theology
developed, he strove to make the practical, governmental

---

[1] Fisher, Notes, pp. 318-319.

[2] cf. William Ladd Ropes, Notes on Park's Lectures on
Systematic Theology (1850-51; ms. in Andover Newton Theological School Library), II, 277-279: "The atonement declares
but does not cause God's grace." Also, it was said not to
"ameliorate" but to render "consistent" the manifestation
of the "whole" divine character in showing "favor to mankind."

[3] cf. Ropes, Notes, II, 295: Christ suffered not "for"
but "in consequence of " our sins.

aspect of the atonement clearer while retaining traditional sacrificial terminology. In a later doctrinal definition (ca. 1875) which he labeled the "best of all," he called Christ's death "a disciplinary sacrifice" which God "substituted for the punishment of men."[1] Here, as his surrounding notes indicate, Park intended to give the terms "sacrifice" and "substitute" a concrete, pragmatic qualification. The atonement was meant as a "disciplinary" demonstration by a loving Father-Governor for the benefit of the public order and the public good.

Neither the term "disciplinary" nor the term "consistent" occurred in Park's most fully developed technical definition of the atonement, however. Its final form, assumed in the mid-1860's, read as follows:

> that sacrifice of the God-man which is substituted for the punishment of men and which therefore forms the sole ground on which God is justified and satisfied, the chief motive by which he is influenced and by which he exerts an influence in directly blessing men.[2]

Here, as indicated by the terms "ground," "motive," and "influence," the emphasis is clearly upon what Park called

---

[1]Park, Lecture Notebook on the Atonement (undated; ms. in Andover Newton Theological School Library), p. 93.

[2]Henry Martyn Tenney, Notes on Park's Lectures on Systematic Theology (1865; ms. in Oberlin College Library), II, 37; see also David Dana Marsh, Notes on Park's Lectures on Systematic Theology (1866-67; ms. in Andover Newton Theological School Library), p. 490; William J. McLean, Notes on Park's Lectures on Systematic Theology (1874-75; ms. in Oberlin College Library), II, 103; and Foster, Genetic History, p. 512.

the "relations" of the atonement. These included the three
important "appeals" of Christ's work to the universe, to the
sinner, and to God himself.[1]

The first of these appeals was most important for a purely governmental approach to the atonement and received primary stress in Park's earlier theology. As already indicated,
Christ's death was, in this case, an appeal for a "disciplinary consistency" in the moral system of the universe. It
protected the general welfare by honoring, without executing,
divine justice. But the other two appeals received increasing emphasis as Park's theology matured.[2] They reflected, in
effect, a tendency on his part to merge governmental and moral
influence motifs in his understanding of the atonement.[3]
Christ's death was more than an objective governmental necessity. It also made a powerful subjective appeal to both the
intellect and the feelings of the sinner to "repent and be
saved."[4] As indeed the "chief motive" through which God exerted "an influence in directly blessing man," the atoning
work of the God-man ran the gamut of human understanding and

---

[1] cf. McLean, Notes, pp. 125-233.

[2] See the successively "improved" definitions of the
atonement in Park, Lecture Notebook on the Atonement (cited
above), pp. 10, 21, and 93.

[3] cf. Charles Franklin Thwing, Notes on Park's Lectures
on Systematic Theology (1877-78; ms. in Case Western Reserve
University Library), II, 72-68 (pagination in alternating
reverse order); see also Park, "The Sorrow of the Redeemer
in Anticipation of His Death," in Discourses, pp. 346-347.

[4] cf. Foster, Genetic History, p. 517; and Park, "The
Power of the Gospel" and "The Prominence of the Atonement,"
in Discourses, pp. 100, 106 and pp. 59-60.

emotion, appealing to man's "love, sense of justice, gratitude, sympathy, reverence," and so on.[1]

As to the appeal of Christ's death to God, this was perhaps the most interesting "moral influence" aspect of Park's atonement theory. The atonement was clearly more than the objective "ground" of divine justification and satisfaction vis-à-vis the universe. It was also the means of removing the divine "motive for punishing the sinner, since the end of punishment had been perfectly gained." And it presented, moreover, "a positive motive for forgiveness."[2] This notion did not imply, for Park, that Christ's death "caused" God's love or benevolence toward the sinner. It meant simply that the atonement not only declared and made possible, but provided a concrete focus for and actively influenced the exercise of divine love in salvation. Herein lies the true import of statements in the Abbot Professor's lectures like the following: "The benevolence of God will never save men unless there be an atonement for benevolence to rest upon."[3] "God will not pardon sin from mere grace or personal feeling...."[4]

There is an interesting interplay here between Park's

[1]G. P. Fisher, Notes, p. 329.

[2]Foster, Genetic History, p. 517; see also McLean, Notes, II, 129.

[3]McLean Notes, II, 103.

[4]Thwing, Notes, II. 76.

atonement theory, with its combination of objective governmental and subjective moral influence perspectives, and
that of Hartford preacher Horace Bushnell. In his lectures,
Park objected to Bushnell's subjective theology of the
feelings as making moral influence the "essence" of the
atonement rather than a "consequence" of it.[1] Bushnell,
in turn, found the "Edwardean" theory of the atonement
too far removed from the personal need of sinners for
salvation. It provided for exhibition but not expiation,
having Christ die, innocently and unjustly, "in no one's
place" and secure nothing but the possibility (or consistency) of forgiveness.[2] Park's response to this
critique, in his review of Bushnell's _Vicarious Sacrifice_,
was to admit the genius of the Hartford divine's subjective
analogies but to insist that they involved the use of old
terms in new ways and reflected an inaccurate conception
of the "New England" theory of the atonement.[3]

Actually, both Park and Bushnell were using old terms
(e.g., sacrifice) in new ways. Language was very important
to both and a chief source of their disagreement. Bushnell
objected to the mechanical, impersonal quality of Park's

---

[1] cf. Ropes, Notes, II, 313.

[2] cf. Horace Bushnell, _The Vicarious Sacrifice, Grounded_
in Principles of Universal Obligation (New York, 1866),
pp. 365-368; see also Bushnell's _God in Christ_ (Hartford,
1849), pp. 194ff.

[3] The review appeared in _Bibliotheca Sacra_, XXIII, 90
(April, 1866), 345-350.

rationalized juridical constructs. And Park found the
Hartford theologian's organic, emotive metaphors needlessly
vague and subjective. These differences in language reflected significant difference of emphasis in regard to
the atonement. An objective cosmic symbol of divine
justice and a suffering identification with the sinner to
renovate his character were by no means the same. And yet,
in the final analysis, there was a striking amount of
common ground on this doctrine between the Andover and the
Hartford divine.

Shared by both, for example, was the conviction that
the atonement originated in divine love and was essentially
non-punitive in character. That is, it was not a device to
appease the Deity, but a revelation of his fundamental
nature in his compassionate efforts to reconcile and save
a fallen humanity.[1] Furthermore, Christ's suffering, for
both Bushnell and Park, revealed the justice as well as the
mercy of God. For Bushnell, a true atonement had to make
man "feel, in the very article of forgiveness, when it is
offered, the essential and eternal sanctity of God's law--
his own immovable adherence to it, as the only basis of

---

[1]cf. Bushnell, Vicarious Sacrifice, p. 73, where the
Cross of Christ was related to an eternal Cross in the
heart of God. See also Thwing, Notes, II, 76, where Park
assured his students that God did not "punish sin merely
for a personal reason" and that the atoning work of Christ
originated "from the nature and character of God and not
from mere expediency."

order and well-being in the universe."[1]   Such a statement
could easily have been written by Park himself.

In addition, though Bushnell was often accused of
viewing the work of Christ too subjectively, he continually
attempted to give it an objective significance as well.
He early found that significance dramatized by Biblical
"altar forms" representing Christ as our "passover," our
"sacrifice," our "sin-offering."[2]   Further dramatizing it
was the "fresh light" incorporated into his later work on
Forgiveness and Law (1874). Published as a modification
of certain sections of The Vicarious Sacrifice (1866), this
work professed a new appreciation of the place of law and
commandment in the redemptive process and found in "human
analogies" a new awareness of propitiation as a pre-condition
of true forgiveness. In Bushnell's words, this new illu-
mination meant that a complete doctrine of the atonement
had to account for "both the reconciliation of men to God
and of God to men."[3]   This balancing of an objective over
against a subjective understanding of the atonement moved
Bushnell closer to Park's position on that doctrine than
perhaps either realized, even though the Hartford divine
continued to give a priority to the subjective side which

---

[1]Bushnell, God in Christ, p. 218; see also The Vicarious
Sacrifice, p. 171.

[2]cf. God in Christ, pp. 246, 260-268.

[3]Bushnell, Forgiveness and Law, Grounded in Principles
Interpreted by Human Analogies (New York, 1874), p. 33.

Park could never accept.

It was ultimately the Andover divine's concern for human freedom, not for the divine moral government as such, that caused his own "modernized" atonement theory to differ significantly from Bushnell's. Both theories incorporated the vindication of the divine law and justice, but Bushnell saw this as indissolubly linked to the renovation of the sinner's character to overcome his basic enmity toward God.[1] The atonement, for Bushnell, was more than a Parkian "appeal" to a free agent to reconcile himself to God. It actually effected that reconciliation and made the human agent free to "repent and be saved." In short, a governmental maneuver which was divorced from any fundamental change in human character was no true atonement in Bushnell's eyes.

Park's obsession with free will caused him to view with deep suspicion any necessary linkage between Christ's death and the sinner's "renovation." Men, declared the Abbot Professor, "live in a system the various parts of which are connected together and influence each other."[2] Adam and Christ form key moral influences within that system, over which the Moral Governor presides. The system thus operates in such a way that "good as well as evil is

---

[1] cf. God in Christ, p. 242; Forgiveness and Law, pp. 10, 56.

[2] Park, "The System of Moral Influences in Which Men Are Placed," in Discourses, p. 217.

disseminated from one person to another." "The glory of the
gospel," Park averred, "is that the good flowing from the
act of the second Adam is greater than is the evil flowing
from the act of the first Adam."[1] Emphasis here is upon the
word "influence." Good and evil do not "flow," are not "disseminated," through necessary connections but through the
voluntary persuasion of "motives."[2]

It is through such motives that God leads men to salvation.[3] Most important to this saving guidance, in Park's view,
was the overarching motive of the divine law. There could be
nothing deterministic about man's response to that law in the
freely governed atmosphere of the divine moral system. "When
God gives a command," Park asserted, "he also gives the power
to fulfill it."[4] In other words, God upholds the individual's
freedom to observe as well as to reject the law. But how absolute could this freedom be in a theological system which
professed to represent "Consistent Calvinism"? On occasion,
relying upon the assumptions of the Scottish Philosophy, Park
could declare, "Consciousness teaches that whenever we choose,
we are able to refuse, and whenever we refuse we are able to
choose."[5] In general, however, he attempted to identify

---

[1]Ibid., p. 233.

[2]cf. Foster, Genetic History, p. 518.

[3]cf. Park, "System of Moral Influences," pp. 217, 226-232.

[4]See Marsh, Notes, p. 380.

[5]cf. Edward Chipman Guild, Notes on Park's Lectures on
Systematic Theology (1855-56; ms. in Harvard Divinity School
Library), III, 136.

himself in some way with the Edwardsean notion that the
will always is "as the greatest apparent good."

He was careful, nonetheless, to interpret this notion
in a non-deterministic fashion: "Between the greatest
apparent good and the choice, there is a certain and infallible connection, but not a necessary one."[1] In other
words, a "motive," whatever its origin, "does not efficient-
ly produce, but merely occasions a volition." A particular
choice "does," not "must," flow from a particular motive;
it always "could" be otherwise.[2] Furthermore, there was,
for Park, "a reciprocal influence of motives and will."
Beyond simply resisting inclinations, "the will itself,"
he found, "has great influence in making an object...the
greatest apparent good."[3]

In short, the Abbot Professor located the certainty
of the will's action not in motives or external constraint
as such but in the will itself. He defined the willing
faculty as "the power of making a choice and the imperative
volition tending to gratify that choice."[4] In other words,
willing involved both choosing and acting, and both these
activities were free of any necessary extrinsic causation.
Did this mean, then, that fallen man, in Edwardsean terms,

---

[1] Ibid., p. 84.

[2] Ibid.

[3] Ibid., p. 85. See also Marsh, Notes, p. 363.

[4] Guild, Notes, III, 69.

had both natural and moral ability to will evil or good?
Park was not willing to go this far. His notion of ability
was "freedom from constitutional obstacles" (including
motives).[1] But this did not mean, for him, "a state of
entire objective uncertainty whether one will act in this
way or that."[2] Exemption from "natural, literal" force or
motivated necessity did not remove the certainty of the
will's actions. True, one always had a "power to the
contrary" or "a power to act otherwise than one does act,"
but that power was certain not to be used.[3]

What Park wanted to make clear, in the final analysis,
was that certainty in volitional acts involved no necessity
whatsoever. Freedom, responsibility, and certainty were
perfectly compatible. The acts of the will were at once
intrinsically free and intrinsically certain. The will
possessed a self-determining power, not in the sense of an
absolute ability "to act or not to act at all," or to
"choose to choose," but in the sense of "a power to act as
distinct from a capacity to receive."[4] That power to act
received important influence from motives but was not passive
in the face of such influence. Man was certain to act
sinfully until regenerated, but his essential identity as

---

[1]Ibid., p. 124.

[2]Ibid.

[3]Ibid., p. 126.

[4]Ibid., p. 127.

a free agent was never lost, whether before, during, or after regeneration. That identity allowed him to exercise secondary causation in his own salvation. Quickened by various motives and means in a moral system upheld by divine grace, the sinner made for himself a "new heart" without the exertion of any irresistible external force.[1]

Given such a degree of freedom for the sinner, one might well wonder about the place of the traditional Reformed emphasis upon human depravity in Park's system. The Andover divine insisted upon defining sin in moralistic terms as the "voluntary transgression of a known law."[2] He usually added that "selfishness" or a "preference of our own good to the greater good" was at the root of such transgression, but he placed the burden of guilt upon individual human acts rather than upon a state, a nature, or even a "preference."[3] Sinful acts constituted, in his view, an obviously universal human phenomenon. But the notion that this phenomenon necessitated a doctrine of total depravity required considerable qualification to hold true.

Park's understanding of depravity centered not upon evil circumstances, or example, nor upon a physically evil human nature, but upon wrong "voluntary preferences."[4]

---

[1] cf. G. P. Fisher, Notes, p. 367.

[2] George Elisha Fisher, Notes on Park's Lectures on Systematic Theology (1847-48; ms. in Andover Newton Theological School Library), p. 135.

[3] Ibid., p. 144; see also Guild, Notes, IV, 25ff.

[4] Guild, Notes, IV, 36.

Such preferences arose from a "disorder in man's nature," but the disorder was not God-given or fundamental. Man's individual created "powers" were good; but "these powers in their relation to each other" were not. Their "equipoise" was disturbed, leaving man with a "disproportion of his sensibilities and capacities--too great a liveliness in some..., too little in others."[1] This disorder in man's nature and the wrong preferences it entailed were fundamentally different from wrong human actions in that the latter were guilty and punishable, while the former remained essentially innocent.[2]

Park was willing to affirm that all human preferences or inclinations were selfish and that they provided the occasion for "uniformly sinful" acts. But the "occasion" of sin was not equivalent to sin itself, nor did it necessitate sin. It was, of course, certain that all men would sin and only sin as soon as they became moral agents. But that a man "will" sin and that he "must" sin were not the same thing; there was always a "power to the contrary." Human beings could never lose their freedom unless their moral responsibility were forfeited as well.[3] Park was not altogether clear as to the manner in which disordered preferences made free sinful acts uniformly certain. Nor

[1]Ibid., p. 83.

[2]Ibid., p. 99.

[3]Ibid., pp. 36, 84-85, 97ff.

was he able to provide a clear explanation of the origin
of man's disordered nature. The former he laid to rest
as a divine mystery. The latter he attempted to relate
in some fashion to Adam.

In general, Park distinguished the individual man's
disordered nature and Adam's Fall as, respectively, the
"immediate" and the "remote" occasion[1] of sinful acts.
He did not like the term "original sin" because it implied
that "the occasion of the first sin was itself sinful."[2]
Since no blame, and hence no repentance, could attach to
such a concept, he sought other, more morally responsible
means of explaining man's relation to the Fall. Rejected
or given figurative interpretations in his search were the
idea of imputation or literal transfer, through hereditary
depravity or otherwise, of Adam's sin to his posterity;
and the notion that all mankind committed sin in Adam.
Viewed most favorably was the concept of Adam as "our
representative" in "consequence of" whose sin, we sin.
This meant that Adam represented us "in respect of the
trial whether we should be constituted and circumstanced
so that we should certainly sin."[3]

There is a hint here of the notion of Adam as a
"federal head" or "covenant representative" of the race.

---

[1] Ibid., pp. 69, 83.

[2] Ibid., p. 101; see also G. E. Fisher, Notes, pp. 168-169.

[3] Guild, Notes, IV, 132.

But Park specifically rejected any literal "covenant-of-works" interpretation of the Fall. Adam, he remarked, was first of all "subject to a law for himself." Only when this was understood could one go on to say that he was also "subject to a peculiar divine constitution in reference to his posterity. If he sinned, they would come into existence inclined to sin and prone to evil."[1] In short, Park divided the responsibility for sin between the individual man's free will and a "divine constitution" which involved two innocent, interrelated "occasions" of sin: Adam and an imbalance in human "sensibilities." The "constitution" did not make sin necessary any more than the atonement made salvation necessary. Each simply "occasioned" certain actions by free moral agents within a divinely governed moral system. It was finally to the needs of that free moral system that all Park's major doctrines, those defining sin, the will, and the atonement, were subject.

*   *   *

What then is one, in the end, to make of this "modern" version of the New England Theology? Did it indeed bear marks of descent from the great Jonathan Edwards or was its true lineage more accurately traced to the thought of

[1]Ibid., p. 138.

Nathaniel Taylor? Certainly in regard to the atonement,
Park's concept of a disciplinary governmental act seemed
closer to the thought of Taylor than to that of Edwards.
A sacrifice which bore only a token relationship to the
immeasurable offense against God of mankind's sin was no
true atonement in Edwards' eyes. And yet his Andover
interpreter was able to discern movement toward governmental motifs not only in early Edwardsean disciples but
in the master himself.

Nevertheless, in regard to the doctrines of sin and
free will, the balance tips rather decisively toward
Taylor. Park actually attempted to put the New Haven
divine's formula of "certainty /of sin7, with power to
the contrary" into the mouth of Edwards.[1] But the Abbot
Professor's rejection of Edwards' understanding of original
sin and his misunderstanding of the Edwardsean distinction
between natural and moral ability tended rather sharply
to divorce him from the "sage of Stockbridge." A moral
inability, or "certainty" of will, not decisively determined
by motives, and a natural ability powerful enough to
respond to "appeals" and make the sinner a "new heart"
were, respectively, much weaker and much stronger concepts
than one finds in Edwards.

But perhaps an emphasis upon Park's divergence from
his heritage does not provide the best perspective for

---

[1]Ibid., III, 126.

appreciating his significance. The nineteenth century
made rigorous apologetic demands upon theologians. Park,
without doubt, failed to comprehend and employ the resources of his Edwardsean tradition as well as he might have
to meet those demands. In some cases, as with Darwinism,
he simply did not recognize the seriousness of the challenge. But he faced the theological situation as he
read it in a highly responsible and heuristic manner.
He was, in the best sense of the word, a "mediating"
theologian. He was interested in reconciling traditional
Christian (particularly Reformed) affirmations with what
he considered the most important scientific and philosophical
thought patterns of the modern world. He was also concerned to reconcile various New England theological parties.
Though the rationalism and moralism of the Scottish
Philosophy tended to dominate his theological method, he
was not unsympathetic to romantic thought patterns and,
at least during part of his career, actively employed them.
His goal was an empirical, scientific theology whose
sources would range over both nature and revelation, both
intellect and feelings.

The latter two sources, when used as tools of
mediation, often proved controversial. Park's opponents
did not like to be told that theirs was a "theology of
the feelings," a figurative way of expressing what his
own "theology of the intellect" conveyed in literal,
exact terms. But, at its best, the intellect-feeling

distinction was much more than a polemical device for
Park. It lay at the heart of his understanding of the
deposit of faith upon which he and all other Christian
thinkers were privileged to labor. Lacking a fully developed historical awareness, he yet recognized a felt
substance of continuity which stood behind the various
intellectual accidents of theological expression of which
he was aware. He was careful to distinguish this recognition, however, from any diminution of the importance of
reasoned language in theology. He had no doubt that the
truth of the Christian faith could and should be captured
in such language, and that it found its most nearly perfect
form in his own version of the New England Theology.

Nevertheless, in content, as in method, the development
of his recension of Edwardsean thought tended to follow
the path of mediation. He began his career with the
intention of speaking to as broad a constituency as
possible. And his work as editor, preacher, and teacher
allowed him to do just that, carrying his influence, in
many cases, far beyond the bounds of New England Congregationalism. To reach such a constituency, which represented
a highly important segment of American Protestantism, he
sought a theology suitable for both pulpit and study. He
wanted constructs which would please both Unitarian and
Orthodox, which would speak to the democratic humanitarianism of the age without unduly abridging the evangelical
emphasis upon sin, salvation, and sovereign divine grace.

That emphasis had to be protected, he maintained, if the all-important missionary and reform activities of evangelical Protestantism were to survive and thrive.

Given the demands of such a theological situation, Park focused upon what he called the "moral system" according to which God governs and saves. That system, he believed, preserved both human freedom and divine sovereignty. It allowed full sway to all sorts of moral and spiritual influences (preaching, reform work, etc.), while at the same time placing God in ultimate charge of things. It provided an eminently reasonable, moral, and evangelical framework within which a Reformed theologian might speak effectively to nineteenth-century America.

The "democratic government" of God and that of America were both founded upon justice and respect for the law. The atonement was in fact the central symbol, for Park, of God's just government of the universe. That Christ's work was "sufficient for all" made it a highly "democratic" as well as evangelical symbol. With such a symbol laid before them, it is not altogether surprising that some of Park's students adopted the "liberal" notion of "future probation." They were, after all, merely extending the democratic divine moral government to the afterlife. Perhaps, in some ways, they proved to be better disciples of the Abbot Professor than either he or they recognized. At any rate, his influence upon the formation of Andover liberalism should not be discounted or regarded as entirely negative. Seeking the way of mediation during much of his career, he became a theologian whose development provides a sensitive and revealing baromenter of an era of revolutionary change in American religious thought.

SELECTED BIBLIOGRAPHY

I. THE NEW ENGLAND THEOLOGY AND ITS INTERPRETERS:
    AN INTRODUCTORY NOTE

Two general critical perspectives have tended to
predominate among expositors of the theological endeavors
of those who, in one sense or another, followed in the
intellectual train of Jonathan Edwards. One of these
might be labeled the "decline" perspective, since its
adherents lament the New England Theology as a progressive
falling away from the inspired vision of Edwards. Perhaps
the most outstanding representative of this point of view
is Joseph Haroutunian's Piety Versus Moralism: The Passing
of the New England Theology (New York: Harper and Row,
1970), a treatment of the post-Edwardsean tradition which
scarcely mentions Park, since Nathaniel Taylor is taken as
the final stage of degradation. Haroutunian directs one to
some important issues and insights. But he tends to support
his theological preconceptions through scattered treatments
of or references to New England theologians whose individual
theological situations and predicaments he seems not always
fully to comprehend.

Following in his footsteps, so to speak, is Kenneth E.
Rowe's Ph.D. dissertation (Drew University, June, 1969)
entitled "Nestor of Orthodoxy, New England Style--A Study
in the Theology of Edwards Amasa Park." Rowe adds Park as
a sort of appendix to Haroutunian's jeremiad of decline.
Much of the dissertation is occupied with unfavorable
comparisons of Park to Edwards or to Horace Bushnell, who
is pictured as a more authentic bearer of the Edwardsean
heritage in the nineteenth century. Park's theological
failures are attributed primarily to his overreliance upon
the Scottish Common Sense Philosophy. Insufficiently
emphasized are the seriousness of the apologetic dilemma
the Andover professor faced and the boldness, reflected
in his theological development, with which he modified his
Edwardsean heritage to meet that dilemma.

A different critical perspective informs the works of
Frank Hugh Foster on Park and the New England Theology.
Adulatory in the manner typical of a protégé is Foster's
Life of Edwards Amasa Park (New York: Fleming H. Revell
Company, 1936). But its author's theological views under-
went fundamental change before the biography reached
completion, and the work fails to do justice to Park's
developing intellectual creativity within the tradition of
the New England Theology. The prevailing image toward
which the biography points is that of a tragic figure of
considerable learning and influence who is unable to accept

the theological wave of the future. Revealing perhaps an unparalleled knowledge of its subject is Foster's Genetic History of the New England Theology (Chicago: The University of Chicago Press, 1907). Far from being a final stage of degradation, Nathaniel Taylor is something of a hero in this volume, and Park's theology occupies a prominent concluding position. But the soundness of Foster's history is seriously undermined by his tendentious concentration upon a particular theory of the will in accordance with which each New England theologian receives arbitrary judgment.

Having significant points of contact with Foster's mature perspective on the New England Theology is John Wright Buckham's Progressive Religious Thought in America (Boston: Houghton, Mifflin Company, 1919). As with Foster's Modern Movement in American Theology (New York: Fleming H. Revell Company, 1939), Buckham's focus is the developing tradition of theological liberalism, represented by Bushnell and the Smyth brothers, among others, which Park came to oppose at Andover. Viewed in relation to that liberal tradition, Park's theology seems to be lacking not because he deviated from pure Edwardsean ideas but because his deviations were not great enough and, in some cases, were moving in the wrong direction. Largely implicit in Buckham and the later Foster, this critical perspective appears clearly and explicitly in Daniel Day Williams' The Andover Liberals (New York: King's Crown Press, 1941).

There, early intimations of liberalism at Andover, including Park's intellect-feeling distinction, receive attention as preliminary background for the central exposition of the book. The New England Theology is valuable in this context only insofar as its adherents were compelled to recognize the inevitable and to diverge from their heritage in the direction of liberalism. Though not treated uncritically, Andover liberalism acquires the appearance of a victory of progress over reaction. That a positive relationship, possibly more fundamental than the negative one, might have existed between Park's theology and that of his pupils is scarcely noticed.

Finally, not displaying a distinctive point of view like Haroutunian's or Foster's are works such as George Nye Boardman's History of the New England Theology (New York: A. D. F. Randolph Company, 1899). Boardman's straightforward expository treatment covers the subject well, but his attempts at balanced appraisal are uninspired. And he cannot find any new developments in the New England Theology after 1830. He thus uses Park as source rather than subject in his theological history.

The present writer has attempted to avoid the imposition of tendentious frames of reference upon his study of Park. Evaluations of the Abbot Professor according to the standard of Edwards or of Andover liberalism produce an unnecessarily negative or one-dimensional image. To avoid such evaluations without falling into a bland "objective" neutrality, the

author has attempted an internal approach to Park's
developing thought. He has tried to see Park's theological
heritage and situation as Park saw them. When this is
done, the creative boldness of the Andover divine vis-à-
vis his Consistent Calvinist tradition becomes apparent.
His movement toward a posture of theological mediation
involving both romantic and rationalistic, both liberal
and conservative elements appears as no small feat in
view of his position at New England's "West Point" of
Congregational Orthodoxy. Internal analysis of that
mediating posture, with all its tensions and difficulties,
points not simply to the weaknesses but also to the
strengths of the New England Theology and its latter-day
adherents within their nineteenth-century context. It
points, too, to the positive as well as negative influence
which Park exerted on later American theology. In short,
viewed from this angle, his mind becomes a highly revealing
window upon an age of revolutionary change in American
religious thought.

II. UNPUBLISHED MANUSCRIPTS

A. Park's notes

1. Notebooks and commonplace books

Commonplace book, 1860?, 1 volume. Andover Newton
Theological School Library.

Commonplace book, 1880's?, 1 volume, ca. 430p.
Many notes about Jonathan Edwards. Andover
Newton Theological School Library.

Lecture notebook on the Atonement, undated,
1 volume, 277p. Andover Newton Theological
School Library.

Lecture notebook on the Church, undated, 1 volume,
359p. Andover Newton Theological School Library.

Lecture notebook on Divine Providence, Book V,
entries dated 1879-99, 1 volume, ca. 300p.
C. R. Park Family Papers.

Lecture notebook on Faith, undated, 1 volume, 82p.
Andover Newton Theological School Library.

Lecture notebook on God, undated, 1 volume, ca. 280p.
Andover Newton Theological School Library.

Lecture notebook on Holiness and Benevolence, undated,
1 volume, 218p. C. R. Park Family Papers.

Lecture notebook on Providential Laws, Natural Laws
/and other subjects/, 1865?, 2 volumes. Brown
University Library.

Lecture notebook on Theology for Bible Classes of
Youthful Students, undated, 1 volume, ca. 70p.
Andover Newton Theological School Library.

Lecture notebook on the Will, 1861, 1 volume, 364p.
C. R. Park Family Papers.

Lecture notebook on the Will (Final Definition of
the Will), undated, 1 volume, 328p. C. R. Park
Family Papers.

Notebook on the Definition of Choice, undated,
1 volume, 220p. C. R. Park Family Papers.

Notebook on the Definition of Moral Ability, Vol. 3, undated, 84p. C. R. Park Family Papers.

Notebook on the Will, No. 1, 1879-1882?, 1 volume, ca. 200p. C. R. Park Family Papers.

Notebook on Edwards on the Will, No. 2, undated, 1 volume, 124p. C. R. Park Family Papers.

Notebook on the Will, Choice, Motives, and Power, undated, 1 volume, 351p. C. R. Park Family Papers.

Notebook on Sensibilities, Feelings, Motives, and the Will, undated, 1 volume, 219p. C. R. Park Family Papers.

Notebook on Theological Subjects, undated, 1 volume. Subjects: church, ministry, sacraments, etc. Brown University Library.

Notebook containing Dr. I. A. Smith's Lectures on Physiology; and Nathaniel W. Taylor's Theological Lectures, New York and New Haven, Winter, 1834-35, ca. 75p. C. R. Park Family Papers.

2. Unbound lecture, sermon, reading, and other notes

Notes on the Associate Creed /1883/, ca. 80p. C. R. Park Family Papers.

Notes on Andover's Associate Creed, unknown hand with revisions by E. A. Park /1883/, ca. 100p. C. R. Park Family Papers.

Notes for proposed book, Andover History and Theology, undated, ca. 150p. C. R. Park Family Papers.

Notes on the Atonement, late 1890's?, 3 p. C. R. Park Family Papers.

Notes on the Atonement, undated, ca. 20p. C. R. Park Family Papers.

Sermon notes on the Atonement, undated, ca. 80p. C. R. Park Family Papers.

Notes on "Power of the Atonement," late 1890's?, 10p. C. R. Park Family Papers.

Notes on Divine Sovereignty in Atonement, late
1890's?, 2p. C. R. Park Family Papers.

Notes on Aristotle's Discussion of Causes, late
1890's?, 8p. C. R. Park Family Papers.

Notes on Causation and Adaptability, undated, 7p.
C. R. Park Family Papers.

Notes on Cause, undated, 8p. C. R. Park Family
Papers.

Notes on History and Causation, late 1890's?, 4p.
C. R. Park Family Papers.

Note sheets on Causation and the Will, undated,
2p. C. R. Park Family Papers.

Notes on Choice and Willingness, undated, 2p.
C. R. Park Family Papers.

Notes for a Definition of the Will, undated, 76p.
C. R. Park Family Papers.

Notes for a Definition of the Will, undated, 103p.
C. R. Park Family Papers.

Notes on the Influence of the Sensibilities on the
Will, undated, 4p. C. R. Park Family Papers.

Note sheets on Reason, Sensibility, Choice, Will,
late 1880's?, 4p. C. R. Park Family Papers.

Notes on the Will, written in pamphlet form, undated,
22p. C. R. Park Family Papers.

Lecture notes on the Will, undated, ca. 100p.
C. R. Park Family Papers.

Notes on Will, Choice, and Volition, undated, 2p.
C. R. Park Family Papers.

Notes on Various Comments on the Will and Edwards,
undated, ca. 46p. C. R. Park Family Papers.

Notes on the Works of Jonathan Edwards (especially
on the Will), undated, ca. 200p. C. R. Park
Family Papers.

Notes on Jonathan Edwards' Attitude toward the Episcopacy, undated, 1p. C. R. Park Family Papers.

Notes on Choice, undated, 96p. C. R. Park Family Papers.

Notes on Choice and Elective Preference, undated, 36p. C. R. Park Family Papers.

Note sheets on Divine and Human Activity, late 1880's?, 2p. C. R. Park Family Papers.

"Notes on the Controversy between Dr. Hemmenway and Dr. Emmons," undated, 20p. Park Family Papers, Yale University Library.

Notes on the Decrees, November 1, 1879, ca. 100p. C. R. Park Family Papers.

Notes on Decrees, Predestination, Election, and Reprobation, undated, 2p. C. R. Park Family Papers.

Notes for discourse, "Was God Obligated to Himself?," late 1890's?, 3p. C. R. Park Family Papers.

Notes on Divine Attributes, written on back of sermon on Divine Justice and the Atonement, undated, 30p. C. R. Park Family Papers.

Notes on Infinite Holiness and Infinite Desirability, late 1890's?, 30p. C. R. Park Family Papers.

Notes on the Trinity, late 1890's?, 10p. C. R. Park Family Papers.

Notes on Punishment, late 1890's?, 22p. C. R. Park Family Papers.

Notes on Sin, Punishment, and Justice, undated, ca. 275p. C. R. Park Family Papers.

Notes on Resignation and Suffering, undated, 2p. C. R. Park Family Papers.

Notes on Belief and Knowledge, late 1890's?, 36p. C. R. Park Family Papers.

Notes for a discourse on the question: "Do we
understand in order to believe, or do we believe
in order to understand?" late 1890's?, 8p.
C. R. Park Family Papers.

Notes on Character Formation, undated, 12p.
C. R. Park Family Papers.

Note fragment on the historical context of the
Old Testament, undated, 1p. C. R. Park Family
Papers.

Sermon notes on the Bible and Inspiration, undated,
ca. 100p. C. R. Park Family Papers.

Notes for "Judas" sermon, undated, ca. 50 folio p.
C. R. Park Family Papers.

Random sermon notes, undated, ca. 40p. C. R. Park
Family Papers.

Notes on Sacred Rhetoric, undated, ca. 13p.
C. R. Park Family Papers.

Notes on "Subjects which are and are not good for
preaching," undated, 6p. C. R. Park Family
Papers.

Notes on the Mind, late 1890's?, 2p. C. R. Park
Family Papers.

Note fragment on Consciousness and Motives,
undated, 1p. C. R. Park Family Papers.

Notes on Orthodoxy versus the Philosophers in
regard to Acts of the Mind, undated, 2p.
C. R. Park Family Papers.

Notes on Natural Theology, undated, ca. 90p.
C. R. Park Family Papers.

Notes on Matter and Penetration; also Selfishness,
late 1890's?, 12p. C. R. Park Family Papers.

Notes on Selfishness, late 1890's?, 8p.
C. R. Park Family Papers.

Notes on Principle, late 1890's?, 1p. C. R. Park
Family Papers.

Note sheets on Reason and Substance, late 1890's?,
  2p. C. R. Park Family Papers.

Notes on Substance and Property, late 1890's?,
  6p. C. R. Park Family Papers.

Notes on Space, late 1890's?, 12p. C. R. Park
  Family Papers.

Notes on Truth, late 1880's?, 6p. C. R. Park
  Family Papers.

"Selected Sentences," miscellaneous notes from
  reading, undated, 75p. C. R. Park Family Papers.

B. Correspondence

Pieces of Park's voluminous correspondence may be found
in a wide variety of libraries and collections stretch-
ing across the eastern portion of the country from New
England to the Carolinas and Tennessee. Most of the
extant letters deal with family affairs, Park's travels
in Europe, editorial matters related to the Bibliotheca
Sacra, and the day-to-day financial and academic affairs
of Andover Seminary. Representative smaller collections
of Park correspondence include the following:

Brown University Library, 10 items.
Case Western Reserve University Library, 3 items.
Drew University Library, 7 items.
Duke University Library, Joseph Cook Papers,
    ca. 65 items.
Harvard University Archives, 2 items.
Harvard University, Houghton Library, 4 items.
Phillips Academy Archives, ca. 6 items.

Two sizable collections of Park   correspondence exist
in the Boston Public Library (ca. 180 items addressed
to Park from American clergymen and authors, relating
to ministerial and editorial matters) and the Library
of Yale University (ca. 175 items, to and from Park,
miscellaneous subjects, in Bacon, Beecher, Dana, Dutton,
Edmonds, Gibbs, Goodrich, Hart, Kingsley, Morse, Park,
Salisbury, Stokes, Thompson, Twombly, and Woolsey Family
Papers).

But perhaps the most significant collection of his
correspondence is in private hands: the C. R. Park
Family Papers, Nashville, Tennessee. Since this
collection is largely uncatalogued, a partial listing
follows:

Letters to and from Park

 Miscellaneous family letters, mostly Edwards A.
    Park to his wife, Anna Maria, 1830's-1840's,
    31 items.

 E. A. Park to Anna Maria, 1838-1855, 11 items.

 E. A. Park to Anna Maria, Journal Letters from
    Europe: 1842-43, ca. 241pp.

 E. A. Park to Anna Maria, October, 1851, 7 items.

 E. A. Park to Anna Maria, Germany, 1862-63, 20 items.

 E. A. Park to Anna Maria, Letters from Europe:
    1869-70, 23 items.

 E. A. Park to Anna Maria, 1874, ca. 15 items.

 Anna Maria to E. A. Park, October 1851, 7 items.

 Mrs. Park to Prof. E. A. Park, in Europe, 1842-43,
    21 items.

 Calvin Park to E. A. Park, 1825-28, 10 items.

 Calvin Park to E. A. Park, 1820-30, ca. 35 items.

 Abigail Park to E. A. Park, undated, 2 items.

 E. A. Park to brother, Andover, February 15, 1847.

 E. A. Park to Edwards /son/, Andover, August 8, 1861.

 E. A. Park to Agnes /daughter/, undated.

 E. A. Park to Ned /grandson, Edwards Albert Park/,
    December 29, 1884.

 Edwards Albert Park to Edwards Amasa Park, May 13,
    1888 to August 4, 1897, 15 items, "Dear Grandpa
    letters."

E. A. Park to Sarah B. Edwards /daughter of Bela
Bates Edwards/, Andover, September 23, 1856.

E. A. Park to Sara/h/, Andover, undated except
for Wednesday, 7 o'clock.

Bela Bates Edwards to E. A. Park, 1837-47, ca. 25
items.

E. A. Park to Bela Bates Edwards, Boston, October 2,
1847.

E. A. Park to Bela Bates Edwards, undated, 2 items.

E. A. Park to Bela Bates Edwards, written by Mrs.
Park as dictated by E. A. Park, December 5, 18--

E. A. Park to Mrs. Bela Bates Edwards, 1857-1892,
30 items.

E. A. Park to the Reverend Benjamin B. Wisner,
Andover, July 22, 1831.

Mrs. Lucy P. Porter to E. A. Park, undated,
probably fall, 1836.

E. A. Park to Mrs. Benjamin Curtis, Andover,
June 2, 1838.

E. A. Park to unknown addressee, London, October 4,
1843; Park is thinking about looking for Edwards
manuscripts in Scotland.

E. A. Park to Mrs. Storrs, Andover, February 5, 1848.

E. A. Park to James Smith, Esquire, Andover,
November, 1853.

E. A. Park to the Reverend Morse, Andover,
December 1, 1853.

E. A. Park to Messieurs S. R. Whipple and
Company, Andover, July 10, 1855.

E. A. Park to Henry Edwards, Esquire, December 21,
1869.

E. A. Park to Daniel L. Furber, August 18, 1871.

Miscellaneous letters to E. A. Park concerning
business matters at Andover, the Bibliotheca
Sacra and events leading to Andover controversy,
undated, probably 1870's and 1880's, ca. 50 items.

Cecil Franklin Patch Bancroft /In behalf of Andover
Trustees/ to E. A. Park, June 29, 1875.

Unknown to E. A. Park, New York, March 23, 1876.

Egbert C. Smyth to E. A. Park, November 7, 1877.

Albert H. Plumb to E. A. Park, Boston, May, 1883.

Albert H. Plumb to E. A. Park, Boston, June 11, 1883.

Albert H. Plumb to E. A. Park, undated.

Kinsley Twining to E. A. Park, New York, June 11,
1883.

Henry M. Dexter to E. A. Park, New Bedford,
Massachusetts, July 18, 1885.

George F. Wright to E. A. Park, Oberlin, October 12,
1888, typewritten.

Letters concerning Andover controversy (copies in Park's
possession)

Daniel T. Fiske, Joshua W. Wellman, Edmund K. Alden
/representing Andover Board of Trustees/ to
Professors Egbert C. Smyth, Joseph H. Thayer,
and Charles M. Mead, Boston, September 3, 1877.

Albert H. Plumb to the Reverend Edward Y. Hincks,
Boston, June 10, 1883.

Albert H. Plumb to the Reverend George Harris,
Boston, June 10, 1883.

Another private collection, the S. P. Scattergood Family
Papers in Philadelphia, contains, among other Park
family correspondence, the following:

Miscellaneous letters, mainly E. A. Park or wife
to William Edwards Park /son/, Sarah E. Park
/daughter-in-law/, or Marion Park /granddaughter/,
late 1860's and early 1870's, ca. 50 items (many
from Europe).

E. A. Park to Bela Bates Edwards, Andover, June 14,
1846; discusses Abbot Professorship and attitudes
toward Moses Stuart.

There is, in the Andover Newton Theological School
Library, a small, uncatalogued collection of letters
pertaining to Park's lecture methods. Requested by
and addressed to the librarian Owen H. Gates, these
letters were written by the following persons:

Mrs. (Wm. J.) Batt, West Concord, Massachusetts,
November 19, 1928.

William R. Campbell, Boston, Massachusetts,
November 15, 1928, typewritten.

Otis Carey, Auburndale, Massachusetts, November 20,
1928, typewritten.

Edward Dwight Eaton, Washington, D.C., November 16,
1928.

George B. Frost, Andover, Massachusetts, undated.

R. A. Hume?, Auburndale, Massachusetts,
November 17, 1928.

Arthur W. Kelly, Auburndale, Massachusetts,
November 15, 1928, typewritten.

F. R. Shipman, Andover, Massachusetts, November 6,
1928, typewritten.

William F. Slocum, Newton Centre, Massachusetts,
November 14, 1928.

Henry A. Stimson, New York City, November 15, 1928.

Charles F. Thwing, Cleveland, Ohio, November 15,
1928, typewritten.

C. Park's sermons

"Centrality of Christ for the Christian Faith,"
I Cor. 2:2, undated, ca. 60p. C. R. Park Family
Papers.

"Christ the Man of Sorrows," South Hadley, 1863, 60p.
C. R. Park Family Papers.

"Eternal Punishment," with notes, undated, ca. 150p.
C. R. Park Family Papers.

"What must I do to be saved?" and other sermons,
undated, ca. 250p. C. R. Park Family Papers.

"A sermon delivered September 17, 1833, at the interment
of Rev. Charles Backus Storrs, President of Western
Reserve College, Hudson, Ohio, who died at Braintree,
Mass., September 15, 1833, aet. thirty-nine years,"
49p. Case Western Reserve University Library.

"Extracts of the sermon delivered at the interment of
Rev. Charles Backus Storrs, President of Western
Reserve College, Hudson, Ohio, who died at Braintree,
Massachusetts, September 15, 1833, aet. thirty-nine
years, by the pastor of the First Church in Braintree,"
46p. Case Western Reserve University Library.

Several sermons on the Decrees, with notes, undated,
ca. 400p. C. R. Park Family Papers.

Six sermons on Law, undated. C. R. Park Family Papers.

Seven sermons on Natural Theology. C. R. Park Family
Papers:
Sermon 1: December 13, 1845,   44p.
Sermon 2: December 13, 1845,   64p.
Sermon 3: December 21, 1845,   30p.
Sermon 4: December 21, 1845,   50p.
Sermon 5: December 28, 1845,   75p.
Sermon 6: January   3, 1846,   42p.
Sermon 7: January   3, 1846,   50p.

Six sermons, mainly on Sin, undated, ca. 200p.
C. R. Park Family Papers.

Seven sermons on Sin and Punishment, undated, each
ca. 35p. C. R. Park Family Papers.

Sermon on Time, undated, ca. 50p. C. R. Park Family
Papers.

Twenty-two sermon outlines on such subjects as taste,
imagination, providence, profitableness of religion,
"old" and "new" school, riches and poverty, unity,
and church union, undated. C. R. Park Family Papers.

Sermon on I Corinthians 6:17, undated, 68p. C. R. Park
Family Papers.

Sermon on Luke 2:52, undated, 68p. C. R. Park
Family Papers.

Eight sermons on various subjects, undated, ca. 350p.
C. R. Park Family Papers.

Notes on sermons delivered by Park and others in the
Andover Theological Seminary Chapel, taken by Mrs.
William F. Snow, 1862, 1866, 1 volume. Park's sermons,
pp. 20-25, 27, 33-34. Oberlin College Library.

D. Park's lectures as recorded in student notebooks

Aiken, Charles Augustus, 1850-51, 3 volumes. Oberlin
College Library.

Alden, Edmund Kimball, 1846-47, 1 volume. Oberlin
College Library.

Allen, Alexander Viets Griswold, 1864-65, 3 volumes,
Andover Newton Theological School Library.

Boies, Charles Alfred, 1862-63, 2 volumes. Harvard
Divinity School Library.

Churchill, Frederic Arthur, 1877-78, 1 volume. Oberlin
College Library.

DeBevoise, Gabriel Havens, 1862-63, 1 volume. Andover
Newton Theological School Library.

Dunning, William Hale, 1861-62, 2 volumes. Andover
Newton Theological School Library.

Fisher, George Elisha, 1847-48, 1 volume. Andover
Newton Theological School Library.

Fisher, George Park, 1850-51, 1 volume. Yale University
Library.

Foster, Frank Hugh, 1875-76, 4 volumes, in shorthand. Oberlin College Library.

Guild, Edward Chipman, 1855-56, 4 volumes. Harvard Divinity School Library.

Howard, James Barber, 1850-51, 1 volume. Yale University Library.

Kelsey, Francis Duncan, 1871-72, 2 volumes. Oberlin College Library.

_____. dated 1873, 1 volume. C. R. Park Family Papers.

Learned, Robert Coit, 1840-41, 1 volume. Andover Newton Theological School Library.

McLean, William J., 1874-75, 2 volumes. Oberlin College Library.

Marsh, David Dana, 1866-67, 1 volume. Andover Newton Theological School Library.

Norton, Smith, 1856-57, 4 volumes. Oberlin College Library.

Peet, Stephen Denison, 1852-54, 2 volumes. Chicago Theological Seminary Library.

Perry, John Bulkley, 1851-52, 1 volume. University of Vermont Library.

Plumb, Albert Hale, 1856-57, 1 volume. Andover Newton Theological School Library.

Ropes, William Ladd, 1850-51, 3 volumes. Andover Newton Theological School Library.

Smith, Moses, 1857-58, 2 volumes. Chicago Theological Seminary Library.

Tenney, Henry Martyn, 1865, 2 volumes. Oberlin College Library.

Thwing, Charles Franklin, 1877-79, 2 volumes. Case Western Reserve University Library.

Wellman, Joshua Wyman, 1847-50, 3 volumes. Congregational Library, Boston.

Williams, Edward Moore, 1866-67, 1 volume. Andover
Newton Theological School Library.

Unidentified, undated, 1 volume. Congregational
Library, Boston.

Unidentified, undated, 2 volumes. Brown University
Library.

Unidentified, undated, 1 volume. Brown University
Library.

Unidentified, 1845, 1 volume. Brown University
Library.

E. Miscellaneous papers

   1. Park's discourses, essays, lectures, translations,
       and other writings

       Discourse on Eternity of God, undated, ca. 60p.
          C. R. Park Family Papers.

       Four discourses on Missions, Atonement, Divine
          Government, and Religious Sensibilities, undated,
          each ca. 50p. C. R. Park Family Papers.

       Transcription of some of the last works of Park;
          notes on the Atonement and the Scottish philosophy,
          1899, unpaged. C. R. Park Family Papers.

       Discourse on Imagination and Association of Ideas,
          undated, 22p. C. R. Park Family Papers.

       "Laws of Nature," undated, 4p. Park Family Papers,
          Yale University Library.

       "O Israel, Where Art Thou?" 2 copies, 4p. each,
          undated. C. R. Park Family Papers.

       "Questions on Remorse, with Answers," undated, 2p.
          C. R. Park Family Papers.

       "Rules and Directions to Instructors," undated,
          8p. C. R. Park Family Papers.

       "Effects of Critical Reviews, a College Exercise,"
          Brown University, 1824, 4p. Brown University
          Library.

"Emmons as a Preacher," undated, 43p. Park Family Papers, Yale University Library.

"Can Anyone Be Saved without a Change of Heart in This Life?" An Essay delivered before the theological society of Brown University, June 26, 1824, 3p. Park Family Papers, Yale University Library.

Translation of Schweitzer's On Eternal Punishment, undated, 74p. C. R. Park Family Papers.

"A Review of the New Theory Regarding the Doctrinal Basis of Andover Theological Seminary," 1886?, 30p. C. R. Park Family Papers.

"Purposes and Present Issues at Andover," undated, unpaged. C. R. Park Family Papers.

Daily scriptural meditation, April and May 1840, 4p. C. R. Park Family Papers.

Family reminiscences of Professor E. A. Park, undated, 15p., typewritten. C. R. Park Family Papers.

Miscellaneous smaller manuscripts, various subjects, 31 articles, undated. C. R. Park Family Papers.

2. Park's reports concerning Andover Seminary

E. A. Park, Alvah Hovey, and E. Robinson, Committee report on conferring honorary degrees, undated, 8p. C. R. Park Family Papers.

Annual reports to the Board of Trustees of Andover Theological Seminary (i.e., Phillips Academy), 1838-1840, 1844-1868, 1871-1874, 1876-1881. Phillips Academy Archives.

Circular concerning state of Andover Seminary, 1850's, 12p. C. R. Park Family Papers.

3. Manuscripts relating to Park or in his possession

Biographical sketch of E. A. Park in unknown hand, ca. 20p., undated. C. R. Park Family Papers.

Abbot, Ephraim, "Answers to Professor Park's Questions," undated, 6p. Park Family Papers, Yale University Library.

Porter, Ebenezer, "Lecture Notes on Sacred Rhetoric," Andover, dated 1823, 3 volumes, each ca. 25p. C. R. Park Family Papers.

"Stories about Professor Park," unsigned typescript, undated, 3p. Harvard Divinity School Library.

Storrs, Richard Salter, Notes for memorial address on Park's life /1890/, 51p. C. R. Park Family Papers.

4. Miscellaneous bound volumes

European Journal Notes, 1842-43 (incorrectly dated 1844), 5 volumes. C. R. Park Family Papers.

"Comments on Mrs. Esther Burr's Journal," 1 volume, ca. 250p. C. R. Park Family Papers.

Scrapbook, undated, 1 volume. Andover Newton Theological School Library.

Index to Miscellany, undated, 2 volumes. Andover Newton Theological School Library.

Large ledger with clippings and comments on Immortality of the Soul and various other topics, undated, 472p. C. R. Park Family Papers.

III. PUBLISHED SOURCES

A. Park's biographical and memorial writings

"Asa Messer," in Annals of the American Pulpit.
ed. William Buell Sprague. New York: Robert Carter
and Brothers, 1860. Vol. VI, Baptists, pp. 327-333.

"Bellamy, Joseph," in A Religious Encyclopaedia; or,
Dictionary of Biblical, Historical, Doctrinal, and
Practical Theology. ed. Philip Schaff. Third
edition. New York: Funk and Wagnalls, 1891. Vol. I,
pp. 236-237.

"Calvin Park," in Sprague, Annals (1859). Vol. II,
Trinitarian Congregationalists, p. 460.

"Characteristics of Edwards," in The Memorial Volume
of the Edwards Family Meeting at Stockbridge,
Massachusetts, September 6-7, A.D. 1870. Boston:
Congregational Publishing Society, 1871, pp. 104-121.

"Charles Backus Storrs," in Sprague, Annals (1859).
Vol. IV, Presbyterians, pp. 488-490.

A Discourse Delivered at the Funeral of Professor
Moses Stuart. Boston: Tappan and Whittemore, 1852.

"A Discourse Delivered at the Funeral of the Rev.
Christopher Minta Cordley, Late Pastor of the
Congregational Church, Lawrence, Massachusetts,
June 26, 1866," Congregational Quarterly, IX, 36
(October, 1867), 375-376. Excerpts only.

"Edwards, Bela Bates, D.D.," in Cyclopaedia of
Biblical, Theological and Ecclesiastical Literature.
ed. John McClintock and James Strong. New York:
Harper and Brothers, 1894. Vol. III, p. 63.

"Edwards, Bela Bates, D.D.," in Schaff-Herzog Encyclopaedia, Vol. II, p. 697.

"Edwards, Jonathan," in McClintock and Strong,
Cyclopaedia, Vol. III, pp. 63-67.

"Edwards, Jonathan, the Elder," in Schaff-Herzog
Encyclopaedia, Vol. II, pp. 697-699.

"Edwards, Jonathan, D.D. /Jr./," in McClintock and
Strong, Cyclopaedia, Vol. III, pp. 67-69.

"Edwards, Jonathan, the Younger," in Schaff-Herzog
    Encyclopaedia, Vol. II, pp. 699-701.

"Emmons, Nathanael," in McClintock and Strong,
    Cyclopaedia, Vol. III, pp. 179-180.

"Emmons, Nathanael, D.D.," in Schaff-Herzog Encyclo-
    paedia, Vol. II, pp. 720-721.

"Homer, William Bradford," in Schaff-Herzog Encyclo-
    paedia, Vol. II, pp. 1010-1011.

"Hopkins, Samuel, D.D.," in Schaff-Herzog Encyclopaedia,
    Vol. II, pp. 1020-1021.

"Jasper Adams, D.D.," in Sprague, Annals (1861).
    Vol. V, Episcopalians, pp. 644-646.

"Joseph Sylvester Clark," The Congregational Quarterly,
    IV, 13 (January, 1862), 1-21.

The Life and Character of Leonard Woods /Junior/.
    Andover: Warren F. Draper, 1880.

"Life and Services of Professor B. B. Edwards,"
    Bibliotheca Sacra, IX, 36 (October, 1852), 783-821.
    Also published as a pamphlet.

"Memoir," in Writings of Professor B. B. Edwards.
    Boston: John P. Jewett and Company, 1853. Vol. I,
    pp. 1-370.

"Memoir," in Writings of William Bradford Homer.
    Andover: Allen, Morrill and Wardwell, 1842, pp. 13-
    136.

"Memoir of the Life and Character of Samuel Hopkins,"
    in The Works of Samuel Hopkins, D.D. Boston:
    Doctrinal Book and Tract Society, 1852. Vol. I,
    pp. v-vii, 1-264.

Memoir of Nathanael Emmons, with Sketches of His
    Friends and Pupils. Boston: Congregational Board
    of Publication, 1861.

"Memorial of Dr. Samuel Harvey Taylor," Bibliotheca
    Sacra, XXVIII, 110 (April, 1871), 366-396. Also
    published as a pamphlet and an essay.

Memorial of Rev. Samuel C. Jackson. Andover: Warren
    F. Draper, 1878.

"Miscellaneous Reflections of a Visitor upon the Character of Dr. Emmons," The Works of Nathanael Emmons. ed. Jacob Ide. Boston: Crocker and Brewster, 1842. Vol. I, pp. cxxvii-clxxii.

"Nathanael Emmons," in Sprague, Annals (1859). Vol. I, Trinitarian Congregationalists, pp. 699-704.

"Notice of /the Death of/ Professor B. B. Edwards," Bibliotheca Sacra, IX, 35 (July, 1852), 654-656.

"Oliver Alden Taylor," in Sprague, Annals (1859). Vol. II, Trinitarian Congregationalists, pp. 728-730.

"Pearson, Eliphalet," in Schaff-Herzog Encyclopaedia, Vol. III, pp. 1781-1782.

/Recollections of Henry Boynton Smith/, in Henry Boynton Smith: His Life and Work. ed. Elizabeth Lee Smith. New York: A. C. Armstrong and Son, 1881, pp. 127-135, 143-144.

"Samuel Harvey Taylor," The Congregational Quarterly, XIV, 53 (January, 1872), 1-27.

A Sermon Delivered September 17, 1833 at the Interment of Rev. Charles Backus Storrs, President of the Western Reserve College. Boston: Perkins and Marvin, 1833.

A Sermon Preached in Braintree, Massachusetts, August 15, 1873, at the Funeral of Rev. Richard Salter Storrs. Boston: Alfred Mudge and Son, 1874.

"Sketch of the Life and Character of Professor Tholuck," in The Biblical Cabinet; or, Hermenuetical, Exegetical, and Philological Library, Vol. XXVIII. Edinburgh: Thomas Clark, 1840.

"Sketch of William Augustus Stearns," Congregational Quarterly, XIX, 76 (October, 1877), 498-500.

"Smalley, John," in Schaff-Herzog Encyclopaedia, Vol. IV, p. 2198.

"Spring, Samuel," in Schaff-Herzog Encyclopaedia, Vol. IV, p. 2234.

"Strong, Nathan," in Schaff-Herzog Encyclopaedia, Vol. IV, pp. 2253-2254.

"Stuart, Moses," in Schaff-Herzog Encyclopaedia,
Vol. IV, pp. 2254-2255.

"West, Stephen," in Schaff-Herzog Encyclopaedia,
Vol. IV, pp. 2497-2498.

"Worcester, Samuel," in Schaff-Herzog Encyclopaedia,
Vol. IV, pp. 2550-2551.

B. Park's historical and theological writings

"Andover Theological Seminary," in Schaff-Herzog
Encyclopaedia, Vol. I, pp. 81-82.

The Associate Creed of Andover Theological Seminary.
Boston: Franklin Press, 1883.

"Connection between Theological Study and Pulpit
Eloquence," American Biblical Repository, X, 27,
s. 1 (July, 1837), 169-191. Also published as an
essay.

"Contributions to Ecclesiastical History," Bibliotheca
Sacra, X, 38 (April, 1853), 418-420.

"Contributions to History--Letters of Dr. John Ryland
to Dr. Stephen West /1814-1816/," Bibliotheca Sacra,
XXX, 117 (January, 1873), 178-187.

"Criticism of the Commission Creed of 1883," in
Joseph Cook, Current Religious Perils. Boston:
Houghton, Mifflin and Company, 1888, p. 401.

"Current Religious Perils: A Letter to Joseph Cook,
Andover, March 23, 1887," in Joseph Cook, Current
Religious Perils. Boston: Houghton, Mifflin and
Company, 1888, pp. 212-215.

A Declaration of Faith. Boston: Thomas Todd, 1884.
Published anonymously. Reprinted numerous times.
Park's name openly linked to creed in 1899.

Discourses on Some Theological Doctrines as Related
to the Religious Character. Andover: Warren F.
Draper, 1885.

"Does Lafayette Deserve More Respect from the Americans
Than Lord Byron from the Greeks?" American Clipper;
A Monthly Catalog of American Literary and Historical
Material, I, 3 (July, 1934), 35-37.

"Dr. Alexander's Moral Science," Bibliotheca Sacra, X, 38 (April, 1853), 390-414.

"Dr. Griffin's Theory of the Atonement," Bibliotheca Sacra, XV, 57 (January, 1858), 132-178.

"Dr. Hodge's Systematic Theology," Bibliotheca Sacra, XXIX, 115 (July, 1872), 553-560.

"The Duties of a Theologian," The American Biblical Repository, II, 4, s.2 (October, 1839), 347-380. Also published as a pamphlet and an essay.

"The Fitness of the Church to the Constitution of Renewed Man," in Addresses of Rev. Drs. Park, Post, and Bacon at the Anniversary of the American Congregational Union, May, 1854. New York: Clark, Austin, and Smith, 1854, pp. 3-54.

"Hopkinsianism," in Schaff-Herzog Encyclopaedia, Vol. II, pp. 1021-1022.

"The Imprecatory Psalms Viewed in the Light of the Southern Rebellion," Bibliotheca Sacra, XIX, 73 (January, 1862), 165-210. Also published as pamphlet under title A Discourse Preached at the Ordination of Rev. Walter S. Alexander over the First Congregational Church in Pomfret, Connecticut, November 22, 1861. Andover: Warren F. Draper, 1862.

"The Intellectual and Moral Influence of Romanism," Bibliotheca Sacra, II, 7 (August, 1845), 451-488.

"John McLeod Campbell's Theory of the Atonement," Bibliotheca Sacra, XXX, 118 (April, 1873), 334-360.

"Judas Iscariot," part 2, in Dr. William Smith's Dictionary of the Bible. ed. Sir William Smith. New York: Hurd and Houghton, 1869. Vol. II, 1498-1503.

"A Layman's View of the New England Puritans," The Congregational Quarterly, X, 1 (January, 1868), 24-37.

"Life of Aristotle," Bibliotheca Sacra, I, 1 (February, 1844), 39-84; 2 (May, 1844), 280-309.

Memorial Collection of Sermons. Agnes Park, compiler. Boston: The Pilgrim Press, 1902.

"Miracles," part 2, in Smith, Dictionary (1870).
Vol. III, 1960-1968.

"The Mode of Exhibiting Theological Truth," The
American Biblical Repository, X, 28, s. 1 (October,
1837), 436-478. Also published as an essay.

"Natural Theology," Bibliotheca Sacra, III, 10
(May, 1846), 241-276. Entire essay written by
"A Society of Clergymen /Park and B. B. Edwards/."

"New England Theology," in Schaff-Herzog Encyclopaedia,
Vol. III, pp. 1634-1638.

"New England Theology," Bibliotheca Sacra, IX, 33
(January, 1852), 170-220. Also published as a
pamphlet.

"Notes /on the Use and Abuse of Creeds/," Our Day,
I, 5 (May, 1888), 370-374.

"President Edwards's Dissertation on the Nature of
True Virtue," Bibliotheca Sacra, X, 40 (October,
1853), 705-723. Entire essay "By an Association."

"The Prominence of the Atonement," in Sermons Preached
at the Dedication of the Broadway Tabernacle, New
York, Sunday, April 24, 1859. New York: N. A.
Calkins, 1859, pp. 9-38.

"The Relation of Divine Providence to Physical Laws,"
Bibliotheca Sacra, XII, 45 (January, 1855), 179-205.

"Remarks of Jonathan Edwards on the Trinity," Bibliotheca
Sacra, XXXVIII, 149 (January, 1881), 147-187; 150
(April, 1881), 333-369.

"Remarks on the Biblical Repertory and Princeton
Review," Bibliotheca Sacra, VIII, 29 (January, 1851),
135-180. Also published as a pamphlet.

Revelation of God in His Works. A Sermon Delivered at
the Installation of the Rev. Jacob M. Manning as
Associate Pastor of the Old South Church in Boston,
March 11, 1857. Boston: S. K. Whipple and Company,
1857. Reprinted several times.

"Richard Baxter's 'End of Controversy,'" Bibliotheca
Sacra, XII, 46 (April, 1855), 348-385.

"A Sermon Preached by Professor E. A. Park, at North Andover, October 11, 1882 at the Installation of Rev. H. H. Leavitt," Congregationalist, XXXIV, 43 (October 25, 1882), 361-362.

"The Theology of the Intellect and That of the Feelings," Bibliotheca Sacra, VII, 27 (July, 1850), 533-569. Reprinted numerous times.

"Theories in Regard to the Nature of the Will," Bibliotheca Sacra, XXIII, 92 (October, 1866), 679-684.

"Unity Amid Diversities of Belief, Even on Imputed and Involuntary Sin," Bibliotheca Sacra, VIII, 31 (July, 1851), 594-647. Also published as a pamphlet.

"Which Society Shall You Join, the Liberal or the Orthodox? A Letter to a Friend," Spirit of the Pilgrim, I, 5 (May, 1828), 234-248. Also published as a pamphlet.

C. Park's miscellaneous writings relative to preaching, education, church affairs, and various evangelical causes and activities

"Address," in Proceedings at the Celebration of the Fiftieth Anniversary of the Ordination and Settlement of Rev. Richard S. Storrs, D.D., Pastor of the First Church, Braintree, Massachusetts, July 3, 1861. Braintree, Massachusetts: First Congregational Church, 1861, pp. 55-68.

Address at the Meeting on the Day of Prayer for Colleges, January 26, 1882. Andover: Warren F. Draper, 1882.

"Address at the Semi-Centennial of Amherst College," in Exercises at the Semi-Centennial of Amherst College, July 12, 1871. Springfield, Massachusetts: Samuel Bowles and Company, 1871, pp. 109-115.

"Address of Professor E. A. Park /at the Andover Alumni Dinner, June, 1882/," Independent, XXXIV, 1753 (July 6, 1882), 7, cols. 1-2.

Address of Professor Park at the Andover Alumni Dinner, June, 1881, Congregationalist, XXXIII, 28 (July 13, 1881), 224, cols. 2-3.

"Address Prepared for the Semi-Centennial of Andover
Theological Seminary," in A Memorial of the Semi-
Centennial of the Founding of the Theological
Seminary at Andover. Andover: Warren F. Draper,
1859, pp. 227-237.

"Character the Main Thing: /Excerpts from/ an
Address before the Senior Class of Abbot Academy,
Andover, Massachusetts," Sunday School Times, XIX,
29 (July 21, 1877), 462-463.

"Conditions of Church Fellowship," The American
Pulpit, III, 3 (July, 1847), 100-102.

"Dignity and Importance of the Preacher's Work,"
Christian Review, IV, 16 (December, 1839), 581-
603.

"The Duty of Professing Religion," The Volunteer,
I, 12 (July, 1832), 353-367. Also published as
a pamphlet.

"The Elocution of the Pulpit," in William Russell.
Pulpit Elocution. Andover: Allen, Morrill and
Wardwell, 1846, pp. 14-21.

"How to Give a Permanent Impulse to Foreign Missions,"
Independent, XLII, 2156 (March 27, 1890), 409-410.

"Hymnology," Bibliotheca Sacra, XVI, 61 (January,
1859), 186-229; XVII, 65 (January, 1860), 134-198.

The Indebtedness of the State to the Clergy. Boston:
Dutton and Wentworth, 1851. Reprinted several times.

"The Influence of the Preacher," in Pulpit Eloquence
of the Nineteenth Century,...Containing Discourses
of Eminent Living Ministers in Europe and America,
with Sketches Biographical and Descriptive. ed.
Henry Clay Fish. New York: M. W. Dodd, 1857,
pp. 13-30.

A Letter on Christian Evidences from E. A. Park to
Joseph Cook, March 17, 1885, Independent, XXXVIII,
1896 (April 2, 1885), 423, col. 4; 424, col. 1.

"Methods of Perpetuating an Interest in Hearing the
Gospel," Bibliotheca Sacra, XXVIII, 110 (April,
1871), 334-365.

"The New England Ministry," in John Dennison
    Kingsbury. Memorial History of Bradford, Massachusetts,
    from the Earliest Period to the Close of 1882.
    Haverhill, Massachusetts: C. C. Morse and Sons,
    1883, pp. 165-171.

"Personal Testimony /from a letter to the Rev. Joseph
    Cook by Professor E. A. Park/," Christian Advocate
    (New York), LX, 39 (September 24, 1885), 619,
    cols. 3-4.

"Plainness as a Quality of Sermons," Christian
    Review, V, 20 (December, 1840), 481-510.

"Power in the Pulpit," Bibliotheca Sacra, IV, 13
    (February, 1847), 96-117.

"Reflex Usefulness of Christian Missions," Baptist
    Missionary Magazine, XXVII, 3 (March, 1847), 65-71;
    4 (April, 1847), 97-104; 5 (May, 1847), 129-135.

"Reinhard's Sermons," Bibliotheca Sacra, VI, 22
    (April, 1849), 300-337; 23 (July, 1849), 507-534.

"The Religious Influence of Theological Seminaries,"
    in Writings of Rev. William Bradford Homer. Second
    edition. Boston: T. R. Marvin, 1849, pp. xi-lix.

"Schott's Fundamental Principles of Rhetoric and
    Homiletics," Bibliotheca Sacra, II, 5 (January,
    1845), 12-48.

"Schott's Treatise on the Structure of a Sermon,"
    Bibliotheca Sacra, V, 20 (October, 1848), 731-750.

"Schott's Treatise on the Subject-Matter of Sermons,"
    Bibliotheca Sacra, III, 11 (August, 1846), 461-499.

"The Structure of a Sermon--the Text," Bibliotheca
    Sacra, XXX, 119 (July, 1873), 534-573; 120 (October,
    1873), 697-728.

"The Text of Hymns," in Austin Phelps. Hymns and
    Choirs; or, the Matter and the Manner of the Service
    of Song in the House of the Lord. Andover: Warren
    F. Draper, 1860, pp. 138-298.

Theological Education. An Address Delivered before
    the American Education Society, at the Anniversary
    Meeting in Boston, May 30, 1865. Boston: T. R.
    Marvin and Son, 1865. Also published as an article.

"Thoughts on the State of Theological Science and Education in Our Country," Bibliotheca Sacra, I, 4 (November, 1844), 735-767. Written by "A Society of Clergymen /Park and B. B. Edwards7."

"The Three Fundamental Methods of Preaching--Preaching Extempore," Bibliotheca Sacra, XXIX, 114 (April, 1872), 339-383; 116 (October, 1872), 720-770.

"The Three Fundamental Methods of Preaching--the Public Reading of Sermons, and the Preaching of Them Memoriter," Bibliotheca Sacra, XXIX, 113 (January, 1872), 157-195.

"The Three Fundamental Methods of Preaching--the Writing of Sermons," Bibliotheca Sacra, XXVIII, 111 (July, 1871), 566-598; 112 (October, 1871), 707-739.

"The Utility of Collegiate and Professional Schools," Bibliotheca Sacra, VII, 28 (October, 1850), 626-649. Also published as a pamphlet and an essay.

"What Can Be Done for Augmenting the Number of Christian Ministers," Bibliotheca Sacra, XXVIII, 109 (January, 1871), 60-97.

D. Park's introductory, editorial and translation works

The Atonement. Discourses and Treatises. ed. Edwards A. Park. Boston: Congregational Board of Publication, 1859.

"Introduction," in Mary Lamson. Life and Education of Laura Dewey Bridgman, the Deaf, Dumb and Blind Girl. Boston: New England Publishing Company, 1879, pp. i-xxx.

"Introduction," in Mary R. Peabody. Memoir of Rev. William A. Peabody. Boston: George Noyes, 1860, pp. v-xl.

"Introduction," in Philena McKeen. Annals of Fifty Years; a History of Abbot Academy, Andover, Massachusetts, 1829-1879. Andover: Warren F. Draper, 1880, pp. v-xx.

"Introduction," in William Gottlieb Schauffler. Autobiography of William G. Schauffler, for Forty-Nine Years a Missionary in the Orient. Edited by his sons. New York: Anson D. F. Randolph and Company, 1877, pp. ix-xxxv.

"/Introduction to an/ Original Letter of President Edwards," Bibliotheca Sacra, I, 3 (August, 1844), 579-583.

The Preacher and the Pastor, by Fenelon, Herbert, Baxter, Campbell. ed. Edwards A. Park. Andover: Allen, Morrill and Wardwell, 1845.

The Sabbath Hymn and Tune Book; for the Service of Song in the House of the Lord. New York: Mason Brothers, 1858. Reprinted numerous times.

Selections from German Literature. ed. and trans. Bela B. Edwards and Edwards A. Park. New York: Gould, Newman and Saxton, 1839.

Tholuck, August. "Remarks on the Life, Character and Style of the Apostle Paul, Designed as an Introduction to the Study of the Pauline Epistles." trans. E. A. Park, in The Biblical Cabinet; or, Hermeneutical, Exegetical and Philological Library, Vol. XXVIII. Edinburgh: Thomas Clark, 1840.

_____. "Sermons on Various Occasions." trans. E. A. Park, in The Biblical Cabinet; or, Hermeneutical, Exegetical and Philological Library, Vol. XXVIII. Edinburgh: Thomas Clark, 1840.

_____. "Theological Encyclopaedia and Method-ology." trans. Edwards A. Park, Bibliotheca Sacra, I, 1 (February, 1844), 178-217; 2 (May, 1844), 322-367; 3 (August, 1844), 552-578; 4 (November, 1844), 726-735.

Ullmann, Karl. "An Apologetic View of the Sinless Character of Jesus." trans. E. A. Park, in The Biblical Cabinet; or, Hermeneutical, Exegetical and Philological Library, Vol. XXXVII. Edinburgh: Thomas Clark, 1841.

E. Park's *Bibliotheca Sacra* reviews

Some four hundred of these, covering a remarkably broad range of subjects, appeared during Park's editorship. A representative sample follows.

Agassiz, Louis. The *Structure of Animal Life*. New York: Charles Scribner and Company, 1866. XXIII, 92 (October, 1866), 698.

Alexander, Archibald. *Outlines of Moral Science*. New York: Charles Scribner, 1852. X, 38 (April, 1853), 390-414.

Allibone, Samuel Austin. *A Critical Dictionary of English Literature and British and American Authors*. 3 volumes. Philadelphia: J. B. Lippincott, 1859-61. XXVIII, 112 (October, 1871), 783-784.

Arnold, Matthew. *Literature and Dogma; an Essay Towards a Better Apprehension of the Bible*. New York: Macmillan, 1873. XXX, 120 (October, 1873), 786.

Augustine. *The Confessions of Augustine*. ed. William G. T. Shedd. Andover: Warren F. Draper, 1860. XVII, 67 (July, 1860), 670.

Bacon, Francis. *Bacon's Essays, with Annotations by Richard Whately*. New York: C. S. Francis and Company, 1857. XIV, 55 (July, 1857), 671-672.

Barnes, Albert. *The Atonement, in Its Relations to Law and Moral Government*. Philadelphia: Parry and McMillan, 1859. XVI, 63 (July, 1859), 655-661.

Beecher, Catharine Esther. *Common Sense Applied to Religion; or, the Bible and the People*. New York: Harper and Brothers, 1857. XV, 58 (April, 1858), 489-491.

Beecher, Edward. *The Conflict of Ages; or, the Great Debate on the Moral Relations of God and Man*. Third edition. Boston: Phillips, Sampson, and Company, 1853. XI, 41 (January, 1854), 186-191.

Beecher, Henry Ward. *Sermons*. 2 volumes. New York: Harper and Brothers, 1869. XXVI, 101 (January, 1869), 201-202.

Beecher, Lyman. The Works of Lyman Beecher. Vol. III. Boston: John P. Jewett, 1853. X, 38 (April, 1853), 417.

Bellamy, Joseph. The Works of Joseph Bellamy. 2 volumes. Boston: Doctrinal Tract and Book Society, 1850. VIII, 30 (April, 1851), 451.

Bushnell, Horace. The Vicarious Sacrifice Grounded in Principles of Universal Obligation. New York: Charles Scribner and Company, 1866. XXIII, 90 (April, 1866), 345-350.

Butler, Joseph. Bishop Butler's Ethical Discourses: To Which Are Added Some Remains Hitherto Unpublished. Prepared as a Textbook in Moral Philosophy, with a Syllabus by Dr. Whewall. ed. Joseph C. Passmore. Philadelphia: Charles Desilver, 1855. XIV, 54 (April, 1857), 442-444.

Butler, William. The Land of the Veda, Being Personal Reminiscences of India. New York: Carlton and Lanahan, 1872. XXIX, 115 (July, 1872), 582-587.

Campbell, John McLeod. The Nature of the Atonement and Its Relations to Remission of Sins and Eternal Life. Cambridge, England: McMillan and Company, 1856. XXX, 118 (April, 1873), 334-360.

Chadbourne, Paul Ansel. Instinct; Its Office in the Animal Kingdom and Its Relation to the Higher Powers in Man. New York: George P. Putnam and Sons, 1872. XXX, 117 (January, 1873), 202-204.

Channing, William Ellery. The Perfect Life in Twelve Discourses. Boston: Roberts Brothers, 1873. XXX, 119 (July, 1873), 589.

Chaplin, Jeremiah. Life of Henry Dunster, First President of Harvard College. Boston: James R. Osgood and Company, 1872. XXIX, 115 (July, 1872), 573-574.

Chatrain, Enkmann. The Conscript; a Story of the French War of 1813. New York: Charles Scribner and Company, 1869. XXVI, 102 (April, 1869), 399.

Clark, James Henry. A Popular Hand-Book. Sight and Hearing, How Preserved and How Lost. New York: Charles Scribner, 1859. XVI, 64 (October, 1859), 890.

310

Clarke, James Freeman. Orthodoxy: Its Truths and
Errors. Boston: American Unitarian Association,
1866. XXIV, 93 (January, 1867), 188-198.

Clement, Clara Erskine. A Hand-Book of Legendary
and Mythological Art. New York: Hurd and
Houghton, 1871. XXVIII, 110 (April, 1871), 415-
416.

Connington, John. The Aeneid of Virgil, Translated
into English. New York: W. J. Middleton, 1867.
XXIV, 95 (July, 1867), 590.

Cooley, LeRoy Clark. A Text-Book of Natural Philosophy;
an Accurate Modern and Systematic Explanation of
the Elementary Principles of Science. New York:
Charles Scribner and Company, 1868. XXVI, 101
(January, 1869), 202.

Cortès, Juan Donoso. Essays on Catholicism, Liberalism and Socialism Considered in Their Fundamental
Principles. Philadelphia: J. B. Lippincott and
Company, 1862. XXIII, 92 (October, 1866), 697-
681.

Cowles, Henry. Isaiah; with Notes Critical, Explanatory
and Practical. New York: D. Appleton and Company,
1869. XXVI, 102 (April, 1869), 389.

Day, Henry Noble. The Science of Aesthetics; or, the
Nature, Kinds, Laws and Uses of Beauty. New York:
G. P. Putnam's Sons, 1871. XXIX, 116 (October, 1872),
788.

Dorner, Isaak August. History of Protestant Theology,
Particularly in Germany, Viewed According to Its
Fundamental Movement in Connection with the
Religious, Moral and Intellectual Life. 5 volumes.
Edinburgh: T. and T. Clark, 1872-1882. XXIX,
113 (January, 1872), 206.

Farrar, Timothy. Manual of the Constitution of the
United States of America. Boston: Little, Brown
and Company, 1867. XXV, 98 (April, 1868), 399-400.

Fisher, George Park. The Beginnings of Christianity;
with a View to the State of the Roman World at the
Birth of Christ. New York: Scribner, Armstrong
and Company, 1877. XXXV, 137 (January, 1878),
202-203.

_____. *Life* *of* *Benjamin* *Silliman*. New York:
Charles Scribner, 1866. 2 volumes. XXIII, 91
(July, 1866), 528.

_____. *Memorial* *of* *Nathaniel* *William* *Taylor*.
New Haven: Thomas H. Pease, 1858. XV, 60
(October, 1858), 884-887.

Gibbs, Josiah Willard. *Philological* *Studies*, *with*
English *Illustrations*. New Haven: Durrie and
Peck, 1857. XV, 57 (January, 1858), 237-240.

Grau, Rudolf Friedrich. *Semiten* *und* *Indogermanen* *in*
ihrer *Beziehung* *zu* *Religion* *und* *Wissenschaft*. *Eine*
Apologie *des* *Christentums* *von* *Standpunkte* *der*
Völker *Psychologie*. Stuttgart: S. G. Liesching,
1864. XXII, 85 (January, 1865), 172-174.

Griffin, Edward Dorr. *Sermons* *by* *the* *Late* *Rev.*
Edward *D.* *Griffin*. 2 volumes. Albany: Packard,
Van Benthuysen and Company, 1858. XV, 57 (January,
1858), 132-178.

Hamilton, William. *The* *Metaphysics* *of* *Sir* *William*
Hamilton. Compiled by Francis Bown. Cambridge,
Massachusetts: Sever and Francis, 1861. XIX,
73 (January, 1862), 237-238.

Hengstenberg, Ernst Wilhelm. *Commentary* *on* *the*
Gospel *of* *St.* *John*. 2 volumes. Edinburgh: T. and
T. Clark, 1865. XXIII, 90 (April, 1866), 349-350.

Hitchcock, Edward. *The* *Religion* *of* *Geology* *and* *Its*
Connected *Sciences*. New edition. Boston: Phillips,
Sampson and Company, 1859. XVII, 65 (January, 1860),
229-230.

Hodge, Charles. *Essays* *and* *Reviews*, *Selected* *from*
the *Princeton* *Review*. New York: Charles Scribner's
Sons, 1879. XXXVI, 143 (July, 1879), 584-589.

Huntington, Frederic Dan. *Human* *Society*; *Its*
Providential *Structure*, *Relations* *and* *Office*.
New York: Carter and Brothers, 1860. XVII, 65
(January, 1860), 235.

Krauth, Charles Porterfield. *The* *Conservative*
Reformation *and* *Its* *Theology*, *as* *Represented* *in*
the *Augsburg* *Confession* *and* *in* *the* *History* *and*
Literature *of* *the* *Evangelical* *Lutheran* *Church*.
Philadelphia: J. B. Lippincott and Company, 1871.
XXIX, 113 (January, 1872), 204-206.

Krummacher, Frederick William. *David, King of Israel*. A Portrait Drawn from the Bible History and the Book of Psalms. Edinburgh: T. and T. Clark, 1867. XXVI, 102 (April, 1869), 394.

Loomis, Elias. *A Treatise on Meteorology, with a Collection of Meteorological Tables*. New York: Harper and Brothers, 1868. XXV, 99 (July, 1868), 590.

Lucretius on the Nature of Things. trans. Charles F. Johnson. London: Sampson, Low, Son and Marston, 1872. XXX, 117 (January, 1873), 196.

Lyell, Sir Charles. *Principles of Geology, or the Modern Changes of the Earth and Its Inhabitants, Considered as Illustrative of Geology*. Eleventh revised edition. 2 volumes. New York: D. Appleton and Company, 1873. XXXI, 124 (October, 1874), 785-790.

McCosh, James. *Christianity and Positivism; a Series of Lectures to the Times on Natural Theology and Apologetics*. New York: Robert Carter and Brothers, 1871. XXIX, 113 (January, 1872), 207-208.

Malcolm, Howard. *Theological Index: References to the Principal Works in Every Department of Religious Literature*. Boston: Gould and Lincoln, 1868. XXV, 98 (April, 1868), 394-395.

Mann, Horace. *Life and Works of Horace Mann*. ed. Mary Mann, Vol. I. Boston: Walker, Fuller and Company, 1865. XXIII, 89 (January, 1866), 172-173.

Marsh, George Perkins. *Lectures on the English Language*. New York: Charles Scribner, 1860. XVII, 66 (April, 1860), 449.

Merle d'Aubigne, Jean Henri. *History of the Reformation in Europe in the Time of Calvin*. New York: Robert Carter and Brothers, 1867. XXIV, 95 (July, 1867), 592.

Morley, John. *Rousseau*. 2 volumes. London: Chapman and Hall, 1873. XXX, 120 (October, 1873), 785-786.

Neander, August. *History of the Planting and Training of the Christian Church*. trans. J. E. Ryland. New York: Sheldon and Company, 1865. XXII, 86 (April, 1865), 350.

Norton, Andrews. Internal Evidences of the Genuine-
ness of the Gospels. Boston: Little, Brown and
Company, 1855. XIII, 50 (April, 1856), 441-442.

Osburn, William, Jr. The Monumental History of
Egypt, as Recorded on the Ruins of Her Temples,
Palaces and Tombs. 2 volumes. London: Trübner
and Company, 1854. XII, 47 (July, 1855), 650-651.

Palfrey, John Gorham. A Compendius History of New
England, from the Discovery by Europeans to the
First General Congress of the Anglo-American
Colonies. 4 volumes. Boston: H. C. Shepard,
1873. XXX, 119 (July, 1873), 582-583.

Pond, Enoch. Lectures on Christian Theology.
Boston: Congregational Board of Publication, 1867.
XXIV, 94 (April, 1867), 389-397.

Porter, Noah. The Elements of Intellectual Science.
New York: Charles Scribner and Company, 1871.
XXIX, 116 (October, 1872), 788-789.

Priestly, Joseph. A History of the Corruptions of
Christianity. London: British and Foreign
Unitarian Association, 1871. XXIX, 116 (October,
1872), 787-788.

Reinhard, Franz Volkmar. Sämtliche Predigten.
43 volumes in 20. Reutlingen, Germany: Fleischhauer
and Kaufmann, 1815-1821. VI, 23 (August, 1849),
507-534.

Schaff, Philip. History of the Christian Church.
3 volumes. New York: Charles Scribner, 1859-68.
XXIV, 94 (April, 1867), 397-398.

Schmucker, Samuel Simon. Elemental Contrast Between
the Religion of Forms and of the Spirit, as
Exemplified in Popery and Puseyism on the One Hand,
and Genuine Protestantism on the Other. Gettysburg,
1852. X, 38 (April, 1853), 420.

Shedd, William Greenough Thayer. Sermons to the
Natural Man. New York: Charles Scribner and
Company, 1871. XXVIII, 112 (October, 1871),
775-777.

Smith, Henry Boynton. Faith and Philosophy; Discourses
and Essays. ed. George L. Prentiss. New York:
Scribner, Armstrong and Company, 1877. XXXV,
137 (January, 1878), 200-202.

314

Stewart, Dugald. The Philosophy of the Active and
Moral Powers of Man. Revised by James Walker.
Cambridge, Massachusetts: J. Bartlett, 1849.
VII, 25 (January, 1850), 191-193.

Stuart, Moses. A Commentary on the Epistle to
the Hebrews. ed. R. D. C. Robbins. Andover:
Warren F. Draper, 1860. XIX, 73 (January, 1862),
235-236.

Taylor, Nathaniel William. Lectures on the Moral
Government of God. 2 volumes. New York: Clark,
Austin and Smith, 1859. XVI, 64 (October, 1859),
884-885.

Theologia Germanica. trans. Susanna Winkworth, with
an introduction by Calvin E. Stowe. Andover:
Warren F. Draper, 1856. XIII, 50 (April, 1856),
456-459.

Tholuck, August. Guido and Julius; or, Sin and the
Propitiator, Exhibited in the True Consecration
of the Sceptic. Translated from the German by
Jonathan Edwards Ryland. Boston: Gould and
Lincoln, 1854. XI, 44 (October, 1854), 842.

Tyler, Bennet. Lectures on Theology. with a memoir
by Nahum Gale. Boston: J. E. Tilton and Company,
1859. XVII, 65 (January, 1860), 217-224.

Ursinus, Zacharias. The Commentary of Dr. Zacharias
Ursinus on the Heidelberg Catechism. Second
American edition. Columbus: Scott and Bascum,
1852. X, 38 (April, 1853), 418.

Wayland, Francis. The Elements of Intellectual
Philosophy. Boston: Phillips, Sampson and
Company, 1854. XII, 46 (April, 1855), 403-415.

Wise, John. A Vindication of the Government of the
New-England Churches, and the Churches' Quarrel
Espoused; or, a Reply to Certain Proposals.
Fourth edition. Boston: Congregational Board
of Publication, 1860. XVII, 67 (July, 1860), 670.

Woolsey, Theodore Dwight. The Religion of the
Present and the Future. Sermons Preached Chiefly
at Yale College. New York: Charles Scribner and
Company, 1871. XXVIII, 112 (October, 1871), 777.

315

F. Intellectual and theological heritage and context

Abbott, Lyman. <u>Reminiscences</u>. Boston: Houghton,
   Mifflin Company, 1935.

Ahlstrom, Sydney E. <u>A Religious History of the
   American People</u>. New Haven: Yale University
   Press, 1972.

_____. "The Scottish Philosophy and American
   Theology," <u>Church History</u>, XXIV, 3 (September,
   1955), 257-272.

_____. "Theology in America: A Historical
   Survey," <u>The Shaping of American Religion</u>. ed.
   James Ward Smith and A. Leland Jamison. Princeton:
   Princeton University Press, 1961, pp. 232-321.

_____,ed. <u>Theology in America, the Major Voices
   from Puritanism to Neo-Orthodoxy</u>. Indianapolis:
   The Bobbs-Merrill Company, Inc., 1967.

"The Alleged Collapse of New England Theology,"
   <u>Bibliotheca Sacra</u>, LXV, 260 (October, 1908),
   601-610.

Atkins, Gaius Glenn. "New England Theology," in
   <u>An Encyclopedia of Religion</u>. ed. Vergilius Ferm.
   New York: Philosophical Library, 1945, p. 561.

Atkins, Gaius Glenn and Frederick L. Fagley. <u>History
   of American Congregationalism</u>. Boston: Pilgrim
   Press, 1942.

/Atwater, Lyman H./ "Jonathan Edwards and the
   Successive Forms of New Divinity," <u>The Biblical
   Repertory and Princeton Review</u>, XXX, 4 (October,
   1858), 585-620.

Bacon, Benjamin Wisner. <u>Theodore Thornton Munger,
   New England Minister</u>. New Haven: Yale University
   Press, 1913.

Baird, Samuel John. "Edwards and the Theology of
   New England," <u>Southern Presbyterian Review</u>, X,
   4 (January, 1858), 574-592.

Barton, William Eleazar. <u>Congregational Creeds and
   Covenants</u>. Chicago: Advance Publishing Company,
   1917.

316

/Beecher, Edward7. "The Theology of New England,"
Congregationalist, II, 11 (March 15, 1850), 42,
col. 1.

Bingham, Millicent Todd, ed. Emily Dickinson's Home:
Letters of Edward Dickinson and His Family. New
York: Harper and Brothers Publishers, 1955.

Boardman, George Nye. A History of New England
Theology. New York: A. D. F. Randolph Company,
1899.

Bowden, Henry W. Church History in the Age of
Science: Historiographical Patterns in the United
States, 1876-1918. Chapel Hill: University of
North Carolina Press, 1971.

Breckinridge, Robert J. "The Relative Doctrinal
Tendencies of Presbyterianism and Congregationalism
in America," The Danville Quarterly Review, I, 1
(March, 1861), 1-23.

Brockman, Henry Caruthers. "Frank Hugh Foster: A Chapter
in the American Protestant Quest for Authority
in Theology." Union Theological Seminary:
unpublished Th.D. dissertation, 1967.

Bronson, Walter C. The History of Brown University:
1764-1914. Providence: Published by the University,
1914.

Brown, Jerry Wayne. The Rise of Biblical Criticism
in America, 1800-1870: The New England Scholars.
Middletown, Connecticut: Wesleyan University Press,
1969.

Buckham, John Wright. "The New England Theologians,"
American Journal of Theology, XXIV, 1 (January,
1920), 19-29.

_____. Progressive Religious Thought in America:
A Survey of the Enlarging Pilgrim Faith. Boston:
Houghton, Mifflin Company, 1919.

Bushnell, Horace. Christ in Theology. Hartford:
Hamersley and Company, 1851.

_____. Forgiveness and Law, Grounded in
Principles Interpreted by Human Analogies. New
York: Scribner, Armstrong and Company, 1874.

_____. God in Christ. Hartford: Brown and Parsons, 1849.

_____. The Vicarious Sacrifice, Grounded in Principles of Universal Obligation. New York: Charles Scribner and Company, 1866.

Cheney, Mary Bushnell, ed. Life and Letters of Horace Bushnell. New York: Harper and Brothers, 1880.

Cherry, Conrad. The Theology of Jonathan Edwards. New York: Doubleday and Company, 1966.

Coleridge, Samuel Taylor. Aids to Reflection. ed. James Marsh. New York: Gould, Newman and Saxton, 1840, c1829.

Cross, Barbara M. Horace Bushnell. Chicago: University of Chicago Press, 1958.

Dahm, John J. "Science and Apologetics in the Early Boyle Lectures," Church History, XXXIX, 2 (June, 1970), 172-186.

Dexter, Henry Martyn. The Congregationalism of the Last Three Hundred Years as Seen in Its Literature. New York: Harper and Brothers, 1880.

Dickinson, Emily. The Letters of Emily Dickinson. ed. Thomas H. Johnson. Cambridge, Massachusetts: Belknap Press of Harvard University Press, 1958. Vol. I, pp. 271-272.

Dwight, William Theodore. Characteristics of New England Theology. Boston: Congregational Board of Publication, 1855.

Edwards, Jonathan. Freedom of the Will. ed. Paul Ramsey. New Haven: Yale University Press, 1966.

_____. Jonathan Edwards, Representative Selections. ed. Clarence H. Faust and Thomas H. Johnson. New York: Hill and Wang, 1966, c1935.

_____. Original Sin (1758). ed. Clyde A. Holbrook. New Haven: Yale University Press, 1970.

Ellis, George Edward. A Half Century of the Unitarian Controversy. Boston: Crosley, Nichols and Company, 1857.

318

Emmons, Nathanael. "Hopkinsianism," in Hannah Adams, Views of Religions. Boston: Manning and Loring, 1801, pp. 127-134.

Ferm, J. Robert. "Jonathan Edwards the Younger and the American Reformed Tradition." Yale University: unpublished Ph.D. dissertation, 1958.

Fisher, George Park. Discussions in History and Theology. New York: Charles Scribner's Sons, 1880.

_____. "Dr. N. W. Taylor's Theology: A Rejoinder to the 'Princeton Review,'" New Englander, XXVII, 105 (October, 1868), 740-763.

_____. "Elements of Puritanism," North American Review, CXXXIII, 299 (October, 1881), 326-337.

_____. "Future Probation and Foreign Missions," Independent, XXXIX, 1998 (March 17, 1887), 338-339.

_____. History of Christian Doctrine. Edinburgh: T. and T. Clark, 1949, c1896.

_____. "The New Congregational Creed," Independent, XXXVI, 1845 (April 10, 1884), 452-453.

_____. "Rev. Prof. Fisher's Discourse Commemorative of Prof. Josiah Willard Gibbs, LL.D.," New Englander, XIX, 75 (July, 1861), 605-620.

_____. "Taylor, Nathaniel William," in Schaff-Herzog Encyclopaedia, Vol. IV, pp. 2306-2307.

Fiske, Daniel Taggart. "New England Theology," Bibliotheca Sacra, XXII, 87 (July, 1865), 467-512; 88 (October, 1865), 568-588.

Foster, Charles Howell. The Rungless Ladder: Harriet Beecher Stowe and New England Puritanism. Durham, North Carolina: Duke University Press, 1954.

Foster, Frank Hugh. "The Benevolence Theory of the Atonement," Bibliotheca Sacra, XLVII, 188 (October, 1890), 567-588; XLVIII, 189 (January, 1891), 104-127.

_____. "The Eschatology of the New England Divines," Bibliotheca Sacra, XLIII, 169 (January, 1886), 1-32; 170 (April, 1886), 287-302; 172 (October, 1886), 711-726. XLV, 180 (October, 1888), 669-694. XLVI, 181 (January, 1889), 95-123.

_____. A Genetic History of the New England
Theology. Chicago: University of Chicago Press,
1907.

_____. The Modern Movement in American Theology.
New York: Fleming H. Revell Company, 1939.

_____. "The Theological Limits of Congregational-
ism," Advance, XXXVII, 1752 (June 8, 1899), 799-
800.

Gardner, Edward Clinton. "Man as Sinner in Nineteenth
Century New England Theology: A Study in the
Challenge of Romantic Humanitarianism." Yale
University: unpublished Ph.D. dissertation, 1952.

Giltner, John Herbert. "Moses Stuart: 1780-1852."
Yale University: unpublished Ph.D. dissertation,
1956.

Gladden, Washington. "The Contribution of Congregationalism to Theology," Ohio Church History
Society, Papers, VII (1896), 119-144.

Gordon, George Angier. Humanism in New England
Theology. Boston: Houghton, Mifflin and Company,
1920.

_____. My Education and Religion: An Auto-
biography. Boston: Houghton, Mifflin Company,
1925.

Grave, Selwyn Alfred. The Scottish Philosophy of
Common Sense. Oxford: Clarendon Press, 1960.

Grotius, Hugo. A Defense of the Catholic Faith
Concerning the Satisfaction of Christ, Against
Faustus Socinus. ed. and trans. F. H. Foster.
Andover: Warren F. Draper, 1889.

Gulliver, John P. Christianity and Science.
Andover, 1879.

Haroutunian, Joseph. Piety Versus Moralism: The
Passing of the New England Theology. New York:
Harper and Row, 1970.

Harpole, Ralph O. "The Development of the Doctrine
of Atonement in American Thought from Jonathan
Edwards to Horace Bushnell." Yale University:
unpublished Ph.D. dissertation, 1924.

Harris, George. "The Rational and Spiritual Verification of Christian Doctrine," Christian Union (June 14, 1883), 469-473.

Hodge, Archibald Alexander. Life of Charles Hodge. London: T. Nelson and Son, 1881.

Hodge, Charles. Systematic Theology. Three volumes. New York: Charles Scribner's Sons, 1872.

Ide, Jacob. "Calvin Park," in Sprague, Annals (1859). Vol. II, Trinitarian Congregationalists, pp. 461-463.

Lawrence, Edward Alexander. "New England Theology Historically Considered," American Theological Review, II, 6 (May, 1860), 209-232.

_____. "New England Theology: The Edwardean Period," American Theological Review, III, 9 (January, 1861), 36-69.

_____. "The Old School in New England Theology," Bibliotheca Sacra, XX, 78 (April, 1863), 311-348.

MacCormac, Earl Ronald. "The Transition from Voluntary Missionary Society to the Church as a Missionary Organization among the American Congregationalists, Presbyterians, and Methodists." Yale University: unpublished Ph.D. dissertation, 1960.

McCosh, James. The Scottish Philosophy. New York: Robert Carter and Brothers, 1880, c1874.

McGiffert, Arthur Cushman. "The Progress of Theological Thought during the Past Fifty Years," American Journal of Theology, XX, 3 (July, 1916), 321-332.

McGiffert, Michael. "Christian Darwinism: The Partnership of Asa Gray and George Frederick Wright, 1874-1881." Yale University: unpublished Ph.D. dissertation, 1958.

Marsh, James. "A Discourse on Conscience," in The Remains of James Marsh. ed. Joseph Torrey. Boston: Crocker and Brewster, 1843.

Mead, Sidney Earl. Nathaniel William Taylor, 1786-1858, a Connecticut Liberal. Chicago: University of Chicago Press, 1942.

Meredith, Robert Dean. The Politics of the Universe:
Edward Beecher, Abolition and Orthodoxy. Nashville:
Vanderbilt University Press, 1968.

Morley, Verne D. "American Congregationalism: A
Critical Bibliography 1900-1952," Church History,
XXI, 4 (December, 1952), 323-344.

Nelson, John Oliver. "Charles Hodge," in The Lives
of Eighteen from Princeton. ed. Willard Thorp.
Princeton: Princeton University Press, 1946.

_____. "The Rise of the Princeton Theology:
A Genetic Study of American Presbyterianism until
1850." Yale University: unpublished Ph.D.
dissertation, 1935.

"The New Theology and the New England Theology,"
Congregationalist, XXXV, 23 (June 7, 1883), 198,
cols. 2-4.

Pond, Enoch. "Hopkinsianism," Bibliotheca Sacra,
XIX, 75 (July, 1862), 633-670.

Pope, Earl Aurel. "New England Calvinism and the
Disruption of the Presbyterian Church." Brown
University: unpublished Ph.D. dissertation, 1962.

Porter, Noah. "Coleridge and His American Disciples,"
Bibliotheca Sacra, IV, 13 (February, 1847), 117-
171.

"President Edwards and New England Theology,"
Panoplist; or, the Christian's Armory, I, 10
(October, 1850), 386-397; 11 (November, 1850),
430-436.

Ramm, Bernard. Witness of the Spirit. Grand Rapids:
William B. Eerdmans Publishing Company, 1959.

Reid, Thomas. "Essays on the Active Powers of Man,"
in The Works of Thomas Reid, Vol. II. ed. William
Hamilton. Edinburgh: MacLachlan and Stewart,
sixth edition, 1863, c1788.

_____. Essays on the Intellectual Powers of
Man. ed. A. D. Woozley. London: Macmillan and
Company, 1941, c1785.

_____. An Inquiry into the Human Mind on the
Principles of Common Sense. Edinburgh: Bell and
Bradfute; and William Creech, sixth edition, 1810,
c1764.

Riley, Isaac Woodbridge. American Thought from
Puritanism to Pragmatism. Gloucester, Massachusetts:
Peter Smith, 1959, c1915.

Rudisill, Dorus Paul. "The Doctrine of the Atonement
in Jonathan Edwards and His Successors." Duke
University: unpublished Ph.D. dissertation, 1945.

Segerstedt, Torgny T. The Problem of Knowledge in
Scottish Philosophy. Lund: C. W. K. Gleerup, 1935.

Schaff, David S. The Life of Philip Schaff. New
York: Charles Scribner's Sons, 1897.

Schaff, Philip. The Principle of Protestantism.
trans. John W. Nevin (1845). Lancaster Series on
the Mercersburg Theology, Vol. I. ed. Bard Thompson
and George H. Bricker. Boston: United Church
Press, 1964.

Schleiermacher, Friedrich. "On the Discrepancy
Between the Sabellian and the Athanasian Method
of Representing the Doctrine of the Trinity,"
trans. Moses Stuart, Biblical Repository and
Quarterly Observer, V (April, 1835), 265-353;
VI (July, 1835), 1-116.

Schneider, Herbert Wallace. A History of American
Philosophy. New York: Columbia University Press,
1946.

Smith, Elizabeth Lee (Allen), ed. Henry Boynton
Smith, His Life and Work. New York: A. C.
Armstrong and Son, 1881.

Smith, Henry Boynton. Faith and Philosophy: Discourses
and Essays. New York: Scribner, Armstrong and
Company, 1877.

Smith, H. Shelton. Changing Conceptions of Original
Sin: A Study in American Theology Since 1750.
New York: Charles Scribner's Sons, 1955.

_____,ed. Horace Bushnell. Library of Protestant
Thought. New York: Oxford University Press, 1965.

Smyth, Newman. Old Faiths in New Light. New York:
Charles Scribner's Sons, 1879.

_____. The Orthodox Theology of Today. New
York: Charles Scribner's Sons, 1881.

_____. Recollections and Reflections. New York: Charles Scribner's Sons, 1926.

_____. The Religious Feeling. New York: Charles Scribner's Sons, 1877.

Stange, Douglas C. "The Third Lecture: One Hundred and Fifty Years of Anti-Popery at Harvard," Harvard Library Bulletin, XVI, 4 (October, 1968), 354-369.

Stein, Stephen J. "Stuart and Hodge on Romans 5:12-21: An Exegetical Controversy About Original Sin," Journal of Presbyterian History, XLVII, 4 (December, 1969), 340-358.

Stoever, William K. B. "Henry Boynton Smith and the German Theology of History," Union Seminary Quarterly Review, XXIV, 1 (Fall, 1968), 69-89.

Stowe, Harriet Beecher. Oldtown Folks. ed. Henry F. May. Cambridge, Massachusetts: Harvard University Press, 1966.

Strout, Cushing. "Faith and History: The Mind of William G. T. Shedd," Journal of the History of Ideas, XV, 1 (January, 1954), 153-162.

Swift, David Everett. "Conservative Versus Progressive Orthodoxy in Later Nineteenth Century Congregationalism," Church History, XVI (1947), 22-31.

_____. "The Future Probation Controversy in American Congregationalism 1886-1893." Yale University: unpublished Ph.D. dissertation, 1947.

Tucker, William Jewett. My Generation: An Autobiographical Interpretation. Boston: Houghton, Mifflin and Company, 1919.

Tyler, William S. A History of Amherst College... from 1821-1891. New York: Frederick H. Hitchcock, 1895.

Van Halsema, Dick Lucas. "Samuel Hopkins (1721-1803), New England Calvinist." Union Theological Seminary: unpublished Th.D. dissertation, 1956.

Walker, George Leon. Some Aspects of the Religious Life of New England with Special Reference to the Congregationalists. New York: Silver, Burdett and Company, 1897.

Walker, Williston. "Changes in Theology Among
American Congregationalists," American Journal
of Theology, X, 2 (April, 1906), 204-218.

_____. The Creeds and Platforms of Congrega-
tionalism. New York: Charles Scribner's Sons,
1893.

_____. A History of the Congregational Church
in the United States. Boston: The Pilgrim Press,
1894.

_____. Ten New England Leaders. New York:
Silver, Burdett and Company, 1901.

Warfield, Benjamin Breckinridge. "Edwards and
the New England Theology," in Encyclopedia of
Religion and Ethics. ed. James Hastings. New
York: Charles Scribner's Sons, 1912. Vol. V,
pp. 221-227.

Williams, George Huntston, ed. The Harvard Divinity
School: Its Place in Harvard University and in
American Culture. Boston: Beacon Press, 1954.

Woods, Leonard. Theology of the Puritans. Boston:
Woodbridge, Moore and Company, 1851.

Wright, George Frederick. The Story of My Life and
Work. Oberlin, Ohio: Bibliotheca Sacra Company,
1916.

G. Theological comment and criticism

A., L. /Review of Park's/ Duties of the New England
Clergy, Christian Examiner and Religious Miscellany,
XXXVII, fourth series II, 3 (November, 1844), 350-
370.

/Abbott, Lyman?/. "Professor Park on Pioneering in
Theology," The Christian Union, XXVII, 22 (May 31,
1883), 427, cols. 1-2.

/Abbott, Lyman?/. "Professor Park's View of an
Important Question," The Christian Union, XXVI,
18 (November 2, 1882), 358, cols. 2-3.

"The Accountability of the Ultra-Conservatives,"
Andover Review, I, 6 (June, 1884), 653-658.

/Allen, George7. The Andover Fuss; or, Dr. Woods
Versus Dr. Dana, on the Imputation of Heresy Against
Professor Park Respecting the Doctrine of Original
Sin. Boston: Tappan and Whittemore, 1853.

An Alumnus of Andover Who Believes in the Catechism.
"Andover Theological Seminary," Congregationalist,
II, 21 (May 24, 1850), 81, col. 2.

"Andover and Danville," Presbyterian Herald,
Bardstown, Kentucky. Volume XXVIII (1850).
Undated extra. 1 sheet.

Andover and Danville: A Reply to an Article in the
Bibliotheca Sacra, for October, 1859, Containing
a View of Breckinridge's Theology. Louisville,
Kentucky: Hull and Brother, 1859.

"Andover Creed," Congregationalist, II, 22 (May 31,
1850), 86, cols. 1-2.

"The Andover Creed," Congregationalist, II, 25
(June 21, 1850), 98, cols. 1-3.

"Andover Seminary and the Puritan Recorder,"
Puritan Recorder, XXXV, 47 (November 21, 1850),
186, cols. 3-6.

/Atwater, Lyman H.7 "Old Orthodoxy, New Divinity
and Unitarianism," Biblical Repertory and
Princeton Review, XXIX, 4 (October, 1857), 561-
598.

Bacon, Leonard. "The Church Review and New England
Theology," New Englander, XI, 1 (February, 1853),
92-111.

_____. "Church Review Theology," New
Englander, XI, 2 (April, 1853), 261-277.

_____. /Review of Park's7 Memoir of the Life
and Character of Samuel Hopkins, New Englander,
X, 39 (August, 1852), 448-472.

Beecher, Edward. /Review of Park's7 Memoir of the
Life and Character of Samuel Hopkins, Bibliotheca
Sacra, X, 37 (January, 1853), 63-82.

Brownson, Orestes Augustus. /Review of Park's7
"Intellectual and Moral Influence of Romanism,"
Brownson's Quarterly Review, II, 4 (October, 1845),
442-540.

Bulfinch, Stephen Greenleaf. /Review of Park's/
Preacher and Pastor, Christian Examiner and Religious
Miscellany, LIII, fourth series XVIII, 2 (September,
1852), 269-283.

Bushnell, Horace. "Christian Comprehensiveness,"
New Englander, VI (1848), 81-103.

_____. "Our Gospel a Gift to the Imagination,"
in Building Eras in Religion. New York: Charles
Scribner's Sons, 1881. First published in Hours
at Home, Vol. VII (1869).

_____. "Spiritual Economy of Revivals of
Religion," Quarterly Christian Spectator, X
(1838), 131-148.

Carleton, Hiram. /Review of Park's/ "Revelation of
God in His Works," Theological and Literary
Journal, X, 3 (January, 1858), 450-480.

A Catholic layman /Cole,?/. A Letter to Professor
Edwards A. Park, Bartlet Professor, Andover
Theological Seminary, Touching His Late Sermon
before the Pastoral Association of Massachusetts.
Boston: Charles Stimpson, 1844.

"The Congregational Board and Its Theology,"
Independent, XI, 539 (March 31, 1859), 4, col. 2.

A Congregationalist. "Andover on Breckinridge--A
Correction," Independent, XI, 577 (December 22,
1859), 2, col. 6.

"The Congregationalist and New England Theology,"
Panoplist; or, Christian's Armory, III, 3
(May, 1852), 104-105.

Cook, Joseph. Current Religious Perils. Boston:
Houghton, Mifflin and Company, 1888.

_____. "What Is New England Orthodoxy?"
Independent, XXXVII, 1894 (March 19, 1885), 358,
col. 4; 359, col. 1.

Cooke, Parsons. The Condition of the Congregational
Board of Publication, Set Forth in a Protest
Against a Recent Vote of Its Executive Committee.
Boston: Crocker and Brewster, 1859.

_____. /Review of Park's/ Atonement, Discourses
and Treatises, American Theological Review, II,
5 (February, 1860), 97-120.

/Cooke, Parsons/. Views in New England Theology.
No. I: The New England Theology Contrasted with
the New Arminianism. Boston: Crocker and Brewster,
1859.

/Cooke, Parsons/. Views in New England Theology.
No. II: The New Apostasy; or, a Word to the
Laodiceans. Boston: Crocker and Brewster, 1860.

Currier, Albert Henry. /Review of Park's/ Discourses
on Some Theological Doctrines as Related to the
Religious Character, Bibliotheca Sacra, XLIV, 173
(January, 1887), 157-162.

Dana, Daniel. Have the Churches the Presence of
Christ? A Sermon Addressed to the Presbytery of
Londonderry, April 30, 1851. Newburyport, Mass-
achusetts: Moses H. Sargent, 1851.

/Dana, Daniel/ Philalethes. "The Andover Creed,"
Congregationalist, II, 25 (June 21, 1850), 98,
cols. 1-2.

/Dana, Daniel/ Philalethes. "Andover Theological
Seminary," Panoplist; or, the Christian's Armory,
I, 5 (May, 1850), 168-170.

/Dana, Daniel/ Philalethes. "Andover Theological
Seminary," Congregationalist, II, 28 (July 12,
1850), 109, cols. 4-7; 110, cols. 1-3.

/Dana, Daniel/ Philalethes. "Human Ability and
Inability," Panoplist; or, the Christian's
Armory, II, 2 (February, 1851), 41-46.

/Dana, Daniel/ Philalethes. "On Creeds," Panoplist,
or, the Christian's Armory, II, 7 (July, 1851),
345-349.

/Dana, Daniel/ Philalethes. "Theological Seminaries,
and Their Creeds," Panoplist; or, the Christian's
Armory, III, 3 (May, 1852), 100-103.

"The Danville Divinity; Its Plagiarisms and Its
Pamphlet," Congregationalist, XII, 8 (February 24,
1859), 30, cols. 1-3.

"Dr. Dana's Communication," Panoplist; or, the
Christian's Armory, I, 9 (September, 1850), 332-
340.

"Dr. Lord's Letter to Dr. Dana," Panoplist; or, the Christian's Armory, III, 5 (September, 1852), 175-182.

"Dr. Lord's Sermon," Panoplist; or, the Christian's Armory, I, 2 (February, 1850), 79-80.

Eells, William Woodward. The Fathers and the Children, Two Sermons Preached on Fast Day, April 6, 1848. Boston: Crocker and Brewster, 1848.

Ellis, George E. "The New Theology," Christian Examiner and Religious Miscellany, LXII, fourth series XXVII, 3 (May, 1857), 321-360.

_____. /Review of Park's/ Memoir of the Life and Character of Samuel Hopkins, Christian Examiner and Religious Miscellany, LIV, fourth series XIX, 1 (January, 1853), 123-130.

_____. /Review of Park's/ Memoir of Nathanael Emmons, Christian Examiner and Religious Miscellany, LXXI, fifth series IX, 2 (September, 1861), 287-291.

Fisher, George Park, ed. An Unpublished Essay of Edwards on the Trinity. New York: Charles Scribner's Sons, 1903.

_____. /Review of Park's/ Memoir of Nathanael Emmons, New Englander, XIX, 75 (July, 1861), 709-730.

Foster, Frank Hugh. "Professor Park's Theological System, Bibliotheca Sacra, LX, 240 (October, 1903), 672-697; LXI, 241 (January, 1904), 55-79; 242 (April, 1904), 272-291; 243 (July, 1904), 511-528.

Gordon, George Angier. "The Achilles of Our Camp, an Acute and Inspiring Characterization of the Late Dr. Edwards A. Park," Congregationalist, LXXXVIII, 24 (June 13, 1903), 840.

Hayden, William B. /Review of/ "Professor Park's Discourse on the Theology of the Intellect and That of the Feelings," New Jerusalem Magazine, XXIV, 1 (January, 1851), 10-21.

Hodge, Archibald Alexander. /Review of Park's/ Associate Creed, Presbyterian Review, IV, 16 (October, 1883), 882-887.

_____. /Review of Park's/ Discourses on Some Theological Doctrines as Related to the Religious Character, Presbyterian Review, VI, 23 (July, 1885), 561-562.

Hodge, Charles. "Professor Park and the Princeton Review," Biblical Repertory and Princeton Review, XXIII, 4 (October, 1851), 674-695.

_____. "Professor Park's Remarks on the Princeton Review," Biblical Repertory and Princeton Review, XXIII, 2 (April, 1851), 306-347.

_____. "Professor Park's Sermon," Biblical Repertory and Princeton Review, XXII, 4 (October, 1850), 642-674.

Holmes, Oliver Wendell. "Jonathan Edwards: An Essay," International Review, IX (July, 1880), 1-30.

A Layman. "Andover Theological Seminary," Panoplist; or, the Christian's Armory, I, 7 (July, 1850), 266-267.

A Layman. "Andover Seminary," Panoplist; or, the Christian's Armory, III, 4 (July, 1852), 138-140.

Lord, David N. "The Congregationalist's Notice of the Review of Professor Park's Discourse /Intellect and Feelings/," The Theological and Literary Journal, III, 3 (January, 1851), 482-514.

_____. "Review of Professor Park's Theologies of the Intellect and of the Feelings," The Theological and Literary Journal, III, 2 (October, 1850), 177-234.

Lord, Nathan. A Letter to the Rev. Daniel Dana on Professor Park's Theology of New England. Boston: Crocker and Brewster, 1852.

McLane, James Woods. /Review of Park's/ Discourse Delivered at the Funeral of Professor Moses Stuart, New Englander, XI, 42 (May, 1853), 247-261.

Marsh, James. "Review of Stuart on the Epistle to the Hebrews," The Quarterly Christian Spectator, Ser. 3, Vol. I (March, 1829), 112-149.

"The New Theology and the Andover Creed," Congregationalist, XXXV, 24 (June 14, 1883), 206, cols. 3-6.

"Orthodoxy in New England," Southern Presbyterian Review, VII, 1 (July, 1853), 52-60.

Pierce, Richard D. "A Suppressed Edwards Manuscript on the Trinity," Crane Review, I, 2 (Winter, 1959), 66-80.

Pond, Enoch. /Review of Park's7 Memoir of Nathanael Emmons, American Theological Review, III, 12 (October, 1861), 632-668.

Porter, Ebenezer. Letters on the Religious Revivals Which Prevailed about the Beginning of the Present Century. Boston: Congregational Board of Publication, 1858, c1832.

"Remarks on the Communication of a Layman," Panoplist; or, the Christian's Armory, III, 4 (July, 1852), 156-157.

/Reply to7 "Lord's Review of Park's Sermon," Congregationalist, II, 41 (October 11, 1850), 162, cols. 1-3.

"Report of Professor Park's Address" ("Taste and Religion Auxiliary to Each Other," delivered at the dedication of the new library at Amherst College), The Hampshire and Franklin Express, Amherst, Massachusetts, December 2, 1853, 3, cols. 3-4.

"Review of Dr. Dana's Sermon 'Have the Churches the Presence of Christ?' 1850," Panoplist; or, the Christian's Armory, II, 6 (June, 1851), 213-220.

Review of Nathan Lord's Letter to the Rev. Daniel Dana, Southern Presbyterian Review, VII, 2 (October, 1853), 299-300.

/Review of Park's7 Atonement, Discourses and Treatises, New Englander, LXVII, 17 (August, 1859), 776-779.

"Review of Park's Discourse on the Theology of the Intellect and That of the Feelings," Christian Examiner and Religious Miscellany, XLIX, fourth series XIV, 2 (September, 1850), 296.

"Review of Prof. Park's Discourse on the 'Theology of the Intellect and That of the Feelings,'" Panoplist; or, the Christian's Armory, II, 3 (March, 1851), 96-118.

/Review of/ The Sabbath Hymn Book. /ed. E. A. Park, et al./, Congregational Quarterly, I, 1 (January, 1859), 89-95.

/Review of/ Selections from German Literature. /ed. and trans. B. B. Edwards and E. A. Park/, American Biblical Repository, second series II, 3 (July, 1839), 198-217.

/Reviews of/ "Prof. Park's Discourse on 'The Theology of the Intellect and That of the Feelings,'" Congregationalist, II, 23 (June 7, 1850), 92, cols. 1-3; II, 41 (October 11, 1850), 162, cols. 1-3.

Sears, Barnas. /Review of/ Selections from German Literature. /ed. and trans. B. B. Edwards and E. A. Park/, Christian Review, IV, 15 (September, 1839), 370-394.

Smith, Henry Boynton. "The Relations of Faith and Philosophy," Bibliotheca Sacra, VI, 24 (November, 1849), 673-709.

_____. /Review of Park's/ Memoir of Nathanael Emmons, American Theological Review, IV, 13 (January, 1862), 7-53.

Smyth, Egbert C. "The Theological Purpose of the Review," Andover Review, I (January, 1884), 1-13.

_____. The Value of the Study of Church History in Ministerial Education. Andover: Warren F. Draper, 1874.

Smyth, Newman. "Orthodox Rationalism," Princeton Review, LVIII, 4 (May, 1882), 294-312.

Stebbins, Rufus Phineas. "The Andover and Princeton Theologies," Christian Examiner and Religious Miscellany, LII, fourth series XVII, 3 (May, 1852), 309-335.

Taylor, Nathaniel W. Concio ad Clerum. A Sermon Delivered in the Chapel of Yale College, September 10, 1828. New Haven: Hezekiah Howe, 1828.

"Taylorism-Bushnellism and Parkism," Independent, II, 84 (July 11, 1850), 114, col. 5.

Thayer, Christopher Tappan. "Heresy in Andover Seminary," Christian Examiner and Religious Miscellany, LV, fourth series XX, 1 (July, 1853), 80-87.

Wallace, David Alexander. The Theology of New England. An Attempt to Exhibit the Doctrines Now Prevalent in the Orthodox Congregational Churches of New England. with an introduction by Daniel Dana. Boston: Crocker and Brewster, 1856.

Warren, William Fairfield. /Review of Park's/ Atonement, Discourses and Treatises, Methodist Quarterly Review, XLII, fourth series XII, 25 (July, 1860), 386-402.

/Williams, John/. "New England Theology," Church Review and Ecclesiastical Register, V, 3 (October, 1852), 349-360.

/Williams, John/. "New England Theology," Church Review and Ecclesiastical Register, VI, 1 (April, 1853), 82-100.

Woods, Leonard. Letters to Rev. Nathaniel W. Taylor. Andover: M. Newman, 1830.

Wright, George Frederick. /Review of Park's/ Discourses on Some Theological Doctrines as Related to the Religious Character, Bibliotheca Sacra, XLIV, 173 (January, 1887), 163-174.

_____. "Science and Religion. Concerning the True Doctrine of Final Cause or Design in Nature," Bibliotheca Sacra, XXXIV (April, 1877), 355-385.

_____. "Science and Religion. The Divine Method of Producing Living Species," Bibliotheca Sacra, XXXIII (July, 1876), 448-493.

_____. "Science and Religion. Objections to Darwinism, and the Rejoinder of Its Advocates," Bibliotheca Sacra, XXXIII (October, 1876), 656-694.

_____. "Science and Religion. Some Analogies Between Calvinism and Darwinism," Bibliotheca Sacra, XXVII (January, 1880), 48-76.

H. Biographical material on Park

"Andover Seminary Confirmation of Professor Park's Appointment," Boston Recorder, XXXII, 16 (April 22, 1847), 63, col. 1.

Bartlett, Samuel C. "How I Was Educated," Forum, II, 1 (September, 1886), 18-26.

Bates, Elisabeth Ballister. "Professor Park Viewed from Another Angle," Congregationalist, LXXXV, 25 (June 21, 1900), 912.

Blau, Joseph Leon. "Edwards Amasa Park," in American Philosophic Addresses, 1700-1900. ed. Blau. New York: Columbia University Press, 1946, pp. 624-626.

Boardman, George Nye. "Professor Park as a Theological Preacher," Bibliotheca Sacra, LVIII, 231 (July, 1901), 540-555.

Bradford, Amory Howe. "Three Great Andover Professors," The Christian Union, XLV, 12 (March 19, 1892), 540-542.

Buckley, James Monroe. "Professor Park," Christian Advocate (New York), LXXV, 25 (June 21, 1900), 999-1000.

Carpenter, Charles Carroll. "Professor Park at Ninety," Congregationalist, LXXXIV, 1 (January 5, 1899), 14-15.

Catalogue of the Theological Library of the Late Professor Edwards A. Park of Andover, Mass. Boston: C. F. Libbie and Company, 1903.

/Cook, Joseph/. "Professor Park's Eightieth Birthday," Our Day, III, 13 (January, 1889),108.

"Death of Professor E. A. Park," Congregationalist, LXXXV, 23 (June 7, 1900), 849.

"Death of Professor E. A. Park," Zion's Herald, LXXVIII, 23 (June 6, 1900), 712.

"Death: The Rev. Dr. Edwards A. Park," New York Times, June 9, 1900, 5, col. 6.

"Edwards A. Park," in History of Essex County, Massachusetts, with Biographical Sketches of Many of Its Pioneers and Prominent Men. ed. Duane Hamilton Hurd. Philadelphia: J. W. Lewis and Company, 1888. Vol. II, pp. 1642-1644.

Edwards, William Henry, compiler. Timothy and
    Rhoda Ogden Edwards of Stockbridge, Massachusetts
    and Their Descendants. A Genealogy. Cincinnati:
    The Robert Clarke Company, 1903.

Evans, Daniel. "Park, Edwards Amasa," Dictionary
    of American Biography. ed. Dumas Malone. New
    York: Charles Scribner's Sons, 1934. Vol. XIV,
    204-205.

Fisher, George Park. "Professor Park as a Theologian,"
    Congregationalist, LXXXV, 24 (June 14, 1900), 871-
    872.

Foster, Frank Hugh. The Life of Edwards Amasa Park,
    Abbot Professor, Andover Theological Seminary. with
    a foreword by Walter Marshall Horton. New York:
    Fleming H. Revell Company, 1936.

_____. "Park, Edwards Amasa," in The New
    Schaff-Herzog Encyclopedia. ed. Samuel Macauley
    Jackson. New York: Funk and Wagnalls Company,
    1910. Vol. VIII, 357.

"The Funeral of Professor Park," Congregationalist,
    LXXXV, 24 (June 14, 1900), 862.

"A Great Man's Wit," Christian Advocate (New York),
    LXVI, 40 (October 1, 1891), 659, col. 1.

"Greetings to Rev. E. A. Park," in Proceedings of the
    Second International Congregational Council, Boston,
    1899. Boston: Samuel Usher, 1900, pp. 8-9.

"A Hero in Our Hall of Fame," Congregationalist,
    LXXXVIII, 24 (June 13, 1903), 833.

Hovey, Alvah and Joseph Cook. "Professor Park as
    Teacher and Preacher," Bibliotheca Sacra, LVIII,
    230 (April, 1901), 338-359. Also published as a
    pamphlet.

"In Memory of Drs. Hamlin and Park," Congregationalist,
    LXXXVI, 2 (January 12, 1901), 75, col. 3.

"The Inauguration of Professor Park," Boston Recorder,
    XXXII, 23 (June 10, 1847), 90, cols. 1-2.

/Kasson, Frank Hatch/. "Professor Park at the Alumni
    Dinner," Congregationalist, XXXIII, 28 (July 13,
    1881), 224, cols. 2-3.

McKenzie, Alexander. Memoir of Professor Edwards
Amasa Park. Cambridge, Massachusetts: John Wilson
and Son, 1901. Also published as an article.

McKenzie, Alexander and Henry Morton Dexter. "Tributes
to Professor Edwards A. Park," in the Proceedings of
the Massachusetts Historical Society, 34, s. 2,
Vol. 14 (1900/1901), pp. 189-195.

Noble, Frederick A. "Professor Park of Andover,"
Advance, 39 (June 14, 1900), 845.

"/Obituary Notice of/ Professor Edwards A. Park,"
Bibliotheca Sacra, LVII, 227 (July, 1900), 628.

"Park and Storrs," Independent, LII, 2689 (June 14,
1900), 1455-1456.

"Park, Edward /sic./ Amasa," Who's Who in America,
1899-1900. ed. John W. Leonard. Chicago: A. N.
Marquis and Company, 1899, p. 547.

"Park, Edwards Amasa," Appleton's Cyclopaedia of
American Biography. ed. James Grant Wilson and
John Fiske. New York: D. Appleton and Company,
1887-1889. Vol. IV, pp. 647-648.

"Park, Edwards Amasa," Concise Dictionary of Religious
Knowledge and Gazetteer. ed. Samuel Macauley
Jackson. New York: Christian Literature Company,
1891, p. 686.

"Park, Edwards Amasa," Encyclopedia of Living Divines
and Christian Workers of All Denominations in Europe
and America. ed. Philip Schaff. New York: Funk
and Wagnalls, 1887, pp. 161-162.

"Park, Edwards Amasa," in Historical Catalogue of
Brown Univeristy, 1764-1904. Providence: Published
by the University, 1905, pp. 147-148.

"Park, Edwards Amasa," Lamb's Biographical Dictionary
of the United States. ed. John Howard Brown. Boston:
Federal Book Company, 1903. Vol. VI, pp. 126-127.

Parkes, Frank Sylvester, compiler. Genealogy of the
Parke Families of Massachusetts. Washington, D. C.:
Presswork of the Columbia Polytechnic Institute
Printing Office, 1909.

Persons, Frederick T. "Park, Edwards Amasa,"
  An Encyclopedia of Religion. ed. Vergilius Ferm.
  New York: Philosophical Library, 1945, p. 561.

"Prof. E. A. Park, D. D.," Congregationalist, XV,
  32 (August 7, 1863), 126, col. 5.

"Prof. E. A. Park," Congregationalist, XXXIII, 27
  (July 6, 1881), 218, col. 4.

"Professor Edwards A. Park," Congregationalist,
  LXXXV, 23 (June 7, 1900), 831-832.

"Professor Park," The Outlook, LXV, 7 (June 16,
  1900), 386-387.

"Professor Park and Dr. Storrs," Congregationalist,
  LXXXV, 24 (June 14, 1900), 865.

Professor Park and His Pupils. ed. D. L. Furber,
  et al. Boston: Samuel Usher, 1899.

"Prof. Park Passes Away," Advance, XXXIX, 1805
  (June 14, 1900), 845-846.

"Professor Park's Ninetieth Anniversary, with Letters
  from Pupils and Friends," Bibliotheca Sacra, LVI,
  222 (April, 1899), 301-326.

Rankin, Jeremiah Eames. "Edwards Amasa Park,"
  Bibliotheca Sacra, LX, 238 (January, 1903), 201-
  222.

_____. "Edwards Amasa Park on His 91st Birthday,
  December 29th /a Poem/," Independent, LI, 2665
  (December 28, 1899), 3494.

Scott, George Robert White. "Edwards Amasa Park,"
  New England Historical and Genealogical Register,
  56 (January, 1902), 11-17.

Stoddard, Charles Augustus. "Professor Edwards A.
  Park," New York Observer, LXXVIII, 26 (June 28,
  1900), 837-838.

"Storrs and Park at Longmeadow," Congregationalist,
  XXXV, 44 (November 1, 1883), 379, cols. 3-4.

Storrs, Richard Salter. Edwards Amasa Park,
  Memorial Address. Boston: Samuel Usher, 1900.

Thwing, Charles Franklin. "Edwards Amasa Park: Apostolic Theologian, Discriminating Teacher," in his Guides, Philosophers and Friends: Studies of College Men. New York: Macmillan, 1927, pp. 369-388.

_____. "Prof. Park as an Editor," Congregationalist, XXXV, 44 (November 1, 1883), 379, cols. 2-3.

"Tributes from Former Pupils in Recent Letters to Dr. Park," Congregationalist, LXXXV, 23 (June 7, 1900), 825.

An Undergraduate. "Professor Park in the Lecture Room," Congregationalist, XII, 10 (March 9, 1860), 37, cols. 5-6.

"Wit Outwitted--an Incident of the Lecture Room," Boston Review Devoted to Theology and Literature, III, 16 (July, 1863), 435-436.

/Wright, George Frederick/. "Professor Park," Bibliotheca Sacra, LVIII, 229 (January, 1901), 187-190.

I. Andover literature

/Abbott, Lyman/. "The Andover Professorship," Christian Union, XXV, 14 (April 6, 1882), 318, cols. 2-3.

/Abbott, Lyman/. "The Outlook," Christian Union, XXV, 23 (June 28, 1882), 521, cols. 2-3; 522, col. 1.

Addresses Delivered at the Service of Induction of the Rev. Daniel Evans, into the Abbot Professorship of Christian Theology and the Rev. Albert Parker Fitch into the Bartlet Professorship of Practical Theology in Andover Theological Seminary in Cambridge, March 22, 1909. Boston: Fort Hill Press, 1909.

"Andover Anniversary September 4, 1850," Independent, II, 93 (September 12, 1850), 150, cols. 6-7.

"Andover Case," Our Day, IX, 49 (January, 1892), 76-77.

The Andover Case: with an Introductory Historical Statement; a Careful Summary of the Arguments of the Respondent Professors; and the Full Text of the Arguments of the Complainants and Their Counsel, Together with the Decision of the Board of Visitors, Furnishing the Nearest Available Approach to a Complete History of the Whole Matter. Boston: Stanley and Usher, 1887.

The Andover Defence. Defence of Prof. Smyth; Arguments of Prof. Theodore W. Dwight, Prof. Simeon E. Baldwin, Hon. Charles T. Russell, and Ex-Governor Gaston; Evidence Introduced by the Respondents, December, 1886, Together with the Statements of Profs. Tucker, Harris, Hincks, and Churchill, January, 1887. Boston: Cupples, Upham and Company, 1887.

"The Andover Disturbance," Independent, XXXIV, 1740 (April 6, 1882), 16.

The Andover Heresy; in the Matter of the Complaint Against Egbert C. Smyth and Others, Professors in the Theological Institution in Phillips Academy, Andover. Professor Smyth's Argument, Together with the Statements of Professors Tucker, Harris, Hincks, and Churchill. Boston: Cupples, Upham and Company, 1887. (Cover title: The Andover Trial).

"The Andover Professorship," Independent, XXXIV, 1739 (March 30, 1882), 17.

"Andover Seminary," Christian Union, XXVII, 24 (June 14, 1883), 466, cols. 2-3.

"Andover Theological Seminary," Congregationalist, XVII, 32 (August 11, 1865), 1, col. 7; 2, col. 1.

"Andover Theological Seminary and the New Departure," Advance, XVIII, 822 (June 21, 1883), 418, col. 1.

"Andover's Opportunity," Independent, XXXIV, 1749 (June 8, 1882), 17.

"Anniversary at Andover," Puritan Recorder, XXXV, 37 (September 12, 1850), 146, cols. 3-4.

/Bacon, Leonard W.7 "Dr. Woods' Position," Independent, V, 258 (November 10, 1853), 178, cols. 2-4.

Bacon, Leonard W. "Andover and Creed Subscription," North American Review, CXXXIV, 307 (June, 1882), 551-562.

Bartol, Cyrus Augustus. The Andover's Bottle's Burst. Boston: A. Williams and Company, 1882.

Bennetch, John Henry. "The Biography of the Bibliotheca Sacra," Bibliotheca Sacra, C, 397 (January-March, 1943), 8-30.

Boardman, Samuel L. "The Bibliotheca Sacra," New England Historical and Genealogical Register, XXXVI, 3 (July, 1882), 339-340.

/Brown, William B.7 "Andover Theological Anniversary," Oberlin Evangelist, XII, 20 (September 25, 1850), 155, cols. 2-3.

/Buckley, James Monroe7. "Is Andover Adrift?" Christian Advocate (New York), LVII, 17 (April 27, 1882), 257, cols. 3-4.

Catalogue of the Library of the Theological Seminary in Andover, Mass. compiled by Oliver A. Taylor. Andover: Gould and Newman, 1838.

Dana, Daniel. A Remonstrance Addressed to the Trustees of Phillips Academy on the State of the Theological Seminary under Their Care, September, 1849. Boston: Crocker and Brewster, 1853.

"The Dismissal of the Andover Case," Andover Review, XVIII, 106 (October, 1892), 421-431.

Dodge, John C. "Calvinistic Theology and the Andover School," Unitarian Review and Religious Magazine, XIX, 4 (April, 1883), 315-321.

Dwight, William Theodore. Before the Board of Visitors of Andover Theological Seminary in the Matter of the Charges Against Professors Egbert C. Smyth, William J. Tucker, J. W. Churchill, George Harris and Edward Y. Hincks. Arguments for Prof. Egbert C. Smyth, Respondent. Boston: Rand Avery and Company, 1887.

Ehlert, Arnold D. "Genealogical History of Bibliotheca Sacra," Bibliotheca Sacra, C, 397 (January-March, 1943), 31-52.

Faulkner, John Alfred. "The Tragic Fate of a Famous Seminary," Bibliotheca Sacra, LXXX, 320 (October, 1923), 449-464.

Fiske, Daniel Taggart. The Creed of Andover Theological
    Seminary. Newburyport, Massachusetts: Moses H.
    Sargent, 1882.

Fuess, Claude Moore. Andover: Symbol of New England;
    the Evolution of a Town. Andover, Massachusetts:
    Andover Historical Society and North Andover
    Historical Society, 1959.

_____. An Old New England School. A History
    of Phillips Academy, Andover. Boston: Houghton,
    Mifflin and Company, 1917.

Funds and Statutes of Andover Theological Seminary.
    Boston: Printed for the Trustees by Fort Hill
    Press, 1909.

Gates, Owen. An Open Door for Andover Seminary.
    Boston: Fort Hill Press, 1929.

General Catalogue of the Theological Seminary, Andover,
    Mass., 1808-1908. ed. Charles Carroll Carpenter.
    Boston: Thomas Todd, 1908.

Gulliver, John Putnam, et al. "Andover Seminary and
    Its New Professor," Christian Union, XXV, 15
    (April 13, 1882), 363, cols. 1-3.

_____. "A Communication from the Andover
    Professors," Independent, XXXIV, 1741 (April 13,
    1882), 17-19.

Hamlin, Cyrus. "The Andover Attack on the American
    Board," Our Day, IX (1892), 709-720.

Herrick, Everett Carleton. Turns Against Home.
    Andover Newton Theological School and Reminiscences
    from an Unkept Journal. Boston: Pilgrim Press,
    1949.

"How about Andover?" Independent, XXXVI, 1768
    (October 19, 1882), 16-17.

Laws of the Theological Institution in Andover.
    Andover: Flagg and Gould, 1827.

Laws of the Theological Seminary, Andover, Mass.
    Andover: Warren F. Draper, 1870.

A Layman. A Review of Dr. Dana's Remonstrance
    Respecting Andover Theological Seminary. Boston:
    Crocker and Brewster, 1853.

McCloy, Frank Dixon. "The Founding of Protestant Theological Seminaries in the United States of America, 1784-1840." Harvard University: unpublished Ph.D. dissertation, 1959.

Massachusetts. Supreme Judicial Court. Egbert C. Smyth, Appellant, v. the Visitors of the Theological Institution in Phillips Academy in Andover, Appellee, before George D. Robinson, Esq., Commissioner /Springfield, Massachusetts, 1889/.

A Memorial of the Semi-Centennial Celebration of the Founding of the Theological Seminary at Andover. Andover: Warren F. Draper, 1859.

Morse, James King. Jedidiah Morse, a Champion of New England Orthodoxy. New York: Columbia University Press, 1939.

Mott, Frank Luther. "The Bibliotheca Sacra," in his History of American Magazines, Part I, 1741-1850. Cambridge, Massachusetts: Harvard University Press, 1938. Vol. I, 739-746.

Pierce, Richard D. "Legal Aspects of the Andover Creed," Church History, XV, 1 (March, 1946), 28-47.

"Professor Park's Successor?" Congregationalist, XXXIV, 10 (March 8, 1882), 82, col. 2.

"Proposed Changes Pertaining to Creed Subscription," Andover Review, XI, 64 (April, 1889), 408-412.

The Question at Issue in the Andover Case: Arguments of Rev. Drs. Joshua W. Wellman and Orpheus T. Lamphear, Complainants in the Andover Case. Prepared for the Hearing before the Board of Visitors, September 1, 1892. Boston: Samuel Usher, 1893.

"Rejection of Newman Smyth," Independent, XXXIV, 1744 (May 4, 1882), 17.

Robbins, Sarah (Stuart). Old Andover Days; Memories of a Puritan Childhood. Boston: The Pilgrim Press, 1908.

Rowe, Henry Kalloch. History of Andover Theological Seminary. Newton, Massachusetts: Printed for the Seminary, 1933.

/Smalley, Elam/. "Examination at Andover," Congregationalist, II, 18 (May 3, 1850), 70, col. 5.

Strong, Edward Alexander. "Anniversary Week at
Andover," Congregationalist, XXIII, 27 (July 6,
1871), 209, cols. 1-5.

Sweet, William Warren. "The Rise of Theological
Schools in America," Church History, VI, 3
(September, 1937), 260-273.

"Unsoundness of Andover Theological Seminary," The
Presbyterian (Philadelphia), XXIII, 12 (March 19,
1853), 46, cols. 3-4.

Vanderpool, Harold Young. "The Andover Conservatives:
Apologetics, Biblical Criticism and Theological
Change at the Andover Theological Seminary."
Harvard University: unpublished Ph.D. dissertation,
1971.

Ward, Elizabeth Stuart (Phelps). Chapters from a
Life. Boston: Houghton, Mifflin and Company,
1897.

/Wellman, Joshua Wyman/. "Progress and Prospects of
the Andover Case," Our Day, IX, 60 (December,
1892), 923-938.

Williams, Daniel Day. The Andover Liberals: A Study
in American Theology. New York: King's Crown
Press, 1941.

Withington, Leonard. "An Essay on Vibrations in
Theology," in Contributions to the Ecclesiastical
History of Essex County, Massachusetts. Boston:
Congregational Board of Publication, 1865, pp. 386-
396.

Woods, Leonard. History of the Andover Theological
Seminary. ed. George S. Baker. Boston: James R.
Osgood and Company, 1885, c1884.

_____. Outline of the Course of Study Pursued
by the Students of the Theological Seminary, Andover,
in the Department of Christian Theology, with
Reference to the Principal Books in the Library
Pertaining to That Department. for the use of
students /Andover: Published for the author, 1840/.